r Eric M. Jackson's

PayPal Wars
Battles with eBay, the Media, the Mafia, and the Rest of Planet Earth

"Way back in 1981 a business book literally kept me up all night reading…Well, it's happened again…Hate to use the hackneyed term, but it's a real page turner, and among other things it gives the best description of 'business strategy' unfolding in a world changing at warp speed."

— **Tom Peters, author,** *In Search of Excellence*

"It's rare that a business book is a page turner, but *The PayPal Wars* is: I read the whole book on one cross-country flight."

— **David Henderson,** *Tech Central Station*

"Reading *The PayPal Wars* is like watching the last two minutes of a championship football game that is tied 21-21—and then goes into sudden death overtime. It's the rare business book that reads like a page-turning exciting novel. *The PayPal Wars* is hard to put down."

— **Skip McGrath, editor, "EBay Auction Seller's News"**

"Eric M. Jackson's *The PayPal Wars* is an absorbing insider's story about two Silicon Valley entrepreneurs…[who] launched an online payment Web site called PayPal. Every School of Business ought to put this book on its must reading list because it is 'case history' analysis at its best."

— **Arnold Beichman,** *The Washington Times*

"Jackson's engaging narrative reads in turn like a spy novel, a business text, and an insider tell-all. One of PayPal's earliest employees and savviest marketers, Jackson documents the full spate of challenges and obstacles faced by start-ups and entrepreneurs, and how visionaries often have to abandon big ideas to keep competitors at bay and to satisfy petty bureaucrats and politicians."

— **Radley Balko,** *Reason Magazine*

THE PAYPAL WARS

BATTLES WITH eBAY, THE MEDIA, THE MAFIA, AND THE REST OF PLANET EARTH

THE PAYPAL WARS

BATTLES WITH EBAY, THE MEDIA, THE MAFIA, AND THE REST OF PLANET EARTH

ERIC M. JACKSON

 WND BOOKS

PAYPAL WARS

WND Books
Washington, D.C.

Jacket Design by Mark Karis

WND Books are distributed to the trade by:
Midpoint Trade Books
27 West 20th Street, Suite 1102
New York, NY 10011

WND Books are available at special discounts for bulk purchases. WND Books, Inc. also publishes books in electronic formats. For more information call (541) 474-1776 or visit www.wndbooks.com.

ISBN: 978-1-936488-59-9

Library of Congress information available.

Printed in the United States of America.

To Beatrice, for standing by me during my PayPal adventures and supporting me as I wrote about them

CONTENTS

FOREWORD TO THE PAPERBACK EDITION

WHEN THE HARDCOVER EDITION of *The PayPal Wars* debuted in autumn 2004, I hoped that PayPal's story might convey some valuable business lessons while also making a broader statement about American entrepreneurship. In assuming the unofficial (and, from eBay's likely point-of-view, unwelcome) mantle of company historian, I sought to illustrate these points by recounting the toils of a small group of entrepreneurs during that quiet moment between the end of the dot-com boom and the beginning of the War on Terror.

In chronicling the past, though, I believe I also painted a decent picture of the future. Since *The PayPal Wars* first appeared PayPal's team has begun to receive the recognition it deserves, in part for the exploits chronicled in this book, but even more so for the amazing new crop of companies started by its alumni. Additionally, the anti-entrepreneurial traits in eBay's culture that I warned about have become more visible to the outside world. In a short period of time, the auctioneer has gone from a Wall Street darling to a company whose stock price and business model are under pressure.

Because it still seems both timely and relevant, the story that I told in the hardcover remains basically unchanged. The most notable exception is a completely new Afterword that summarizes the unfolding challenge that Google now poses to PayPal and eBay. I've also made a few updates on the current activities of PayPal alumni in the Conclusion.

In writing this narrative, I went to painstaking efforts to produce an accurate account. I drew upon my personal recollections and records, discussions with former colleagues, and extensive research using the media sources and SEC filings listed in the Notes section of this book. While I've endeavored to produce a thorough and precise account, any errors or omissions are entirely my own responsibility.

PayPal's financial and customer data referenced in this narrative come from readily available public sources, including PayPal's IPO prospectus and eBay's quarterly reports; given this, I opted to spare the reader from the scores of repetitious notes that would have ensued had I documented each figure individually.

It should be added that while I've been careful to supply background information for the reader whenever appropriate, this narrative's focus is on the events surrounding PayPal and not eBay, PayPal's erstwhile competitor and current owner. Lest I be accused of dehumanizing eBay for the purpose of constructing a foil to PayPal, interested readers are enthusiastically referred to Adam Cohen's *The Perfect Store: Inside eBay*, (New York: Little, Brown, and Company, 2002) for an engaging account of eBay's creation.

ACKNOWLEDGEMENTS

I AM INDEBTED TO EVERYONE at World Ahead Publishing for bringing this paperback edition of *The PayPal Wars* into existence. It is my pleasure to have worked with Norman Book, Judy Abarbanel, Ami Naramor, and Cara Eshleman on updating and revising this book. I owe them all my heartfelt gratitude, as I also do Brandi Laughey, Ken Hassman, Gilbert Kalombo, Hank Terry, Alexander Hoyt, and Anu Hansen. Daniel J. Bramzon, Thorvin Anderson, and Jeff Giesea have likewise been welcome advisors along the way. I must also acknowledge Gail Kump, who long advocated this paperback release, and Eric Kampmann, a fellow entrepreneur, for believing in World Ahead.

Prof. Michael New, Candice E. Jackson, Alec Rawls, Rod and Sherri Martin, Jonathan New, Nancy Humphreys, and Sharon Goldlinger remain in my gratitude for their assistance with the creation of the hardcover edition. And thanks must go to David Boaz of the Cato Institute, Prof. Bill Anderson, Ina and David Steiner from AuctionBytes, David Nott of the Reason Foundation, and *The Right Balance* host Greg Allen for their enthusiasm and support following the hardcover's release.

Family and friends were no less crucial in bringing this book into being. Above all others, I must acknowledge my wife, Beatrice, whose skill in her second language (English) humbles me only slightly less than her devotion and love. Boundless gratitude is also owed to my sister, Kristina, for reviewing my early manuscript, to my brother-in-law, and to my parents, Ron and Teresa, for always believing in their son. My thanks go to Victor Dominguez for his perpetual enthusiasm and support, and to Nick Vander Dussen for the many volumes of books he has given to me over the years. I must also thank my grandmothers, Pauline and Marie, who so often took the time to read to their grandson. I could not have done it without all of you.

Finally, I must express my gratitude to my PayPal compatriots for serving as the source of inspiration for this book. It was my privilege to have worked alongside all of you. "World domination" or not, the planet is still better because of what you have done.

INTRODUCTION

PAYPAL'S STORY is one of war. Not conflict with guns or tanks, but a mighty business struggle waged with ingenuity, determination, and plenty of midnight oil. When PayPal's online payment service debuted toward the end of the dot-com boom, it set in motion a chain of events that would ultimately pit the company's talented entrepreneurs, revolutionary technology, and bold vision for global currency change against one of the fiercest series of challenges ever endured by a Silicon Valley startup.

At the risk of giving away the ending, PayPal managed to survive the onslaught—but just barely. After several years of erratic ups and downs, the venture reached profitability, registered 40 million users, became the first Internet company to stage an IPO following the 9/11 terrorist attacks, and eventually sold out to a much bigger firm. While this is an impressive track record by most standards, it's far short of what our group initially hoped to accomplish.

I may not have fully appreciated it when I accepted the CEO's invitation to join what was then a tiny startup, but it stands to reason that the creation of most technology ventures is by necessity a tumultuous process. Joseph Schumpeter, a Harvard economist, dubbed the process of entrepreneurs unleashing new innovations into the marketplace as "creative destruction" because it invariably shakes up the existing economic order.[1] Looking back, this term is certainly appropriate to describe what PayPal set out to do, and it also hints at the turbulence that accompanied our efforts.

Vigorous competition provided one source of that tumult. A torrent of competitors, including multinational banks and established Internet players, also saw the profit potential of our startup's payment system and raced to construct their own versions. This slew of entrants into a brand new market touched off a furious race for dominance, one which ultimately led to a bruising one-on-one confrontation between PayPal and an unlikely rival.

Intense internal debate, coupled with clashes over the direction of the company's strategy, was another tumultuous challenge. Entrepreneurs attempting to do something that no one else has done often lack a precedent to guide their choices and are forced to grapple with each decision. Fortunately PayPal's founders instilled in the company a culture that accommodated this reality and even tried to turn it into an asset.

With hindsight, competition and uncertainty could be said to be par for the course for innovators attempting to launch a potential-laden service like PayPal. Others will want to beat your team in the race to the prize, and the best course of action is not always clear at any given moment. But what proved less predictable, and ultimately far more dangerous to PayPal's prospects, were the challenges completely unrelated to the marketplace that emerged out of nowhere as soon as PayPal stood on the threshold of success.

Scheming Mafioso, capricious regulators, opportunistic lawyers, savvy online identity thieves, volatile capital markets, an antagonistic press—collectively these external challenges proved more daunting than we could have ever foreseen. The modern business environment itself turned out to be more hostile to our band of entrepreneurs than even our fiercest competitor. While Schumpeter intended to imply a certain level of instability when he coined the phrase "creative destruction," he didn't mean to suggest that entrepreneurs should have to worry more about these non-competitive threats than about the products they wanted to bring to market. And yet, as PayPal's experience suggests, today's innovators must often do just that.

These daunting threats and the blood, sweat, and tears they extracted make PayPal's story all the more important to tell. While this book documents the amazing exploits of the talented men and women I had the pleasure of working alongside, it is primarily a cautionary tale told firsthand from the high tech trenches.

I hope you enjoy it.

CHAPTER ONE

THE NEW RECRUIT

NOVEMBER—DECEMBER 1999

MY ENTREPRENEURIAL summons came with an abrupt qualification: "You need to start this Friday."

"W-what?" I stammered in reply. "Are you serious?"

Peter Thiel smiled and nodded. Evidently my reaction amused him.

"No, no. Look, it's already Sunday," I responded, shaking my head. "That would only be four days notice—I can't possibly quit my job with Andersen that quickly! We're in the middle of a project."

The chief executive officer of Confinity, Inc., didn't find that argument exceptionally compelling. "We expect to close our next round of financing at the end of this week, so the strike price of the options will go up. Now, let's see…" he paused, his hawkish nose pointing upward as the computer housed under his short, sandy hair rattled off a series of calculations. "Given your stock options, if you wait two weeks then it's going to cost you another $8,000."

I shivered as we continued our walk next to the bay. The gusts of wind whipping under the Golden Gate Bridge sliced through my light jacket. San Francisco sees plenty of gray skies and blustery weather year round, and this December afternoon was no exception. The chill distracted me as I tried to follow Peter's rapid train of thought— something many found difficult to do under the best of conditions.

"Eight thousand dollars?" I had no idea how he had calculated the figure. In fact, I had no idea how stock options even worked. I was a babe to such startup matters. The only thing I knew for sure was that startup stock options made people rich. Very rich.

Northern California on the eve of the millennium was the geographic epicenter of the dot-com boom. Young people in their early twenties, including many of my Stanford classmates, fled their old economy jobs in droves to cast their lots with Internet companies. Leaving behind stodgy, seniority-based firms they turned to small companies that let them make important decisions and bring their dogs to work while they earned IPO riches. Or so I'd heard.

Eight thousand dollars certainly didn't mean much to these people, but it did to me. I worked for the oldest of the old economy firms, the buttoned-down Arthur Andersen, which at the time was still viewed as one of the world's most trusted and respectable professional services companies. The partners running the firm called it a privilege for people my age to have the opportunity to start out at such a venerable institution, and in return they paid stingy salaries to match.

Peter made sure I would not mistake Confinity for another Andersen. He was offering me stock options and an increase in salary even though he wasn't sure exactly which position I'd fill. It didn't matter, he assured me, since Confinity had just launched its software product and needed talented people as quickly as possible. The product let people exchange money for shared expenses such as dinner bills and utilities, a novel idea that seemed poised to catch on despite its silly name — PayPal.

"Yes, an extra $8,000," Peter chirped, refocusing my attention. "Now, let's see, you could always ask Andersen if they're willing to pay you the $8,000 to stay another two weeks," he added, smiling.

He had me and he knew it.

◊

My PayPal journey began when I met Peter Thiel five years earlier at Stanford University. At an activities fair during my first week on campus I joined an independent student newspaper named the *Stanford Review*. Founded by Peter in 1987, the paper ardently defended the value of classical education and had itself received a good deal of media coverage over the years. Peter, a philosophy major, shepherded the *Review* with editorial guidance and fundraising during its lean early days and helped to transform it into a campus institution that attracted dozens of student members every quarter.

Peter left California for New York following his graduation from Stanford's law school in 1992. After working for the Wall Street law firm Sullivan & Cromwell for a year, he took a position trading derivatives for CS First Boston. He then began collaborating with another former *Review* editor, David Sacks, on *The Diversity Myth*, a book critical of recent changes to Stanford's curriculum. Shortly after I joined the *Review* an upperclassman introduced me to Peter, who needed someone to do legwork on campus as he put the finishing touches on his research for the book. I assisted him for several weeks, and the two of us remained in casual contact during the remainder of my time at Stanford.

When I graduated in 1998 I took an economics degree and a pile of student loans with me. I set out to tackle the world of finance, accepting a consulting job with Arthur Andersen in nearby San Francisco. I thought it would allow me to get hands-on experience with multiple clients in a variety of industries, preparing me for business school and a gradual-but-certain climb up the corporate ladder. In the process I'd pay off those loans, make a name for myself, and earn the respect of my peers in the financial world. At the time I had no way of knowing that meeting Peter Thiel would eventually derail those plans and change my life in a way I could never have imagined.

◊

Soon after my departure from Stanford, Peter returned to the campus to deliver a guest lecture on the link between market globalization and political freedom. It was a topic dear to his heart. A libertarian wary of concentrated government power, Peter's philosophical underpinnings were influenced by accounts of totalitarian oppression such as the works of Aleksandr Solzhenitsyn. Peter had recently moved back to the San Francisco Bay Area to set up his own hedge fund, and the lecture opportunity enabled him to discuss an issue he knew well. The animated speech Peter delivered inspired a twenty-four year old programmer in the audience to introduce himself afterward.

Max Levchin had good reason to show interest in Peter's remarks. Growing up as a Jew in the Soviet Union, he and his family faced limits on opportunities for education, housing, and employment because of their religion. When they emigrated from Kiev to Chicago in 1991 they made the most of their newfound freedom by buying Max a used computer. Max went on to graduate from the University of Illinois at Urbana-Champaign and formed a startup called NetMeridian that focused on automated marketing tools. After selling NetMeridian to Microsoft, Max moved to Silicon Valley on the lookout for his next startup idea.

Peter and Max hit it off. After several lunchtime discussions over the following weeks, the pair decided to launch a company with a security focus allowing users to store encrypted information on Palm Pilots and other personal digital assistant (PDA) devices. They settled on the name Fieldlink, since Palm devices use infrared ports to link up and beam information to each other. Peter initially agreed to help finance the venture with seed money from his fund, but with additional persuasion from Max he consented to becoming the company's full-time CEO.

Although digitized Palm security appealed to the privacy-loving instincts of the company's founders, the commercial applications appeared limited. Who would need to encrypt information on their handheld PDA device, and for what? And how would it generate revenue for the company? As the duo fleshed out the business model for the venture, its *raison d'être* began to evolve. Peter's background in finance prompted him to suggest money as a potential area of focus. It immediately felt like a good fit.

The need for making payments was universal, but the marketplace had yet to offer technology that addressed every form of that need. In prior decades the credit card and ATM networks had vastly expanded the payment options available to consumers, but these infrastructure-heavy systems also had significant shortcomings. Only merchants could obtain the permission and equipment necessary to accept credit cards, and ATMs were often not physically present at a given moment when a consumer needed one. With such limitations, neither network met the needs of one consumer wishing to make a payment to another. Without exact cash on hand, a consumer's only option was to write a check, a cumbersome form of payment that required a trip to the bank and a wait of several days before the check cleared and the recipient could take possession of the funds. Peter and Max surmised that technology had yet to offer a viable alternative to cash for person-to-person payments.

Fieldlink, they reasoned, could be positioned to develop a solution. Palm Pilots, designed to travel with their owners, would be an ideal platform for a digital wallet. The convenience of such an invention could earn Fieldlink's product the status of killer application, especially if the software behind it could be beamed through infrared ports from one Palm user to the next. But privacy and security, Fieldlink's original focus, were just as important as convenience—no digital wallet could be successful without addressing these two concerns. This is where Max's original encryption idea came into play. Encrypted data on a digital device theoretically could not be stolen, making it more secure than cash carried in a wallet.

The only problem was the Fieldlink name itself. While not exactly a misnomer for a payments company, it failed to hint at the new strategy. Peter and Max settled on a new name, Confinity, a combination of "confidence" and "infinity."

With Peter at the helm and the business plan centered on payments, Confinity began to look for talent. Max recruited three engineers from the University of Illinois while Peter brought over Kenny Howery, a former *Review* writer and classmate of mine who worked for Peter's hedge fund. Marty Hellman, the inventor of public key cryptography, joined the company's advisory board, and Bill Melton, the founder of VeriFone, provided his backing, as well.

Of course a startup with no revenue, much less a working product, needs more than talent. Attracting investments is critical, and selling private equity through a round of venture financing is how most Silicon Valley startups receive cash infusions. At a hyped press conference in July, 1999, a year after Peter and Max first met, representatives from Nokia Ventures and Deutsche Bank used a Palm Pilot to "beam" $3 million in venture funding to Peter in front of a gaggle of media onlookers. It was a public relations hit. *Wired* magazine published a glowing profile of the company's product demo, and the *International Herald Tribune* quoted an analyst predicting that millions of Palm users would sign up for the service.[1]

With cash in the bank, a quickly increasing number of employees on staff, and a new set of offices just down the street from Stanford University, Confinity hummed along at full speed developing its software. It was not long after this that I entered the scene.

◊

White fog shrouded Arthur Andersen's thirty-fifth floor offices in a haze. Indian summer typically arrives late to San Francisco and lasts through October. It's a pleasant time of year but all too brief. When it ends, the jackets come out and the fog comes back as it did on this dreary November afternoon.

Boredom made the day all the more downcast. An intense litigation support case that had filled my time for several months had just abruptly concluded when the client grew upset over Andersen's ever-mounting fees. While I had little historical perspective on it at the time, this was just another instance of the company's obsession with aggressively growing its lucrative consulting practice beginning to backfire. It was the same obsession with consulting fees that would eventually lead to Andersen's downfall in a cloud of auditing scandals three years later.[2]

What I did have ample insight into was Andersen's disillusioning treatment of its younger employees. The company's partners and managers, sequestered behind glass-walled offices, shipped staff consultants from one assignment to the next, giving the staffers little view of the big picture facing the firm — much less any control over their own career paths. When their current project ended staffers unceremoniously re-entered the internal labor market. Their names were added to the list of unassigned consultants while they sat in the office from nine to five, surfing the Net and waiting for a manager to swoop in to claim their idle time. Lucky staffers were able to get plucked for a new assignment in just a couple of days; unlucky ones might have to wait several weeks before being asked to join another job.

It was an exasperating process for young employees who took pride in their work, much less those who thought they might contribute to the making of any decisions. Andersen rigidly adhered to hierarchy to the point where title meant more than skills or experience. A total lack of ownership and frequent bouts of inactivity frustrated the entrepreneurial members of the young staff, and that frustration manifested itself in the form of constant cynicism. It was little wonder then that many of them over the past year had headed south to work for Silicon Valley startups. The thought had certainly crossed my mind more than once, especially on days such as this when I idly sat by waiting for something to do.

This early-November lull proved fateful. Cranky and dejected, I decided to waste some of the long day by catching up on personal correspondence. It was when I opened the inbox of my personal e-mail account that I came across an unusual message. The e-mail's subject line curiously exclaimed "PayPal User Beamed You Money!" The title sounded like spam—I had never heard of PayPal before. But given the lack of competing demands for my time at that moment, I opted to see what it was about. "Ken Howery has just Beamed you Money!" the message's text read. "You now have $1.00 waiting for you at PayPal. Visit www.PayPal.com to set up your PayPal account today!"

At this point I realized that this had to be the money transfer service that Confinity was developing. Evidently the site had just launched, and Kenny had sent a buck to everyone in his address book to get them to try out the service. This was the first time I'd heard their digital wallet software referred to as "PayPal," a name that struck me as a little juvenile compared to Confinity's futuristic and sophisticated corporate name. But the e-mail piqued my interest, so I clicked on the link to visit the PayPal Web site.

The site surprised me. When I'd last heard from Peter and Kenny a few months earlier their company specialized in Palm Pilots, but here was a fully functional online money transfer service that operated with or without a PDA device. The site advertised that anyone could instantly open an online account; all that was needed was an e-mail address and a credit card. The e-mail address was the critical ingredient—PayPal used it as a unique identifier, meaning that a person wanting to pay someone else only had to know his e-mail address to send him money. After a payment was sent it was credited to the recipient's PayPal account and he received an e-mail notice. The money could then be withdrawn from the account by requesting a check, initiating an electronic transfer to a bank account, or by using it to pay someone else.

The online service, I later learned, came as an afterthought. Since users of the Palm software would need to upload their encrypted financial transactions to the PayPal Web site anyway, Peter, Max, and the development team agreed that it made sense to create an online account that could work with or without a Palm. This enabled Confinity to expand PayPal's appeal beyond just the 3 or 4 million Palm owners in the U.S. to include everyone with access to the Internet. If the Palm Pilot wallet did turn out to be a killer application, online accounts would at least let consumers without Palms take advantage of the service while the penetration of PDAs continued to grow.

Whatever the source of inspiration, the system was brilliant. It was both simple to understand and to use. Better yet, Confinity offered it free of charge. The Web site explained that Confinity earned interest from the "float," the funds that users kept in their PayPal accounts. By placing this money in the bank, Confinity secured interest while keeping the funds liquid so customers could use them to send payments or withdraw them at any time.

But PayPal wasn't just a free service—its promotional bonus program rewarded all new account holders with a $10 deposit just for registering and linking a credit card to their account. And that wasn't all. Confinity would also pay users $10 for every new customer they referred to the service who completed the registration requirements! It was an obvious ploy to gain new customers, but an effective one. I spent the remainder of that gray afternoon blasting dollars into my friends' inboxes.

◊

My '88 Merkur looks out of place, I thought as I slammed the door of my little white coupe and strolled past a fleet of Beamers and Benzes parked in the lot around the corner from the restaurant. Not that these high priced examples of European engineering came as a surprise— they were just a sign of the times. Il Fornaio, an Italian eatery in downtown Palo Alto, attracted many of the Valley's wheelers and dealers, people flush with cash from the Internet boom. In fact, I had driven down here on a Friday evening in early December to have dinner with two of them.

Peter had extended the invitation to thank me for brokering an introduction. I'd placed him in contact with a former colleague, Steve Kuo, when I heard that Confinity sought to hold another financing round. Steve joined the growing exodus of Andersen staffers after our head partner unceremoniously shipped him off to a multi-week assignment in Brunei a few weeks after he proposed to his girlfriend. This pushed Steve out the door, prompting him to take a position as a senior analyst for a medium-sized venture capital firm. Following my introduction, the discussions between Steve's company and Confinity progressed quickly. Impressed by Confinity's management team and product, the venture capitalist sought to pull together a syndicate of other investors to support the startup, good news which Peter felt deserved celebrating.

Entering the restaurant, I spied Peter and Steve at a table toward the back. We exchanged greetings and settled in for dinner.

"I've got to come clean," Steve said with a grin. "Peter, did you know that my fiancée started working for you today?" Steve went on to confess that Confinity's new marketing hire, Jennifer Chwang, was also his bride-to-be. After learning about Confinity, Steve had encouraged her to apply for an opening posted on the company's Web site. Careful to avoid a conflict of interest, she interviewed for the position without revealing her relationship to a potential investor.

"I guess that's quite a vote of confidence in the company," Peter replied with a broad smile. "We've really been ramping up our staffing quite a lot lately. It's been a challenge to get people in fast enough." I'd seen evidence of Peter's hiring push firsthand. He had recently lured in several more of our associates from the *Stanford Review*, including David Sacks, his friend and *Diversity Myth* co-author.

Steve then steered the conversation back to me. "So, Eric, how are things back at Arthur?" he asked, exchanging a glance with Peter. "I hear you've been working with the Troll."

At that moment I realized that I'd been set up. The Troll, as I'll call him, was a hard-driving senior manager who thought the road to becoming an Andersen partner was paved with the burnt-out bodies of staff consultants. He was rumored to have a wife and kids, but most of us felt he'd never been outside of the office long enough to acquire either. Because of his penchant for demanding long hours and assigning inane tasks, Andersen staffers didn't ask people working for the Troll how things were going—they knew what the answer would be.

I settled for a euphemism. "It's been busy." Steve clicked his tongue and stated what a shame that was, given Andersen's salary stinginess.

Peter had his opening and he wasted no time. "You know, you should come work for us. We have a couple of new positions that you'd be good at."

Out of the blue this Italian dinner morphed into a pivotal moment in my young life. And pivotal moments are something I tend to take seriously. I generally consider myself a left-brained, analytical type who weighs his options carefully before passing judgment. But this time I had a ready answer. Maybe it was because of my disappointing stint working in the old economy. Perhaps it was a little greed set off by all those German cars sitting out in the parking lot. Or, most likely, it was because I was young and naïve. Whatever the reason, deliberation went out the door and I immediately offered a confident answer to Peter: "Yes, that definitely sounds interesting. Let's do it."

"Great! On Sunday I'm going to be up in the city to meet with some potential Japanese investors," Peter replied. "Let's meet around one o'clock in the Marina."

And so it began, innocently enough, over a plate of ravioli. Within forty-eight hours I had received and accepted a verbal offer from Peter and agreed to start the following Friday.

◊

Monday afternoon I left Andersen early to head south along Highway 101 to Palo Alto. Peter suggested I stop by a few days before beginning work so he could introduce me to my new colleagues. After giving notice at Andersen that morning, I looked forward to seeing a few welcoming faces. The Troll actually surprised me by offering congratulations on my decision, but our group's head partner turned red with rage and roared that I had burned my bridges. I was rashly giving up a chance to acquire marketable skills, he sputtered, to chase after fool's gold. His strong reaction left me shaken—it was only at this point that I realized I didn't even have a written offer, much less a job description.

The scenery along 101 at least provided enough distraction to keep my mind off the morning's conflict. Flashy billboards littered both sides of the highway with endless pitches for Internet companies. I tried envisioning how to make a large, prominent display for "PayPal.com by

Confinity" stand out from the legions of online pet food and herbal health services. I'd heard that billboards along this route commanded as much as $100,000 per month, but for a company like Confinity that would soon pull in additional millions in venture capital financing this was small potatoes. Maybe we should rent two?

My little daydream ended as I exited the highway onto Palo Alto's swank University Avenue and made my way to Confinity's office. *My new office*, I thought, my heart racing.

Marked only by a vinyl banner with Confinity's name, the offices were located on the upper floor of a two-story building above a bike store and a coffee shop. Though it looked like many other unassuming beige buildings on this shady downtown street, 165 University had a good track record—Internet search engine Google and mouse designer Logitech previously leased the same location.[3] But startup karma had less to do with Peter's choice than good old fashioned supply and demand. The Internet boom had made commercial real estate hard to come by, and when Confinity outgrew its old offices just down the street Peter was able to offer equity to this building's landlord to obtain a lease.

I parked my car nearby and headed through the front door. A wide but slippery interior staircase covered in glazed terra cotta tiles led up from the ground level entrance to a small exterior courtyard surrounded on all sides by the Confinity offices. Ascending up this treacherous staircase and then winding up outdoors again in the bright light was visually disconcerting—it took me a minute to locate the unmarked door that opened up to the lobby.

I introduced myself to the receptionist, who had no idea that I was expected. She quickly circled the office only to conclude that Peter was not in the building. Her call to his cell phone went straight into voice-mail, prompting her to ask if I wanted to come back later. I began to feel uneasy—I had just burned my Andersen bridges for an unspecified position without so much as an offer letter because Peter said I needed to start immediately, and now he was nowhere to be found.

"Could I meet with Kenny Howery, then?" I asked, thinking that my friend and Peter's right hand man surely would have heard about my job offer.

I was wrong. "Oh, really? That's great," my buddy said with his mild Texan accent, looking up from his computer with a slightly bewildered expression. Evidently he knew less about my job offer than I did, but he mused aloud that the company's sole human resources specialist should be in the loop.

"Lauri, have you heard about Eric?" he asked as he walked to a cubicle on the other side of the compact room. I trailed a few feet behind, hoping that this latest person would have some answers. "He said Peter told him he's starting this week." Lauri, I later found out, only oversaw Confinity's human resources operations on the side; she also managed a host of legal and financial matters and reported directly to the CFO. This very busy woman responded to Kenny's inquiry with a quizzical frown—she had no clue who I was. She asked which position Peter had hired me for, which of course I couldn't answer.

My concern grew. Three people in the company who should have known about my job offer seemed completely stumped. Could Peter have changed his mind? Why then did he press me to join immediately? I had no idea what was going on.

Kenny clearly needed to get back to his desk to resume working, but my friend made a point to give me a quick tour around the office to meet a few people. "This is Jamie Templeton; he's our product manager and works with the engineers...And you know Sacks, don't you?"

I first met David Sacks, whom everyone called by his last name, several years earlier when he visited Stanford to promote *The Diversity Myth*. Hearing his name he looked up from his computer and commented that it was great to have me on board. He instantly asked for my cell phone number which he entered into his own cell's memory, prompting his neighbor to quip, "Uh oh, once you're in there, you're always on call!" Sacks ignored the joke and got back to work, leaving Kenny to figure out what to do with me.

After checking on his availability, Kenny handed me off to Luke Nosek, the company's vice president of marketing. A lanky young man with wavy, dirty blonde hair, Luke popped up from his chair. "Hi! I'm Luke," he said, the first zestful greeting since I'd walked in the door. But my own enthusiasm was short-lived. "And what position are you interviewing for?"

"Actually Peter just hired me," I replied, a little dumfounded by both the question and this bouncy twenty-four year old vice president. "He said I could do either marketing or press and investor relations."

"Oh," Luke exhaled, settling back into his chair sideways with his legs draped over one of its arms. "So why do you want to work at

Confinity?" he continued, displaying a genuine smile and interest in whatever my response would be.

Before I could answer, a loud "ding" sound rang out from Luke's computer. "Another one!" Luke said. "Take a look at this!"

On Luke's monitor was a rectangular pop-up box labeled the "World Domination Index." It was a counter linked to the PayPal database that refreshed every few minutes. The number inside the box stood at 2,413.

"Isn't that great?" Luke asked. "I just always have to check whenever I hear it go off. It's gone up so much in the past week alone."

The counter's name caught my attention. I liked the concept of a tool to let employees keep a close eye on how well the business was doing, but a name like that was sure to set people's expectations pretty high. At Andersen we used tools with names like Knowledge Space or Risk Management Matrix, but nothing so megalomaniacal as a World Domination Index. This kind of swagger could at least make Confinity an interesting place to work—assuming I really did have a job, of course.

The index dinged several more times that afternoon as Luke "interviewed" me. Peter never turned up and I ended up leaving Palo Alto more confused and concerned than when I'd arrived. My angst lasted through the evening until I finally managed to catch the CEO on his cell phone; he explained that unforeseen events had forced him to be out of the office and he assured me that everything would be in order for my first day on Friday. Despite the false start, my journey into the new economy was indeed under way.

◊

If I'd expected to see a little more structure on my first day on the job than during my introductory visit, this notion was quickly dispelled. Following Peter's suggestion I reported for work at ten that Friday morning. This struck me as a little late to get started, but I reasoned that the extra time would allow my new colleagues to get ready for my arrival. After ascending the slippery stairs and crossing the tiny courtyard into the reception area it became apparent that my expectations were again off the mark. Except for a pair of engineers who walked past me evidently on their way home to sleep, the stillness and darkened hallways hinted that I was the only person in the office.

I breathed a sigh of relief when Kenny bound through a side entrance twenty minutes later and rescued me from the eerie silence of the small lobby. A handful of employees had begun to trickle in by this point, one of whom turned out to be the company's lone tech support specialist. The young man shrugged when Kenny inquired about my computer, responding that no one had bothered to mention my arrival to him, and even if they had it wouldn't matter since the company had no empty desks. After exchanging a few ideas on what to do, the pair decided to deposit me at the unoccupied desk of a customer service representative whose shift began several hours later.

What have I gotten myself into? I pondered as I tested the password to my new Confinity e-mail account on a borrowed computer. I had no job description, my colleagues didn't know who I was, and there wasn't even a desk for me in the building! At least Andersen gave its new hires places to sit.

The appearance of another familiar face provided a welcome distraction from the doubts now surfacing about my career choice. Dave Wallace, a fellow Stanford alumnus, extended a friendly handshake as he took a seat in the customer service bullpen next to me.

I had previously met Dave—a wiry and meticulous man with neatly trimmed brown hair—at several *Stanford Review* functions. He had gone into journalism after graduating in the early nineties, and following a stint as a reporter for the *San Francisco Examiner* he became an editor for a weekly paper in Palo Alto. I half expected him to tell me Peter had tapped him to write content for Confinity's Web site or deal with media inquiries. Instead I was surprised to hear from him that he was the company's director of customer service.

As Dave booted up his computer and went about his duties, I mused that his journalism background seemed an odd match for his role with the company. Journalism and customer service have little in common. As anyone who's been around reporters knows, a journalist often has to be persistent and sometimes a little scheming to get the story he's after—skills that are the opposite of what a company presumably looks for in an employee tasked with helping exasperated customers deal with their problems.

While this apparent miscasting of a journalist might have seemed like another haphazard action on the part of my new employer, as I met additional colleagues it turned out there was more of a pattern to Confinity's staffing decisions than I initially realized. Many employees, like Dave, had pasts that bore little resemblance to their present. Peter would later tell me that he preferred talent over experience when looking for people to take jobs within the company, a philosophy that certainly explained why he hired me. In the case of Dave, he saw an intelligent, well-educated man whom he trusted to work hard and make good decisions. Even though Dave's background had nothing to do with customer service, Peter valued these known traits more than the experience some unknown candidate might have brought to the table.

And at the moment that work ethic was on clear display. The director of customer service had fielded a phone call with a customer who worked at Hewlett-Packard and had trouble getting the PayPal software on his Palm Pilot to synchronize with our servers. "I'll be sure to look into it for you, sir, and call you back," Dave reassured him while jotting down some notes. "I don't think you can synch up your Palm from behind a firewall, but maybe there's a workaround that I can come up with." It seemed like a labor intensive assignment for the team's director to worry about, but he dealt with the inquiry in stride.

Watching Dave address a matter that was beneath his position in a field in which he had no experience at least suggested that I wasn't the only person in the company whose responsibilities were not set in stone. Employees' roles at Confinity were certainly more free-flowing than at Andersen, a firm that treated its own internal hierarchy with as much deference as the U.S. military. This stark difference and the flexibility it demanded would take some getting used to.

The morning crept along and I kept busy on my borrowed computer doing some odd tasks that Kenny had asked me to tackle. Nearly a month had passed since PayPal's launch and Confinity was gearing up for its first online advertising campaign. In need of somebody to do the initial legwork for the campaign, Kenny thrust the contact information for a dozen Internet advertising companies under my nose and requested that I call them to find out what their CPM rates were. I had no idea what CPM even stood for, but by this point I was happy just to have a role to play, even if that role meant sounding like a complete idiot on the phone with total strangers.

A few minutes later my impromptu orientation guide returned again, this time to announce triumphantly that he had located a spot for my desk and it only needed a small amount of work. I followed Kenny out into the central courtyard and back through the reception area, where we turned right into a darkened room I had not seen during my earlier tour around the office. "Here it is," he exclaimed as he flicked on the lights, "the ping pong room!"

I looked around at a twenty-by-twenty-foot room that sported no windows, one door, and a solitary piece of furniture—a folding ping pong table. Clearly the least desirable room in an otherwise open and bright office, the fact that such a tiny box had only earned the status of a seldom-used recreation space didn't surprise me.

"Great," I said, shrugging my shoulders. "But don't I need a desk and a computer?"

"Scott's going to bring you a computer in a couple of minutes," Kenny replied, referencing the IT guy. "As for a desk, I think they've ordered some more, but for now we're going to borrow a table."

The table in question turned out to be a banquet-sized rectangular slab of wood ensconced in the CFO's office. The CFO—David Jaques, a British national and the former treasurer of Silicon Valley Bank—remained at his desk, immersed in signing what appeared to be hundreds of checks by hand. He greeted us in a proper upper-class English accent but barely looked up as Kenny and I lumbered out of his office with the giant table.

The massive plank served as my makeshift workstation until I finished assembling my own particleboard desk over the weekend. With the help of several engineers, the displaced ping pong table made its way into David Sacks's cube. Taped to it was a copy of a commentary he had penned for *The San Francisco Chronicle* extolling the virtues of firms that empower young employees by giving them stock options and letting them do informal things like play ping pong. The engineers gleefully noted that since they had never actually seen the Chicago School of Law graduate set foot in the ping pong room, they wanted to help Sacks out by bringing the game to him.

◊

My unnerving hiring experience and disorderly first day on the job suggested that Confinity wasn't exactly a structured environment. While a young company with few resources devoted to HR and IT can be forgiven for not planning an orientation session for its new employees, this apparent chaos was still a little unsettling. As much as I didn't want to entertain the thought of it, by mid-afternoon on that first day I found myself wondering if my blind trust in Peter and eagerness to make a quick buck had led me into committing a terrible mistake.

Glancing around at my new physical surroundings, this was a reasonable conclusion to draw. The interior didn't look at all like Andersen's staid high-rise arrangement of staff consultants' nondescript cubicles sitting opposite their managers' glass encased offices. Heck, it didn't even resemble the dot-com work environments with vaulted ceilings and postmodern furniture shown in television commercials. Instead it felt more like a dorm. Board games, especially "Risk," littered the floors. Engineers collected old Domino's pizza boxes on their desks. Employees wore shorts and T-shirts to work, convenient attire when the occasional water gun fight broke out in the hallways. A ratty couch with sagging cushions sat next to the entrance of Max Levchin's office, which he shared with two other coders. Could anything but chaos come out of such a setting?

I had plenty of time during the afternoon to mull over that question as I sat largely ignored behind my mammoth desk. Might the youth of Confinity's employees be the source of the company's erratic behavior? I wondered. After all, the company's average employee was about twenty-five years old. At thirty-two, Peter was the second oldest person, and the rest of the business side of the company was around three to six years younger. Max was twenty-five, and most of the engineers that he had hired were either college classmates or people who were in the same age group. Only David Jaques, the CFO, could claim more than four decades. Maybe Confinity didn't act like a real company because too few of its people were old enough to know any better?

My musings were mercifully cut short when the receptionist—my first visitor in over an hour—stuck her head into the ping pong room and announced that Peter had called a company meeting. I gleefully sprung up and shot through the lobby toward the corner of the building where my twenty-six colleagues were beginning to congregate. Already some of them were lined up in both of the perpendicular aisles leading up to the space, with several employees opting to sit on the desks of nearby cubicles for a better view.

Peter stood in a small corner and chatted with David Jaques as he waited for people to arrive. When a sufficient number of his employees had sauntered in, Peter cleared his throat to quiet the din and began the impromptu assembly.

"It's been a little while since we've had one of these, and I think a lot of people have joined us since then," the CEO said. "Let's go around the room and have everyone say your name, when you started, and something about yourself." I did my best to memorize as many names as possible while thinking of a quip about my tenure with the old economy to introduce myself to my new colleagues.

"Now, for another piece of news," Peter casually added when the introductions wrapped up. "It looks like it's going to be a few more days before we close the next financing round." My jaw dropped—the imminence of the financing round, after all, was the reason I hastily left Andersen. "But don't worry, we're just haggling over details and we're oversubscribed. Everyone wants to invest in this company!

"And why not?" he went on. "We're definitely onto something big. The need PayPal answers is monumental. Everyone in the world needs money — to get paid, to trade, to live. Paper money is an ancient technology and an inconvenient means of payment. You can run out of it. It wears out. It can get lost or stolen. In the twenty-first century, people need a form of money that's more convenient and secure, something that can be accessed from anywhere with a PDA or an Internet connection.

"Of course, what we're calling 'convenient' for American users will be revolutionary for the developing world. Many of these countries' governments play fast and loose with their currencies," the former derivatives trader noted, before continuing, "They use inflation and sometimes wholesale currency devaluations, like we saw in Russia and several Southeast Asian countries last year, to take wealth away from their citizens. Most of the ordinary people there never have an opportunity to open an offshore account or to get their hands on more than a few bills of a stable currency like U.S. dollars.

"Eventually PayPal will be able to change this. In the future, when we make our service available outside the U.S. and as Internet penetration continues to expand to all economic tiers of people, PayPal will give citizens worldwide more direct control over their currencies than they ever had before. It will be nearly impossible for corrupt governments to steal wealth from their people through their old means because if they try the people will switch to dollars or Pounds or Yen, in effect dumping the worthless local currency for something more secure.

"Granted, that's still some time off," Peter continued, glancing around at the faces transfixed on him. "In the meantime our great Palm and Internet products are making quite a splash closer to home. Our user growth continues to ramp up nicely. I think we're going to generate a lot of media buzz in the next few weeks. I have no doubt that this company has the chance to become the Microsoft of payments, the financial operating system of the world." Everyone around me burst into a combination of laughter and applause. Though most had evidently heard a similar version of Peter's speech before, they still seemed to enjoy it.

For my part, I stood there with a reaction bordering on awestruck. I knew Peter was a deep thinker who held a strong sense of vision for the world, but when convincing me to join the company he spoke primarily of its great product and omitted any mention of these global aspirations. Now, hearing him articulate such a grand, sweeping mission for our little startup at an otherwise routine company meeting set me aback. Bold vision and corporate management don't always go hand-in-hand—the few Andersen executives who bothered to attend company events invariably had seemed content to stick to a few platitudes about excellence and empowerment, two qualities in short supply at that firm. Peter, on the other hand, offered a grandiose but specific vision for his company without mentioning the milestone most dot-com CEOs dwelt on—an initial public offering. Why would he? His talk about changing the very workings of international commerce made an IPO sound small by comparison.

There is a cynical interpretation to the speech, of course. Every successful company needs some form of a big-picture vision to guide its decision-making processes. Management teams also need to motivate their employees by making them feel that their company is somehow special. Both cases certainly applied to Confinity. But those observations alone don't diminish the magnitude of Peter's vision. Even though he never used the exact words, he was pledging to turn Confinity into nothing less than an initiator of the "creative destruction" that Joseph Schumpeter described sixty years earlier. He genuinely seemed to believe that this little startup had the ability to upend the world's financial systems by giving consumers unparalleled power over their own finances.

Say what you will about this vision's credibility, but in the days that followed his speech I became convinced that Peter wasn't the only person in the office who believed it. The company's Web site designer created a T-shirt that showed God and Adam from Michelangelo's Sistine Chapel ceiling exchanging cash with a pair of Palm Pilots. Many of the engineers carried around copies of *Cryptonomicon* by Neal Stephenson, a novel about the offspring of World War II army coders who conspired to build an offshore haven for encryption-protected data in Asia. In between the dings of the World Domination Index emitting from their computers, employees laughed that paper money was passé and insisted on using PayPal to settle their lunch bills and office pools. As a colleague in programming put it, why move atoms in order to exchange bits?

This belief that Confinity was developing something far more important than the standard e-commerce site that peddled groceries or pet food encountered little internal dissent. My colleagues genuinely thought that PayPal could change the world, and they spent far more time talking about this prospect than growing rich from a public stock offering. While I may have been lured out of the old economy by a longing for a more rewarding workplace and the promise of wealth, most employees only seemed concerned with creating something new and different—and in this case, that something held the potential to have a positive impact on the lives of millions.

It was this potential that made Confinity's vision of "world domination"—which might have been more appropriately called "world liberation"—all the more credible. The recent currency crises in Asia, Russia, and Latin America had shown that people around the globe really did need increased control over their own money. Many of the bouts of contagion that plagued currency markets in the late nineties were caused by governments trying to manipulate both exchange and interest rates. When investors caught on to these governments' slight-of-hand practices they began selling off the local currency, putting downward pressure on the exchange rate as countries doled out their reserves of U.S. dollars to traders who no longer wanted the local money. These sell-offs forced many countries to devalue their currencies by lowering their official exchange rate against the dollar, an action that effectively made the local currency worth less by weakening its global purchasing power. This in turn caused local prices to skyrocket which decreased the value of money held in savings accounts.

Whenever this scenario played out, the citizens of these countries—especially the poor and middle class, who seldom had access to offshore banking options—were always hit the hardest. If PayPal could find a way to empower these people to move and transfer money with the click of a mouse, then we would indeed be on the verge of creating something far more revolutionary than just a new way to split up dinner bills. As the use of the Internet spread, even the lower classes could theoretically whisk their money away to safety by exchanging it for a more stable foreign currency and storing it far away from the reach of their own floundering governments.

I may not have appreciated this potential when I hastily fled Andersen to join what at first seemed like a disorganized and chaotic startup, but in the days following Peter's speech I gradually began to understand its implications. A company staffed by young entrepreneurs who had set out to upend the world financial system couldn't be bothered with putting desks together or conducting formal orientations. Peter wanted to recruit good people—and fast. He needed them to help him pull off a technological revolution, and the specifics would just have to be sorted out later.

◊

As the days went by the details regarding my own ambiguous role with Confinity eventually became clearer. Early the following week I officially received a title—marketing manager—and a department. Along with Kenny Howery and Jennifer Chwang, the fiancée of my venture capitalist friend, I became a member of Confinity's new marketing group reporting to Luke Nosek.

The direct mail campaign that Kenny had tossed to me during my first day on the job turned out to be more than just busywork. PayPal's well-publicized launch and bonus promotions had steadily increased the number of users, and by this point in mid-December we had several hundred registering daily. But with an imminent infusion of cash from the upcoming venture round, Peter wanted to use some of the funds to scale up PayPal's user base even faster. In meetings with his team, Luke echoed this strategy. Growth, he insisted, was critical for a startup at this stage to deter potential competitors and position us to implement a business model that would begin to generate serious revenue.

With this focus, Luke tasked our team with introducing a combination of advertising banner and direct mail campaigns to acquire new customers. Caught up in this push, my transition from financial consultant to junior marketer didn't take long. Soon I found myself surfing direct marketing sites and calling smoozy salesmen to ask about their clickthrough rates and opt-in lists, terms I hadn't even known a few weeks earlier.

Meanwhile, David Sacks, collaborating with a public relations agency, worked on refining Confinity's image in advance of this major marketing push. Inspired by an article titled "Beam Me Up Some Money, Scotty" that profiled our Palm wallet, Sacks suggested that the company hire Star Trek actor James Doohan as Confinity's spokesman.[4] It sounded like a good idea—Scotty was a recognizable character and the beam branding complemented our Palm product. The Star Trek celebrity spokesman route had also served another dot-com well. Priceline, the online travel service, rocketed in popularity when it unveiled a series of commercials featuring William Shatner (Captain Kirk) reading Beat poetry that described the benefits of its Web site. If Priceline could venture to the final frontier, then why not Confinity?

Within a few days our agency inked a deal with Doohan to endorse PayPal. However, Scotty would not be following Captain Kirk back onto the TV screen—at least not initially. Forthcoming venture capital infusion or not, Confinity's cash on hand was in the millions, not hundreds of millions, so a Super Bowl commercial remained out of the question. Peter and the other executives harbored a basic mistrust of television's ability to generate Internet users. The TV ads used by so many other dot-coms, they maintained, were generally expensive, untargeted, and—because they required a viewer to remember a particular Web site when he later sat down at a computer—less cost effective than online promotions. Instead we opted to have Doohan preside over a media event to kick off PayPal's growth campaign. Scotty would use his "beam me up" message on our Web site and e-mails to introduce our futuristic service to potential customers.

But before work on the user acquisition campaign shifted into high gear, the company paused to collect its breath. If "world domination" was to be the eventual outcome, Peter realized camaraderie and team-work were necessary ingredients. He scheduled an afternoon for the company's holiday offsite party so employees could relax and bond away from the office before making a final pre-holiday push.

Employees caravanned over from the office to the party, held at a meeting facility on Sand Hill Road in adjacent Menlo Park. For anyone not familiar with the reference, Sand Hill is to venture capital what Wall Street is to the stock market. A broad, ambling road in the undeveloped foothills behind Stanford University, Sand Hill houses many of Silicon Valley's top venture capital firms and provided four-fifths of the funds that poured into California startups during the late 1990s. This might be hard to guess just by looking at the road itself; most of the buildings nestled along it could not be called noteworthy. Typically two or three stories with wooden facades and nondescript signs, the offices convey a message of frugality to visiting entrepreneurs in search of money.

The afternoon began with drinks and appetizers served by a blazing fireplace in a large lounge. After mingling over cocktails for a half-hour, the group migrated into a private dining room occupied by large, round tables. Looking around, I realized I still had not met all of my colleagues. In just the week that I had been with the company another six employees had joined, and the list of open positions posted on the Web site was still long and growing.

A few minutes passed before Peter picked up a microphone and headed to the front of the room. After thanking the employees for their hard work, he mentioned that Confinity had added many new faces. Instead of calling on each person to introduce himself as he had done at the company meeting, this time Peter went around the room and gave the name and job of each employee. When he arrived at David Sacks, someone playfully cried out "old huff and puff!" to the amusement of the engineers. Sacks, who did often gallop through the office on his way to the desk of an unsuspecting victim for an impromptu meeting, grumbled back, "I hope that branding doesn't stick."

After finishing with the last table, Peter gestured toward a man standing in the back. "Finally, for those of you who don't know him, I'd like to introduce Reid Hoffman," he said. "Reid is the founder of SocialNet.com and is a member of our board. Starting next week, Reid is going to come on full-time as president, reporting directly to me. He'll be in charge of operations and day-to-day matters, letting me spend more time on setting our strategic vision and financing."

Compared to Peter's thin profile, Reid sported a wide frame and a smile to match. His curly hair and glasses gave him a friendly, approachable look which he reinforced with a couple of brief remarks. "Thanks, Peter. Now, I haven't officially started yet, so it's going to be a couple of weeks before you will see me around the office all day. I've met some of you already, and over the next few days I'll try to stop by and get to know everyone personally."

I hadn't met Reid before, but I later learned that he and Peter were old friends from Stanford, meaning he was a person whom Peter could trust. While this development surprised many of the people in the room, I certainly understood why Peter envisioned Reid in this operational role. Confinity's internal growth could benefit from full time supervision, and, considering Peter's background in finance and his hands-off approach to management, it seemed logical that he'd want some assistance in running this company.

From my workstation near the office's reception area, I saw firsthand how much of Peter's time went into securing financing for the company. In the days following the holiday party a steady stream of potential investors trotted in and out of our offices. Yet even the Japanese businessman whom an engineer accidentally struck in the head with a remote-controlled dirigible went away undeterred.

The parade continued for several more weeks until Peter finally closed the company's second round; it was a full month after the expected date, but with $23 million in cash in the bank, it seemed worth the delay. Goldman Sachs and IdeaLab Capital Partners, the investing arm of a startup incubator service, provided the bulk of the money.[5] Although Steve Kuo's company ended up backing out when they couldn't pull a syndicate together, from the vantage point inside Confinity we still did quite well by lining up a large infusion of cash from such prestigious partners. Or so it seemed at the time; a couple of months later actions by one of our investors would force us to conclude otherwise.

◊

In the days following the holiday party we scrambled to finalize the Scotty promotion. Sacks, Luke, and I settled on a plan to have Scotty use the upcoming press event as a publicity stunt to beam $1 million to randomly selected recipients all over the Web using PayPal's Palm Pilot application. The news would hit the media, we thought, and over the weeks to come Internet users across the country would eagerly look for an e-mail from Scotty telling them they had cash waiting at PayPal's Web site. I would use our online direct mail campaign to distribute these notices from Scotty, allowing us to bank on our new spokesman to drive tens of thousands of people to our site.

The entire event came together in about a week. We booked the posh Westin Saint Francis hotel in San Francisco's Union Square. Our PR agency began calling media outlets to drum up interest. And the press release Sacks and I drafted described the event with dot-com flair:

> PayPal.com introduced James Doohan—widely known for his role as "Scotty" on Star Trek—as the company's official spokesman. "I've been beaming people up my whole career," Doohan quipped, "but this is the first time I've ever been able to beam money!" While remarking on PayPal.com's cutting-edge technology, Doohan also stressed how easy it is to use… [H]is "Scotty" character may have explored the frontier of space, [but] James Doohan and PayPal.com are heralding a new frontier of wireless, person-to-person payments.[6]

The stunt seemed foolproof. We were an up-and-coming dot-com with a celebrity spokesman. We'd planned an attention-grabbing display of our product, and we had a great facility reserved for the show. The media would surely eat this up—it seemed nothing could go wrong. That is, until Scotty actually touched down in Palo Alto.

James Doohan was spry and full of life—for his age. When Sacks had his brainstorm about hiring Star Trek's Scotty to be PayPal's spokesman no one had realized that the star was now well into his eighties.

Though alert and happy in his new role as corporate pitchman, Doohan knew little about the Internet, PDAs, encryption, and PayPal. This glaring problem became evident when he arrived at our office and Jennifer tried explaining our service to him. While he gregariously handed out autographed Scotty magnets to the staff, it dawned on us that we might have a problem. In twenty-four hours this man would be paraded in front of the inquisitive press at a media event where he was supposed to use a Palm to beam $1 million all around the globe and he had no idea what PayPal did.

Ironically, it didn't matter.

The following day our extravagant room at the Saint Francis was sparsely populated. Confinity employees outnumbered the media four-to-one. And none of the half-dozen reporters who stopped by to munch *hors d'oeuvres* went on to write about the event. Doohan and Peter ultimately went through the motions of beaming $1 million with a pair of Palm Pilots, and Peter used the moment to give an impromptu pep talk to his employees.

Encouraging words and upscale surroundings did little to hide the truth—our Scotty event flopped. For a startup full of young people who believed they were on the verge of changing the world, failure was a new and unwelcome experience. While PayPal had the potential to overhaul the global financial system, until we could develop a succinct message of how people could use it for their everyday lives, our futuristic vision and Star Trek spokesman weren't going to attract the kind of attention we wanted.

My crestfallen colleagues and I gradually trickled out of the mahog-any-lined hotel lobby into the chilly San Francisco air. It was only one minor setback, but for the first time since hearing Peter's speech I realized that the road to "world domination" would be a long one.

CHAPTER TWO

BREAKTHROUGH

IF WE HAD INTENDED the Scotty event to herald the start of PayPal's journey to a new payments frontier, imagine our surprise when we learned that another company was racing with us to the same destination. The week after our botched press conference, and just six weeks after the launch of Confinity's payment platform, a copycat version of PayPal burst onto the scene.

I first caught word of it while getting a second cup of morning coffee from Confinity's well-stocked kitchen. The considerable hours I suddenly found myself spending at work, coupled with my hour-long drive to and from San Francisco, had forced me to cut back on my sleep time dramatically. As I rummaged through the refrigerator looking for half-and-half my late morning caffeine jolt, David Sacks and Luke Nosek strode the hall in a heated discussion about a project Sacks called the "dotBank features." From the tone of their voices, I could tell something significant had happened.

Coffee in hand I shot out of the kitchen, crossed the tiny courtyard and returned to my desk in the ping-pong room. I anxiously typed "dotbank.com" into my Internet browser, my heart skipping a beat as I looked over the clean, blue Web site that appeared on my monitor. DotBank's service mimicked the basic PayPal payment functionality, allowing users to input a recipient's e-mail address and fund their transactions with a credit card. Displaying another familial trait, dotBank was taking advantage of customer referrals by giving away $5 to anyone who opened an account or referred a friend.

I slumped at my desk, crestfallen. After a week and a half with Confinity I had just begun to appreciate the brilliance of PayPal's product. The Web site and Palm versions of our person-to-person payment services were both easy to navigate and useful. Watching several hundred new customers sign up each day, I couldn't help but begin to believe we were on the cusp of something revolutionary. But suddenly here was another dot-com ripping off Peter and Max's amazing idea. With Confinity's patent application for using an e-mail address as a unique identifier still in its early stages, any legal remedy would be years away. There was nothing we could do to prevent dotBank from entering our market.

In some respects dotBank did more than just copy PayPal; aspects of its service were better. While it did not have PDA software for Palm Pilots, dotBank did have a pair of online features that promised to enhance its growth prospects. A money request feature enabled its users to send an electronic invoice to a third party. The e-mail would tell the recipient the requested amount, give him a list of instructions for using dotBank to pay the bill, and provide a link to the dotBank site. A second feature for group payments allowed a user to send a money request to several people at once and track who made a payment. It was an intuitive way to facilitate payments for club dues or dinner bills with large groups, the kinds that we'd been touting as uses for PayPal. Both of these features would increase the ease with which dotBank's customers could conduct payments with others, and in the process attract non-users to dotBank's site.

The presence of a competitor capable of putting together such a slick Web site sent shock waves through our office. Outrage quickly turned to urgency as Peter ordered product manager Jamie Templeton to get the engineers working on a response. If there was any consolation to dotBank's launch, it was that its features could be replicated. In fact, both the money request and group payments tools had been on Confinity's planning list for a while but development had been delayed to pursue other matters. No longer. Peter instructed Jamie to have the engineers get the "dotBank features" live on PayPal's site before anyone took time off for Christmas, by then less than a week away.

The programmers tackled the assignment with an intensity and focus that I could not have imagined during my traumatic first day on the job. The whiff of chaos that shaped my initial impressions of Confinity remained undetected this time. To the contrary, although the engineers debated with Jamie and Max over the best way to execute specific points of the strategy, everyone knew the role they were being asked to assume and plunged into it with fervor. A challenge had been placed in front of them, and the company's needs—to keep PayPal a step ahead of the competition—were clear. Unlike the minions of Andersen, for whom assignments seemed to be randomly handed down from on high, this youthful team of coders knew it had an important task to address and felt empowered to influence the way that job would be done. This caused them to band together and pour their energy into finding a response to this competitive threat.

But even as our programming team raced to build an answer to dot-Bank, two days later another challenger sprouted up from an unexpected place. X.com, an ambiguous financial Web site with a name to match, launched its own payments service. If dotBank's launch concerned Peter, X.com's entrance into payments made him livid. Up until Confinity's move to 165 University Avenue a few months earlier, the two companies had been neighbors in a building just down the street.

Elon Musk founded X.com in early 1999 after selling his previous company, an online map service named Zip2, to Compaq for $307 million.[1] He set up his new venture in a small suite of offices overlooking a bakery that shared common space with Confinity. Although the two companies had no reason to communicate formally, the employees often bumped into one another in the entrance and restrooms. When Confinity relocated six months later, X.com expanded into the space formerly occupied by its neighbor.

Though the name might suggest otherwise, X.com's original business plan had nothing to do with pornography or Generation X. Its goal was to become the ultimate one-stop financial portal where users could take care of all their cash and investment needs. X.com made a media splash when Elon lured Bill Harris, the former CEO of software maker Intuit, to head the venture. Harris bragged to *The Wall Street Journal* that he had received CEO offers from more than one hundred startups but chose X.com because he saw it as "a blank canvas upon which to write new rules on the delivery of financial services."[2]

X.com also generated some additional buzz toward the end of 1999 with a no-fee, no-minimum balance S&P 500 index fund, the only one of its kind.[3] This loss leader product had been rationalized as a way to attract new users who could be up-sold to X.com's other financial products, including its bond and money market funds, interest-bearing checking accounts, and low APR credit lines. X.com certainly seemed eager to become a financial services supermarket, but Confinity had not seen any sign that it held an interest in following PayPal into person-to-person payments.

Yet here it was. Sometime over the previous month, X.com had quietly built an e-mail-based payment feature on top of its existing bank account service and had turned itself into a formidable competitor. With banking functionality that allowed account holders to write checks, withdraw funds at ATMs, and enjoy a $500 overdraft credit line, X.com accounts had far more financial bells and whistles than our payments-only service. X.com also doubled PayPal's new user bonus by tempting would-be customers with a $20 deposit for opening an account. Referrals earned $10, the same as PayPal, but X.com made getting the word out to friends and family easier by providing its users with a customized URL they could forward through e-mail. Anyone who clicked on the link and signed up would be credited as a referral to the user's account.

X.com, just like dotBank, launched its payments service with many features designed solely to spur user growth. PayPal had a race on its hands, and it became clear there would be no prize for second place.

◊

Peter Thiel often claimed that growth was the most critical objective for a business like Confinity. Our CEO maintained that creating a successful payments service could only happen if we achieved something called a network effect. An interactive, inter-connected system, he explained, could exist only if it conferred value on the people who voluntarily chose to join it. The more people participating in it, the more beneficial the network would become since all the members could interact together. Hence a large, established network is very valuable to enter and very costly to leave; in essence it locks in its members and prevents would-be competitors from getting off the ground.

Telephones are a good example of a network. The first pair of phones used by Alexander Graham Bell and Thomas Watson offered little value beyond demonstrating a new technology. But as telephones began to proliferate over the following century, the benefit of having one increased exponentially as the number of people and companies that could be reached using it also grew. The more people who had phones, the more people wanted phones. Now telephones are so ubiquitous that many of us carry a mobile one at all times.

Similarly, the advantage of participating in a payments service like PayPal increases as the number of other users goes up. If only a handful of people in the world accept money through PayPal, there is little benefit to taking the time to create an account. But if PayPal can be used to pay millions of people, the account is much more valuable. Robert Metcalfe, the inventor of Ethernet and founder of 3Com, coined Metcalfe's Law as a way of understanding the power of networks. He claimed that the value of a network equals the square of its users, implying that a network with twice as many users as a competitor is four times as valuable.[4]

Given Peter's firm belief in the importance of quickly scaling up our network, it didn't surprise anyone that the calmness he displayed at the disappointing Scotty event was absent following the dotBank and X.com launches. He pushed hard on the engineering team to add dotBank's money request and group billing features to our site before Christmas, and later to duplicate X.com's customized referral link. Peter acted as if the future of PayPal hung in the balance during those stressful days in mid-December, and the engineers rose to the occasion and met his deadlines.

The marketing team also received the call from Peter to play a role in responding to the launch of our competitors. We kept the user acquisition plan that Luke had laid out earlier in the month but expedited its timeframe. My own small piece of the puzzle, the online direct mail campaign, fell into place just as our new competitors revealed themselves. After interviewing a score of opt-in subscription services, I chose a mailing company that offered lists with tech-loving "early adopters," including Palm users and college students.

I wrote the campaign's makeshift e-mail promotion to sound as though it came from Scotty. Utilitarian and a far cry from any best practice, this was Confinity's first significant marketing effort since employees sent money to everyone in their address books eight weeks earlier. And, coming as it did right after the unveiling of two competitors, I knew management would closely scrutinize the results from my first project with the company.

Things went better than I'd hoped. The next day's daily user update from Jamie Templeton showed that our sign-ups had spiked to several times their normal level. Employees expressed awe as the World Domination Index ratcheted up by more than 1,000 customers overnight. The promising results attracted Peter's attention and prompted him to call Luke, Sacks, and me into his austere office to discuss them.

"What did the cost per user acquisition work out to?" Peter asked, getting quickly to the point by collecting the data he believed was needed to make a decision.

"A little less than $20 per account, but we'll see that come down a little over the next few days as more recipients read the e-mail and sign up," I noted.

"That's really good," Peter replied, leaning back in his chair and pausing to calculate some figures in his head. When he finally opened his mouth again, the words that came out surprised me. "We need to scale this up quickly. How fast can you spend $1 million?"

"One million?" I parroted. For someone used to dealing with managers who demanded that subordinates submit two forms with an attached receipt just to get a $5 reimbursement, being asked to spend $1 million was new territory. I told him I'd have to do some quick research and get back to him.

"How about in the next two weeks?" The CEO shot me a smile, but I could tell he was serious.

The impromptu meeting disbanded and I left knowing that I had my work cut out for me. Over the following days I scoured the demographics of every reputable Web-based direct mail service that I could locate. I booked dates for as many early adopter mailing lists as possible, but with each e-mail costing between 5¢ and 10¢ I concluded that there might not be enough technology geeks in the country to spend the entire amount Peter had authorized. I needed additional groups to target, but selecting those groups was not going to be an easy task. Our young company lacked any significant market research capabilities. To meet Peter's mandate to grow our user base quickly, I'd be on my own in selecting new demographics.

Online auction shoppers immediately came to mind. Ironically, I had never even bid on an online auction, much less taken the time to list an item for sale. But like all observers of the Internet, I was well aware that they were fast becoming a pop culture phenomenon. The sector had received a fair amount of media buzz since industry leader eBay's IPO in September 1998, and lately I had noticed that even my non-technical friends were turning to auctions to hunt for bargains and hard-to-find collectibles alike.

Acting on this hunch, I pointed my browser to eBay's Web site. A cursory glance instantly dispelled my misconception that auctions were only for kitschy collectibles like Beanie Babies and Furbies—the site had books, clothes, videos, and even computer equipment for sale among its millions of listings. This simple, brightly colored site was facilitating a lot of commerce and at the same time attracting a diverse group of users. And from the looks of things, these users stood to benefit greatly from a person-to-person payment service like PayPal.

Unlike shoppers on major e-commerce sites like Amazon.com, the vast majority of eBay's buyers could not use a credit card to pay for their purchases. Most of the service's sellers either hawked their wares part-time or otherwise recorded too few sales to qualify for a merchant's credit card processing account. This meant that buyers typically had to mail checks or money orders to their seller in the amount of their winning bid. The time the payments spent in the mail, plus the time required for personal checks to clear, added about a week to the waiting period that high bidders had to endure just to receive their treasure. It was a clumsy process for an Internet service, one that PayPal could clearly improve.

Yet even though my hunch that auction users had a need for an instant payment service like PayPal seemed right, it didn't necessarily follow that PayPal needed these auction users. In fact, I had been told by one member on the executive team that auction traders would not make good PayPal users. Being less tech-savvy than Palm users and college kids, this logic went, they'd be too cautious to sign up, much less be willing to keep balances in their PayPal accounts. If I made the call to invest a significant amount of funds to pursue this demographic, while it might help me meet Peter's ambitious marketing target, it would also leave me vulnerable to criticism for pursuing a demographic the company didn't want.

In search of information to help me decide if this gamble was worth taking, I stumbled across the message board section of eBay's site. Filled with hundreds of online discussions between community members, the message boards contained lively and wide-ranging conversations on a variety of topics, many of them business-oriented. Reading the posts prompted me to conclude that these users were more sophisticated than the popular perception gave them credit for; not only would they understand how to use PayPal's service, but they'd also eagerly adopt it. If Peter wanted us to pursue rapid growth, this crowd looked like a good candidate. I decided to add auction users to the campaign and apologize later if my hunch turned out wrong.

When the data from the campaign came back later in the week the results were encouraging. Auction users registered with roughly the same frequency as technophiles, so I made them a fixture in my future campaigns as I pressed on with my charge of getting as many users as $1 million could buy.

As the clock struck 2000 and people from around the world celebrated the Millennium, PayPal seemed to be firing on all cylinders. The combination of the site's referral bonuses, engineering's new features, and marketing's advertising campaigns helped speed up our daily registrations, propelling us past the 10,000 account mark less than two months after launching the service. Like everyone else, I was merely trying to carry out my duties to the best of my ability with the hope of generating the account growth that Peter sought. And I did so having no idea what the consequences of my minor act of rebellion would be.

◊

Luke Nosek and David Sacks were PayPal's odd couple. Luke, a Chicago transplant who'd moved to the U.S. from Poland as a child, was outgoing and creative. His focus, much like his wavy hair, had a habit of bouncing from place to place without much warning. Yet unlike so many intellectuals who seem to care more about ideas than people, Luke took an active interest in those around him. A graduate of the University of Illinois at Urbana-Champaign's computer science department, Luke possessed a genuine love of technology and seemed equally comfortable talking with engineers as with strategists. This was a major reason Max sought out his former schoolmate when he started Confinity—he felt Luke could serve as a go-between for the business and technical sides of the company.[5]

Sacks, on the other hand, exuded focus. A lot of focus. Everyone in the company knew of his tendency to descend on a colleague out of nowhere and initiate an in-depth conversation. With short, dark hair, wire glasses, and a habit of making sweeping gestures, Sacks came across as intense, especially in Confinity's informal office. He certainly didn't seem as interested in socializing as Luke. Though an avid movie buff, this law graduate spent jaw-dropping amounts of time at work. He seldom left the office before three o'clock in the morning and generally found his way back by eleven.

Given their contrasting styles and mannerisms, most of us found it ironic that Luke and Sacks wound up sharing a very compact office. However much these two young vice presidents clashed in approach and temperament, it was out of their six-by-six-foot room that one of the most pivotal realizations in PayPal's history emerged. Shortly after I began my marketing campaign, Sacks received an e-mail from a customer seeking the company's permission to use the PayPal logo. Sacks followed a link in the message that took him to an eBay auction. The user had created an HTML banner for PayPal to display in his auction. The banner featured PayPal's logo and linked back to our Web site. The auction's owner evidently thought that adding this homemade banner into his listing would be an easy way to earn a few extra $10 referral bonuses from PayPal.

As Sacks looked at the customer's auction, something clicked. He called over to Luke. Studying it together, they realized this seller had turned his auction into far more than a format to receive bids—he had created an advertisement for PayPal. A quick search showed that this wasn't the only listing featuring PayPal. When Sacks typed "PayPal" into eBay's search engine, it revealed that several thousand of eBay's nearly 4 million listings also mentioned our service.

As it turned out, including a reference to PayPal in an eBay auction was simple. While the top of an eBay auction is a standardized header that includes the auction's title, the seller's feedback rating, and the high bid amount, the body of the listing is customizable. With some simple HTML a seller can design unique backgrounds and images for his listing. Item descriptions can be long and detailed, often running the length of several screens, or as terse and direct as just a couple of sentences.

Most of eBay's frequent sellers develop a template for their auction descriptions. Using a basic layout multiple times cuts down on the administrative hassle required in posting dozens—sometimes hundreds or even thousands—of items on eBay's site. As well as saving time, this gives all of the seller's auctions a consistent look and feel, a critical step for any small business selling through eBay that seeks to develop a brand and customer base of its own.

As he scoured the Web site, Sacks found that eBay sellers were incorporating PayPal into their auction descriptions in different ways. Most included clickable hyperlinks to our homepage, a few pasted in copies of the PayPal logo, and some even wrote lengthy stylized narratives describing how to sign up for PayPal. These sellers had seized onto PayPal as a convenient way to get paid for their auctions and they were happy to steer their buyers toward it. And if anyone looking at their listing read their commentary about PayPal and decided to sign up, the $10 referral bonus didn't hurt, either.

PayPal also proved a hot topic on eBay's discussion boards, with the conversation topics varying from the practical to the paranoid. Is PayPal safe? How do I get my money out? How many referral bonuses have you earned? What happens to my money if PayPal shuts down?

A couple of weeks after I had gambled marketing dollars by sending a promotion to auction users, Sacks had stumbled onto proof that PayPal was beginning to take root in eBay's online community. Even if our executive team had initially wanted to avoid this demographic, some combination of PayPal's easy-to-use service, Confinity's generous referral bonuses, and my marketing campaign had already planted the seed. Now it was time for us to help it grow.

◊

"This is the Internet," Luke proclaimed solemnly, scribbling on a white board in Confinity's lone conference room. At his request, about ten people from the business side of the company had assembled at the office for an emergency Saturday afternoon meeting in mid-January.

Luke gesticulated with his free hand as he jabbed dozens of blue dots at random intervals around the board. "People on the Internet are spread out all over the place," he said, simultaneously adding to the flurry of blue dots and trying to explain his thinking to a puzzled crowd. Then, connecting some of the dots by drawing lines between them, he went on: "There are a few people over here, and they interact with their group—and there are more over here, and they interact with each other. But the problem is all these little groups are scattered across the Net." He stepped back to look at the several small clusters of dots and lines.

"Our model has always called for PayPal to rely on viral growth—spreading like a virus from one person to the next as they pay each other. But it's tricky because people are so dispersed." By this point Luke had become quite animated and was swinging his arms in big circles. Sensing that he was about to go off on a tangent, my mind started to wander.

This better be worthwhile, I thought, regretting that I had left my girlfriend Beatrice to wrestle with boredom back at my desk. Days off had become few and far between since I joined Confinity, so listening to our vice president prattle on about abstractions seemed like the least appealing way I could think of to spend a Saturday.

But Luke did have a point, and it was a crucial one.

"So what I've drawn is the Internet overall, but now this is eBay." Luke began jabbing the center of the white board repeatedly with his blue marker. As he spoke, the dozens of blue dots began to overlap and form a dense ball. "It's the busiest place for person-to-person interactions on the Internet. People from all over the Web come here to use this site. So, for PayPal to grow rapidly and expand all over the Internet, the quickest way to do that is to first grow on eBay!"

Luke went on to explain that since dotBank and X.com were now competing with Confinity, Peter and the management team believed that we needed to find the fastest way possible to scale up PayPal's customer base. If we could increase our number of accounts to reach critical mass before our competitors, the resulting network effect would freeze out any opponents. Potential users would not waste time signing up for multiple accounts with different payment services if PayPal were ubiquitous. But if we failed and another service outpaced us, then there probably would be nothing we could do to catch up.

Although stopping short of defining how many users constituted critical mass, the management team did agree that customer acquisition had to take on a higher importance than profitability in the short run. We couldn't worry about whether eBay users would keep large balances in their PayPal accounts—we just had to concentrate our efforts on this popular auction site where there was an obvious need for faster and easier person-to-person transactions. We would build PayPal's payments network on top of eBay's marketplace.

"For the next several months," Luke continued, "all of our work is going to focus on eBay. For marketing, all of our direct mails should be to auction users. And, since we can't buy advertising directly on eBay's site, we'll get online banners and magazine ads in other places where eBay users go.

"For engineering, we're going to freeze the other projects we're working on." At this point, Jamie Templeton, knowing what this would do to engineering morale, groaned. Luke went on: "We've got to make it easy for auction sellers to earn referral bonuses by driving sign-ups. We'll design a tool that sellers can use to put PayPal referral logos in all their auctions for them. That way everyone who looks at their listings can learn about PayPal, and all they have to do is click on the logo to register."

Some in the room may not have completely appreciated it at the time, but Luke's animated description painted an accurate picture of eBay's amazing size and reach. The four year old service boasted 10 million registered users by the end of 1999, a 350% increase from the 2.2 million on file just a year earlier.[6] By the second half of 1999, analysts estimated that the site averaged 3 million live listings every day and accounted for 70% of the year's approximate $4.5 billion in online auction sales. With Gomez Advisors forecasting that the size of the auction market would swell to $15.5 billion by the year 2001, eBay's phenomenal growth seemed poised to accelerate.[7]

EBay's financial success masked its humble origins. When Pierre Omidyar created a site called AuctionWeb over the course of Labor Day weekend in 1995, he didn't view it as the start of an e-commerce juggernaut but rather as a simple hobby.[8] Wary of the entrance of big business into cyberspace, Omidyar wanted to build a site where the little guy had a chance to buy and sell wares on a level playing field. He announced the service by posting on several newsgroups, and by mid-September users listed a total of thirty items for sale on his site. It was after successfully selling his own broken laser pointer through the service that Omidyar first realized that AuctionWeb looked like a viable business. He soon started charging sellers a percent fee on their sales and his fledgling company immediately became profitable.

As the service grew, Omidyar tried to foster a sense of community with its users. Commerce should exist alongside community, he reasoned, and to facilitate that he set up message boards to allow users to talk directly to one another and answer each other's questions. Proclaiming that his company believed that "people are basically good," he asked his users to take advantage of this platform to make new friends but to never forget to "treat others the way you want to be treated."[9] Fortunately this hippy-capitalist mantra about the innate goodness of people didn't stop Omidyar from introducing a policing mechanism to his site; in order to encourage the community to play by the rules, he built a user feedback system to display public reports of deal-breaking.

Omidyar's site turned into a growing company, and that company went on to evolve a great deal over the following years. A name change, a veteran CEO, and a public stock offering later, eBay looked nothing like the business Omidyar ran from out of his house, although it still retained some of its original community characteristics. The thirteenth most trafficked Web site in late 1999, visitors to eBay held longer sessions and returned more often than the customers of any other e-commerce location.[10]

It was on this mammoth, community-centric auction site that Peter, Sacks, Luke, Max and Reid had decided to one-up my marketing campaign and gamble PayPal's future. If we could use eBay to propel our service past dotBank and X.com, we would be well on our way to revolutionizing the field of payments and achieving "world domination." But if the gamble failed we had no backup—it would be all or nothing.

◊

Confinity wasted no time mobilizing. In a shift every bit as significant as Fieldlink's move away from Palm security, overnight we changed PayPal's focus from payments between friends to online auction transactions.

While our Scotty event had bombed in part due to our inability to offer a succinct description of what PayPal should be used for, we now had a single message to convey. The company's solitary HTML designer overhauled the PayPal Web site and placed a large "Auction Payments" link at the top of the homepage, just under the PayPal logo. He also added a new auction tab to the site's navigation to explain PayPal's benefits to buyers and sellers. Reflecting their decreased importance, the request money, group billing, and Palm Pilot features—which just a few weeks before seemed critical to the future of our service—were given second billing and lumped together under a "Personal Payments" section.

The marketing team shifted all of its customer acquisition efforts to auction users. Kenny Howery inventoried a list of several dozen auction-related services comprised largely of niche specialty sites such as Numismatists.com and aspiring mini-eBays like BoxLot to inquire about advertising space. Jennifer Chwang placed ads in a variety of collectible magazines, and I continued in my efforts to spend $1 million on direct mail. (After maxing out every reputable direct mailer, I ultimately came up about $600,000 short.)

Jamie and the engineers set out working on an auction logo insertion tool. By providing eBay sellers with a clickable HTML logo to put in their auctions, we hoped to make it easier for them to educate their bidders about PayPal. Besides giving them a more efficient way to prompt their winning bidders to use our service, the logos would allow sellers the opportunity to make money off all other visitors to their auctions by earning $10 referral bonuses. As sellers used their listings to train buyers to look for PayPal, buyers would in turn learn to ask sellers who weren't using PayPal if they could pay with our service. PayPal customers in eBay's community would recruit other users for us—it was viral growth in its most basic form.

Engineering finished the auction logo insertion tool in a matter of days. Named AutoLink because it automatically linked to existing eBay auctions and added a PayPal logo to the bottom, the feature could be activated by customers from the PayPal Web site. The only catch was that since eBay's Web site required users to first log in before updating an auction, AutoLink needed the PayPal customer to submit his eBay username and password to be activated.

This requirement ultimately didn't deter customers from using AutoLink; since they trusted PayPal to handle their money, most of them realized they could trust PayPal to insert a logo for them. The feature caught on and the impact was immediately evident. We ran daily searches with eBay's search tool for the word PayPal to estimate how many auctions accepted our service. This figure started out around 1%-2% of auction listings but began to grow rapidly. Our "listing share," as we called it, marched steadily upward toward around 6% by February.

Just as we began to roll out our auction strategy and quantify our position in our new market, PayPal reached a significant milestone. In late January we registered our 100,000th account. As a countdown to the event, our receptionist pasted a large thermometer made out of white construction paper to the wall of our lobby. Each day she used a red marker to fill in another portion of the thermometer and the company watched as we drew closer to the 100,000 figure at the top. When PayPal finally reached the mark, we held a party complete with six cakes—one sported the number "1" on top, and the other five each had a "0."

While 100,000 users might have been somewhat short of our ill-defined goal of critical mass, it was still a major accomplishment. During the eight weeks since the day Luke introduced me to the World Domination Index while interviewing me for a job I already had, the number of PayPal accounts had increased by over 4,000%.

Unfortunately the euphoria from our customer acquisition success proved short-lived. X.com, watching every change on our Web site, followed us onto eBay within a matter of days. Our competitor soon launched its own version of an HTML logo for auction sellers, and banner ads for its service began to appear on some of the very same auction sites that Kenny had called just days before. X.com also re-vamped the content on its homepage, toning down the "all your financial services in one place" messaging in favor of descriptions touting its ability to conduct auction payments.

X.com's decision to duplicate Confinity's actions was fair play. We had done the same thing with dotBank's features just a month before. And, even if the X.com team hadn't grasped the value of entering the eBay auctions market on its own, Elon Musk's company did understand what Confinity was up to before we could seize a commanding lead. In an online world where all it takes is several hundred lines of code and a handful of HTML pages to overhaul an entire business, being able to adapt to competitive changes is critical for survival, something I would see demonstrated again and again in the years to come.

By contrast dotBank, a company that had appeared nimble by developing money request and group billing features for its launch just six weeks before, chose not to join Confinity in the pursuit of eBay. Whether it was a breakdown in the company's ability to execute, a lack of funding, or a failure to see the value in building a payments network on top of eBay's existing marketplace is unclear, but dotBank did not roll out any significant campaigns to enter the auction market. Instead, dotBank limited itself to providing users with a couple of Web site logos while muddling its referral program to try to make it appear as if new users received $500 for registering.[11] It came as no surprise that our daily queries to determine eBay listing share showed that while X.com was beginning to grow and trailed PayPal's total by about 2%-3%, dotBank gained no traction on eBay at all.

For now, X.com was the only competitor facing down PayPal in the battle for eBay. And we were determined to stay a step ahead.

◊

As Confinity and X.com revamped their strategies to pursue growth on eBay, both companies did so without an official business relationship with the auction giant. This wasn't necessarily a problem since eBay tended to treat its site as an open marketplace, meaning it took an agnostic view toward the tools and third party services used by customers so long as they did not provide an unfair advantage or impede the operation of its Web site. This was in keeping with Omidyar's philosophical leanings. An engineer who disapproved of well-connected players obtaining advantages unavailable to the little guy, Omidyar thought that eBay should be a level playing field that allowed all manner of buyers and sellers to compete.

And yet there was a reason to suspect that this level playing field might not always exist for PayPal. In May 1999 eBay announced the acquisition of a credit card processing firm called Billpoint. Billpoint, itself a startup still in product testing mode at the time of purchase, was lauded by Mike Wilson, the head of eBay's product development, as a way to speed up transactions on its Web site by cutting down the time necessary to exchange money.

Facilitating credit card payments, however, also exposed eBay to a risk previously borne only by its users—transaction fraud. If a transaction somehow went wrong or involved fraud on the part of one of the parties, eBay could find itself on the hook for the funds. Entering into auction payments of course meant this was also true for Confinity, but our focus on growth dictated that we would have to confront this problem as we went along. But eBay, a publicly traded company that took pride in being profitable since its first month of operations, felt it needed to make sure that any risk was minimized. "Billpoint and others have developed technology to detect fraud in this area," Wilson said at the time, trying to reassure investors and the media, "and we view it as a small risk that we would be managing carefully."[12]

Wilson, whom CEO Meg Whitman later stripped of his role as head of engineering for failing to keep her in the loop on key technological issues,[13] understated the problems that eBay faced. Developing the tools that eBay considered sufficient to manage the risk—not to mention updating Billpoint to work with eBay's auctions—proved arduous and time-consuming for a company focused on improving its site stability in the wake of several lengthy outages. EBay shut down the Billpoint Web site soon after completing the acquisition to work on development. More than eight months had since passed without word as to when or if Billpoint-powered credit card payments would become available to sellers on eBay's site.

Sacks did not view the possibility of payments competition from eBay as a reason not to move forward in the auction market. "It could be months before they ever roll out that service," he once said to me, speaking of Billpoint. "We could have millions of customers by then." For their part, Sacks and the rest of the management team stressed the need to focus on live opponents like X.com and dotBank and not worry about hypothetical future competitors. And the way to beat those opponents was simply to outgrow them.

◊

"So I've got this idea on how to kill X.com and get more sellers to start accepting PayPal," Luke said to me from across my desk. Since recovering from the initial shock of coming to such an unstructured environment, I had begun to realize just how much Confinity's informal culture encouraged all employees to put proposals on the table. In fact, the culture didn't just allow employees to think big—it demanded it. With everyone striving

to come up with ways to make PayPal better, simply going throug|
motions of a job's requirements was impossible.

But while everyone took advantage of this intellectual freedom a|
time or another, no one managed to be as routinely prolific as my b|

"There's no reason for auction sellers not to take PayPal," Luke
tinued. "They get their money so much faster than checks, and they
earn a $10 referral bonus just for signing up a buyer. I bet that r|
pads their profit margins!" He paused. "Hmm, I guess if you're clea
$5 or $6 on a $20 Beanie Baby, you'd already be getting decent mar|
so adding another $10 would—"

"So, you said you'd thought of a way to reach sellers," I interru|
trying to bring him back from a world of small stuffed animals. V
very different people, I had hit it off with Luke over the past two mc
and had grown to respect his intellect. His creativity and abili|
generate far-flung ideas exceeded my own, but he seemed to valu|
left-brained approach and often vetted his thoughts with me.

"Oh, yeah. So what we need to do is go out and start buying stu
eBay and insist on using PayPal to pay for it."

"But there are over three million auctions on eBay—we don't |
that much money!" I rebutted.

"Well, we don't need to buy every auction," Luke replied. "|
sellers list multiple items at a time. Instead of buying all their item
we need to do to introduce them to PayPal is just purchase one."

"So how do we do this? How do we buy something from |
seller on eBay?"

"OK—there are a couple of ways we could try. First, have you |
of the Web farms in Asia?" I shook my head to indicate I had not.

"Oh, my gosh! It's amazing. People have these entire Web f
with employees sitting at computers all day. And they sign them u
these 'pay to surf' programs like AllAdvantage where they'll pay |
dime an hour if you keep their toolbar open while you surf the Inte
The toolbar flashes ads, and that's how they can afford to pay y|
surf because they're being paid by advertisers to show the ads. S
people running these Web farms just have their employees sur
Internet all day and they collect the money from the 'pay to
company since the accounts are in their name. And since it's Asi|
Web farm just pays their employees a portion of the money the|
from the 'pay to surf' company and makes a huge profit."

As Luke paused to come up for air, I asked, "So you want us to open a Web farm to buy eBay auctions?"

"Yeah—but we don't have to start our own. We could just use one that's already there." Noticing my frown at the thought of PayPal being publicly associated with a digital sweatshop, Luke casually brought up an alternative plan. "Either that, or we could build a 'bot."

"A 'bot?"

"A robot—a script that could spider eBay's site looking for certain types of auctions." Luke smiled, patiently explaining simple Web terms to an Internet newbie. "And then when it finds them, it could make a bid just like a human and try to win the auction and pay for it with PayPal. The seller might even think he was dealing with a human buyer."

"So the 'bot would act just like a human and buy auctions using PayPal?"

"Yeah, that's it!" Luke replied.

"What if the seller doesn't want to accept PayPal?" I asked, highlighting the kind of minor complication that Luke sometimes overlooked.

"Hmm, that could be an issue," he conceded. "I guess we'll have to think about that."

Within a day we figured out the answer—the 'bot would bid on items for charity. We'd have our charity robot identify itself to sellers before it placed a bid, sending an e-mail that said it was collecting goods that would be donated but it could only pay with PayPal. The e-mail would then tell the seller that if he didn't mind transacting with a computer program and accepting PayPal he could reply to the e-mail and a bid would automatically be placed. We thought most sellers would accept this offer since it was a win-win for them—bids from the robot would allow them to participate in a charitable cause while also ensuring that their auction price went higher. From our perspective, even if our 'bot didn't win the auction, at least the seller would have been exposed to PayPal.

Though admittedly a bit far out, the charity robot idea also had merit. We wanted to put some extra breathing room between PayPal and X.com, and this would be a marketing campaign that our competitors could not easily detect, much less duplicate. And, while aggressive, the plan benefited from aiding charity, an attribute that would shield Confinity from community criticism for using a robot on eBay's site.

For its part, eBay was no fan of 'bots. In 1997 a competing auction site named Onsale, run by Silicon Valley veteran Jerry Kaplan, used 'bots to harvest users' e-mail addresses directly from eBay's site in order to send them promotional materials. In response to Onsale's affront eBay instituted a ban on robotic activity and incorporated 'bot-blocking defenses onto its site.[14] Information-stealing competitors weren't eBay's only incentive to ban 'bots. Since the purpose of robotic scripts is to call up page after page of content in rapid succession to record data, they placed excessive demand on eBay's already burdened Web site. Allowing even benign third parties to run such programs for the purpose of observing trends or collecting market data risked the fragile stability of eBay's site.

This made the stakes of the charity robot particularly high. If eBay uncovered our 'bot it would be justified in blocking PayPal's ability to access its site, crippling our AutoLink feature. But if it didn't, the robot could help give us a critical edge in the race to build a payments network.

◊

Potential opposition from eBay itself notwithstanding, Luke sold the other executives on the plan's merits. The risk of X.com or dotBank catching PayPal, they concluded, exceeded the risk of eBay punishing us for the 'bot. The project took on an air of importance when Max Levchin claimed direct ownership of it. Confinity's CTO, who typically spent his time focusing on security and network scalability issues while leaving specific features to Jamie and the engineers, wanted to create the 'bot personally.

Soft-spoken but intense, Max was well aware of his own technological genius and only assigned himself jobs that merited his skills. Already a startup veteran, Max had perfected the ability to grind through forty-eight hour periods of uninterrupted work during his previous ventures, and he seemed more than happy to tackle a cool and slightly subversive project like this. But development of our secret weapon would be no easy task. Software that pulled data from another company's Web site—especially one as large and dynamic as eBay's—had to contend with many variables such as missing pages, broken links, and updates that change the flow of site pages. The 'bot would also need to interact seamlessly with humans and avoid any misunderstandings to protect Confinity from criticism.

As Max worked on bringing the robot to life, Luke asked me to locate a charity willing to take custody of the countless Pokemon cards, comic books, and ceramic frogs that would soon start pouring in. My first choice was the American Red Cross, a universally respected group that people would be eager to aid. Not surprisingly, though, the national charity seemed unconvinced that it should partner with a little-known dot-com seeking to send an unknown quantity of in-kind donations. A publicist referred me to the local chapter. After a bizarre cold call in which I convinced the skeptical branch manager to accept the random knickknacks that would be arriving in the mail, Confinity had its charitable partner.

With the Red Cross's participation secured, we moved forward with tests to simulate the charity robot while Max continued working on the real thing. Jennifer Chwang created a company e-mail account as "charityrobot@paypal.com" and contacted several dozens auction sellers, masquerading as an automated robot asking the seller for permission to place a bid. The vast majority were more than happy to help out a charity and receive an extra bid that would increase the price of their item.

As her oddball eBay purchases began to trickle in, Jennifer's alternative e-mail alias also provided some much needed levity in our intense work environment. Jennifer occasionally forgot to toggle back and forth between the simulation e-mail account and her personal one, resulting in her sending long and detailed e-mails to colleagues under the pseudonym "The PayPal Charity Robot." Even Max laughed when mockingly congratulated on his remarkable achievement in artificial intelligence.

◊

As we moved forward with the development of PayPal's secret weapon, the competitive landscape in the online payments market shifted once more. In late February another startup entered the fray, again stunning our young company.

PayMe was not a new online presence. A service had been located at the PayMe.com URL since December 1998.[15] The nascent Web site provided visitors with a free referral to collection agencies for organizations with accounts receivable problems. The new offering at the PayMe.com address was very different. Featuring rotating images of college students asking mom and dad for a few bucks, PayMe introduced its own version of free accounts to send money to anyone with an e-mail address. While not especially ground-breaking in terms of its technology, PayMe roiled our company in a way that no other competitor had. PayMe was funded by Idealab, the corporate owner of Idealab

Capital Partners, which was one of the lead investors in Confinity's January venture capital round.

Idealab CEO and founder Bill Gross created his company as an all-purpose incubator to "turn innovative ideas into successful businesses."[16] Founded in 1996, the Pasadena, California-based Idealab claimed to have perfected the managerial algorithm of transforming other people's ingenuity into viable businesses. Or, as its Web site spun it, "Once an idea is prototyped, Idealab shares with the fledgling business its market-tested knowledge and expertise, supporting its initial growth and development."

By early-2000 it looked as if Idealab was onto something. Its portfolio of incubated companies included a long list of dot-com high fliers such as eToys (an online toy store that boasted a larger market cap than Toys 'R Us), DotTV (a URL registration firm for the ".tv" domain), and NetZero (a free Internet service provider that sponsored network television coverage of the NBA). Gross, a trustee at Cal Tech, opened an Idealab office in Silicon Valley and drew up plans to take his own company public.

Even though Idealab proper never provided Confinity with managerial guidance or support, Peter had welcomed its subsidiary's participation in our second venture round because of the credibility and name recognition it brought to the table. But from our perspective it now looked as if our investment partner liked what it saw during its due diligence so much that it decided to double down with another payments startup.

Like X.com two months before, PayMe launched with a media splash. Founder Dan Grigsby trumpeted his service as a technological breakthrough that solved "the awkward situation of collecting money from friends," and Idealab proudly hailed PayMe as the first company launched by its Silicon Valley office.[17]

Responding to what he viewed as an act of corporate betrayal, Peter vehemently pushed Gross either to shutter his new venture or to sell back Idealab's stake in Confinity. Gross refused, remaining an estranged shareholder in our company and an owner of yet another competitor to our young venture.

◊

As the online payments arena grew more crowded, Confinity continued to increase its ranks. I was officially the twenty-seventh employee when I reported for my to-be-defined job on December 10; at that point,

Confinity had been in existence for twelve months. Just over two months later, toward the end of February 2000, we had reached fifty employees and given up counting when new bodies showed up in the office.

The majority of our new hires joined our customer service team. As PayPal ramped up from several hundred daily registrations to over 10,000 per day, the trickle of customer inquiries had become a torrential flood. Despite every effort to keep the Web site as clean and simple as possible, customers contacted Confinity for assistance on everything from linking a credit card with their PayPal account to security questions about whether or not our service had ever been hacked.

If the avalanche of e-mails and phone calls wasn't sufficient proof of our need for more customer service personnel, additional data points began to present themselves. From my desk in the old ping pong room, I noticed a steady stream of irate account holders showing up in the nearby reception area, typically because they had trouble using our online form to request a check for their account balance. One sunny afternoon an elderly man clad in blue jeans, brown leather boots, and a white ten gallon hat with a broad rim strode into our lobby, proclaiming loudly, "Howdy! My wife and I just drove in from Arizona and we want to get our money out of PayPal." Someone from the CFO's office quickly cut him a check, and the next day we removed our address from the Web site.

Customer service personnel weren't the only new recruits in our quest for "world domination." In an attempt to attract desperately needed software engineers, Max took out an eye-catching ad in the daily student newspaper at Stanford that read "Tuition hike? Ask your mom to e-mail you the money." This was followed by the PayPal logo and an even more provocative question: "Think kick-ass stock options in a cool startup are worth dropping out of college? We are hiring right now!"

Although the ad only brought in a few engineering students in search of summer jobs, it did produce results from a different academic department. A junior history major named Paul Martin arrived at the office at midday later that week for a meeting with Peter. A blonde Arkansas native with a tall and muscular frame, Paul was the *Stanford Review*'s business manager and a runner on the university's track team. He wanted to speak to Peter about an internship for the upcoming summer, but similar to my own hiring experience, locating Peter proved difficult. Since I had previously met Paul through our mutual friends at the *Review* and didn't want him to go away without at least learning something about the company, I invited him to join me for lunch instead.

"Take a look at this," I said, handing Paul a printout of an upward-sloping, hockey stick-shaped graph. "That's a chart of the total number of PayPal users. We've gone from around 2,000 when I started to over 150,000 today."

"Wow, that's amazing," he replied, taking the graph and studying it in silence.

"And it's picking up," I continued, enjoying the chance to make a point. "You see, our system is powered by viral growth. The service is so easy to use that each customer can send us more new ones.

"That's why we offer $10 referral bonuses, to encourage our users to go out there and get their friends to open accounts. It's cheaper than what it costs to acquire customers through TV commercials and mass media, and it's a great way to help people understand what our service is all about."

Paul hung on my every word as I prattled on about viral growth, network effects, and PayPal's potential to revolutionize world currency markets. I didn't realize it at the time, but I was giving Paul my own version of the "world domination" speech that Peter had given at the company meeting ten weeks earlier.

After lunch, we tried one last time to track down Peter. After Paul finally located the CEO and discussed terms for his future internship, I gave him my business card and he headed back to campus.

I had put the entire event out of my mind by the time my phone rang early the next day. "Eric, it's Paul," the speaker on the other end said in his distinguishable southern twang. "I've been thinking a lot about what you said yesterday, and I realize this is something that I want to be a part of." I appreciated his unsolicited feedback on my lunchtime speech—evidently I had become an effective cheerleader for the company. But I couldn't have guessed just how good: "I want to drop out of school and start working full time now."

To my surprise, he told me that his family and his girlfriend supported him in his decision. I paused for a minute, wondering what I should recommend. On the other end of the line was a young man from rural Arkansas who I suspected had borrowed money to finance his Stanford education. All he knew about PayPal was what I had told him, and that was enough to convince him to put his schooling on hold and roll the dice. While Stanford's re-enrollment polices were flexible, dropping out of one of the world's elite colleges to join a startup that had not booked a dime in revenue was still a gamble.

"Go for it," I told him.

That evening around midnight Paul came in to meet with Luke. Luke seemed apprehensive about bringing another inexperienced employee onto the marketing team, but my recommendation convinced him to talk with Paul. I headed home to San Francisco before Paul arrived; I typically started my fourteen hour workday early, and in the evenings I tried to leave before ten o'clock just to squeeze in an hour with Beatrice before catching a few winks of sleep. Luke, however, was a night owl who thought nothing odd about holding an interview into the wee hours of the morning.

Paul won Luke over. He earned his offer and eagerly became a twenty year old college dropout later that week. It would prove to be a mutually fateful decision, both for Paul and for PayPal.

◊

Despite PayPal's accelerating growth rates and my sunny optimism, with hindsight the future of the startup that Paul joined was far from certain. The slew of dot-coms that followed us into the online payments market made for a very competitive landscape. Our daily searches on eBay showed X.com's listing share had increased and trailed us by only a couple of percentage points. And the development of our secret weapon, the charity robot, stalled when getting it to select random auctions on eBay's site proved more difficult than originally anticipated.

Then there was the matter of cash. Despite raising $23 million the prior month, our rapid user growth meant that we were paying out over $100,000 per day in bonuses to our customers. Meanwhile, revenue from the float of funds re-circulating through the PayPal system failed to materialize as most recipients withdrew their funds upon receipt. Worse still, since few users kept account balances the vast majority of them used credit cards to fund their payments, a decision costing Confinity a 2% fee to the credit card associations on each transaction. Every time someone signed up and used PayPal, we lost more money.

All of this meant that while Confinity was in no imminent danger of running out of money, we had a limited runway for operating in cash-burning mode. We needed to grow our network to critical mass and banish our competitors soon if PayPal was to survive.

CHAPTER THREE

MEGA-MERGER

FEBRUARY—MARCH 2000

"ARE YOU SITTING DOWN?" Luke breathlessly asked me over my phone on a Sunday evening in late February.

"No," I answered. "What's going on?"

"You should sit down." I frowned but didn't respond. After a brief pause, Luke continued, "We're merging with X.com."

The wind momentarily knocked out of me, I sat down.

After giving me a moment to grasp what he had just said, Luke went on. "Yeah, we're merging with X.com. It's going to be a fifty-fifty merger of the two companies. Don't worry about your job or anything— there's enough work to keep everyone busy."

"OK," I finally muttered, at a loss for words. "But, w-why?"

"This will help us to grow and take over the online payments space. There's a lot of synergy between what we're both trying to do, and now we won't have to waste time and money competing with each other.

"The merged company is going to be called X.com," he added, "but we'll keep offering the PayPal service. PayPal is going to be the way we acquire accounts—it's easier to sign up for it than an X.com bank account and doesn't require the user to give his Social Security number. Then once customers are registered with PayPal we'll upsell them to X.com financial services to bring in revenue."

"Yeah, I see," I grumbled, the shock beginning to wear off, replaced by consternation. For some reason I didn't understand, a feeling of betrayal began to creep into my head at the thought of allying with this former enemy. "So, who, who's going to be CEO?" I stammered.

"Bill Harris," Luke replied. "He's a really big name and used to be CEO of Intuit, the company that makes Quicken and QuickBooks."

I inhaled a deep breath. So in this merger we'd agreed to give up both our company's name and leadership—how was this a merger and not an acquisition? "What about Peter?" I asked.

"Peter's going to be senior vice president of finance, since that's really his strong suit and Bill is so well known," Luke responded without any hint of reservation. "Elon Musk, the chairman of X.com, will be chairman of the new company since he's the biggest shareholder. And Max will stay on as CTO.

"Everyone else is still going to be doing roughly the same thing they were doing before. The teams from the two companies complement each other pretty well; they have more financial expertise, and we have more marketing and engineering.

"I think this will work out very great," Luke added. "With Bill Harris we'll have no trouble raising more money, and we'll definitely be able to take the company public now!"

That last promise quelled my unease a little—at least there was some upside to this merger after all. But I still had little to say to Luke as my mind raced frantically to grasp what I had just been told. "Let's talk about this more tomorrow. I need to try to call a few more people to tell them the news," Luke said, slipping in his goodbye.

I stood up from my desk, haphazardly dropped the phone back in its cradle, and walked over to the edge of the sofa—a short distance in my cramped San Francisco studio. "What happened?" asked Beatrice, who had been trying to follow my end of the conversation with Luke.

I shook my head as I searched for the right words to convey that the company I was just beginning to fall in love with might very soon no longer exist.

◊

For the rest of the evening I struggled to come to grips with our management team's decision. While the benefits of removing a leading competitor were obvious, Confinity was giving up a lot in order to do so. Abandoning our company's name and handing over the reins to X.com's chairman and CEO for all intents and purposes was not a merger of equals, even with Peter and Max retaining executive positions. Young as I was, I knew enough to realize that companies aren't always led by consensus; having the X.com name on the marquee with X.com executives running both officer and board meetings meant that Peter and Max's influence would be limited. How could we know that the new managers would share Confinity's vision for revolutionizing payments or commitment to an open and informal culture?

What I knew about the people at X.com also concerned me. While I had not interacted directly with anyone there, X.com's officers projected a haughty image to the media. After all, the same Bill Harris now lauded by Luke had publicly bragged about receiving more than one hundred job offers. And Elon Musk seemed even more brash. After striking gold from the sale of his previous startup, the young millionaire plowed his assets into his new company but had enough left over to outbid fashion mogul Ralph Lauren on a McLaren F1 roadster which he happily showed off to the press.[1] Now he crowed that X.com would land a bigger IPO than online grocery service Webvan, which had ended its first day of trading with a market cap of $7.9 billion, saying that his financial services supermarket was "going to be the super-Webvan."[2]

Taken together, these uncertainties made the proposed merger difficult to warm up to in spite of its benefits. After a night of fitful sleep, I anxiously went into the office the following morning looking for some answers. In typical Confinity-style, no one had thought to schedule an office-wide meeting to discuss the agreement and some employees were still not aware of the news. Around mid-morning I grabbed Luke as he made the rounds, trying to track down uninformed colleagues.

"Luke, we need to talk—in private," I implored him. "I'm trying to understand why we would want to merge and give up control of the company."

We ducked outside into Confinity's small, central courtyard, a frequent site for meetings in our increasingly crowded offices.

"I guess I see why you'd be concerned. Look, this isn't a bad deal for us. For one thing, they actually have almost two hundred thousand users, about as many as we do!" Luke confided. "They were careful not to make it public, but as part of the due diligence we found this out. I guess that $20 bonus they were giving out to people to sign up really worked!

"Also, with all of the financial services like money markets, index funds, and debit cards that they offer, each of their accounts is probably worth a lot more than ours," he continued. "And since we were beginning to burn through cash pretty quickly and will have to do some more financing soon, merging with our top competitor will help us raise a lot more funds.

"Plus, Peter felt that there was probably only a market for one player in this space to go public, and whoever had an IPO first would have enough resources to crush the competition. And with their management team, user base, and cash on hand they'd have had a good chance at beating us to that IPO finish line."

"But what about auctions?" I countered, citing a market where PayPal had the upper hand. By this point roughly 8%-9% of eBay's listings on any given day featured PayPal, as compared to 4%-6% for X.com.

"That's true, we were certainly beating them on eBay," Luke said with a smile to acknowledge my personal attachment to that market. "And that was the reason they were willing to accept a fifty-fifty merger, because they could see how well we're doing in auctions." He paused, and added, "Thanks in no small part to our marketing team, of course!

"By the way, have you seen Paul Martin? I still need to tell him the news." With that Luke scampered off to drop this bombshell on more unsuspecting colleagues.

I mulled over Luke's points. X.com posed more of a competitive threat to Confinity than its lack of public disclosure had suggested. Even if our success on eBay was accelerating PayPal's growth, X.com's flashy launch and generous bonuses had given it a strong early burst. More disconcerting, though, was the prospect of competing with X.com in the capital markets. Our large but rapidly shrinking cash reserves meant that without the merger we'd have to bet PayPal's future on beating out X.com in an effort to raise a massive amount of new capital. And since its founder was a multimillionaire, X.com had the leg up in this department.

While none of this new information overrode my reservations about Confinity abdicating control of the merged company, it exposed the motivations behind the deal. And, regardless of my lingering concerns, I wasn't in a position to impact the decision one way or the other.

One of the people behind that decision stopped by my desk later on that day. Peter sported a smile on his face, something we had seen infrequently during the recent stressful weeks. Checking to make sure that his lieutenants had succeeded in getting the word out, he asked "So, have you heard about the merger yet?" I answered and he replied, "Good, good," before pausing and finishing his thought, "You know, I think this is going to go very well. This combined company will just blow everyone else away!"

Optimism ruled the day. It wasn't until much later that I realized that all of my initial concerns were justified.

◊

Four weeks after the agreement was struck the employees of both companies sat on folding chairs in an otherwise empty building, looking at Bill Harris, Elon Musk, and Peter Thiel—dubbed the "Big Three" by Vince Sollitto, Confinity's fast-talking director of public relations. By now the merger was nearly finalized, and employees from both companies had already been shuffled between our two offices on University Avenue.

On this Thursday afternoon we were being given a literal and figurative preview of the future of the company. The setting, a sprawling one-story building in an office park on the outskirts of Palo Alto, bordered the San Francisco Bay marshlands just east of Highway 101. The edifice previously housed Bill Harris's old company, Intuit, and his new company had just signed a multi-year lease. Although the spackle was still wet and few cubicles had been installed, we would be moving in within a matter of weeks.

After several minutes passed and employees finished filing in, Bill Harris strolled to the front of the group and took the microphone. In his mid-forties with slightly graying hair, designer glasses, and a neatly pressed dress shirt, Harris could have easily passed for an Andersen partner.

"Thanks everyone for coming to our future offices," he began, looking at ease in front of this crowd of over one hundred people. "For those of you who haven't met me before, I'm Bill, the CEO." Everyone chuckled. Harris exuded a natural confidence and charisma that could immediately warm up an audience. Charming and polished, he seemed like an old economy executive who believed in the value of appearance—all the more so standing next to Peter, who wore shorts and a Confinity Sistine Chapel T-shirt.

Even before the deal officially closed, the corporate structure of the new X.com had begun to crystallize. As planned, Peter took over the finance and investor relations divisions of the company. David Jaques, Confinity's CFO, retained his position but reported to Peter. As CTO, Max answered to Harris and had the combined engineering staffs of both companies under his supervision. But beyond engineering and accounting, Harris instituted little integration of the other departments from the two pre-merger companies. He grouped Confinity's marketing, business development, customer service, and operations teams together into a "Payments" division headed by Reid Hoffman, Confinity's president. Luke, who remained VP of marketing and reported to Reid, continued to oversee the lean marketing team comprised of Paul Martin, Jennifer Chwang, and me.

With Peter, Max, David Jacques, and Reid occupying leadership positions, Confinity personnel dominated the next tier of the org chart below Harris. It was a compromise meant to ensure continued influence in the new firm by Confinity's executives. Despite my fears about Confinity's management team losing the ability to impact the merged company's strategy, for the most part our execs appeared to fair well in the merger.

David Sacks was a notable exception. Sacks saw his role as Confinity's vice president of strategy reporting to the CEO transformed into that of VP of Web site design answering to Reid. Besides suffering the effective demotion, the move came as a double surprise since Sacks had little experience in the field and found himself overseeing a half-dozen Web site designers. Shortly following his reassignment, I bumped into him carrying a copy of *HTML for Dummies*. When I glanced at the book he held in his hands, it prompted him to reply, "I guess I should learn some of this stuff."

Continuing his speech, Harris painted an optimistic picture of the potential for the combined company. After the merger we had realized immediate cost savings, he reminded everyone, by eliminating X.com's $20 new user bonus and cutting PayPal's bonus in half to $5. Despite this reduction, PayPal continued to attract new accounts at an accelerating rate; a staggering 12,000 people were signing up each day, proving that PayPal was the perfect account acquisition tool for the new company. X.com bank account registrations, on the other hand, dramatically tapered off following the demise of the bonuses and the de-emphasis of the service.

Shifting gears, Harris focused on what he saw as the company's vision. After users registered for PayPal, he said, we would be able to upsell them to X.com's supermarket of financial services. When they received money from a friend through PayPal, we'd entice them to invest it into the no minimum-balance S&P 500 fund. For sending money to make an auction purchase, we'd offer them an X.com line of credit with a lower APR than their credit card. If their local bank wasn't paying enough interest, a mere click of a button could transfer their checking or savings balance over to their new X.com account. Finally, if they needed to have cash, they could pull out their X.com debit card or checkbook. With PayPal's easy sign-up process and viral money transfer technology getting customers in the door, the X.com suite of financial products would make them profitable. In contrast to Peter's plan for revolutionizing world currency markets, Harris saw PayPal as the perfect loss leader.

Of course, at that point the company actually did not have a way to upsell the ever-increasing number of PayPal users. The smattering of financial products that Harris discussed fell far short of a financial supermarket, and, to complicate matters, only the accounts in the X.com database could access these financial services. The X.com and PayPal platforms remained completely separate, although Harris indicated he eventually planned to merge them.

Harris readily admitted that we had a lot of work to do before we could start earning income off PayPal-driven traffic. But, in the meantime, the company would continue acquiring accounts in the auction market while using business development deals to break into fledgling new sectors in need of online payment capabilities.

As Harris concluded his remarks on the vision of our new company, he warmly welcomed Elon Musk to the microphone. Elon seemed uncomfortable and fidgety speaking in public and, in following Harris, he'd been dealt a tough hand to play at the podium. The twenty-eight year old multimillionaire had a youthful face but thinning hair, and appeared to smile while speaking in short and precise sentences.

Elon spoke briefly of how far X.com had come and how many challenges it had faced, but as he continued it became clear to me that he was not talking about the company created by the merger with Confinity. In fact, he made no mention of Confinity. He announced that X.com, the world's most mnemonic URL, would soon be the most highly trafficked as well, and that "X-Finance" and "X-PayPal" services were on the path to becoming household names. The term "X-PayPal" sounded jarring—it was the first time that anyone had used "X" as a prefix in front of PayPal's name.

Peter stepped up to speak last. Looking fairly relaxed, it was evident that he had not prepared any statement prior to the meeting. Instead, he went into detail on a specific topic that he knew was of interest to Confinity employees, their stock options. "Let's see, every old share of Confinity is now exchanged into shares of X.com," he said. "That's roughly, hmm..." he paused, looking upward for a second, "about 2.0207 shares of X.com stock for every share of Confinity." Bill Harris laughed hard at the fact that his senior vice president could do division to the ten-thousandth decimal place in his head.

Peter finished his brief set of remarks giving everyone an update on the company's forthcoming financing plans. The goal, he said, was to raise $100 million in venture capital, one of the largest financing rounds ever, and to do it in record time. Fortunately, with the NASDAQ composite looking hale and hearty at 5,000 and record amounts of capital flowing into Silicon Valley, no one envisioned this would be difficult for a company registering 12,000 new customers every day.

◊

"I need to tell you something," Luke said in a subdued tone. Over the past three months I could not think of many instances in which Luke could be characterized as subdued about anything, so his approach came as a surprise.

The marketing team, along with business development and finance, had recently moved down the street from the former Confinity office to the X.com one. This had been a homecoming of sorts for Luke. When Confinity and X.com were neighbors the prior year Confinity occupied the southern side of the building, and now Luke found himself sitting in approximately the same location as his original desk.

For my part, I longed for the ping pong room after moving into the cramped offices at 394 University. Most employees' workstations were clustered into bullpen configurations, and marketing was positioned by a rear window that overlooked a communal dumpster. The building's faulty air conditioning meant that the window stayed open most of the time, causing a pungent odor to fill the room. The office had only one large conference room for its fifty or so employees, meaning that any private conversation required going down the steps and out the back door to chat in an alley next to the stinky dumpster.

After following Luke down this path, he turned to me and announced solemnly, "I'm leaving the marketing group."

In the past three months I'd already been bowled over by my fair share of heavy news, but this still shocked me. Working under Luke, even as unpredictable as he could be, had been a source of stability during the merger, and now that was being withdrawn.

"Reid's asked me to work directly for him as VP of strategy," Luke replied. "It will give me a chance to spend more time thinking of new directions for the company to go in." Reid's rationale seemed clear. Management wasn't the young executive's strongest point, but he possessed boundless creativity. By putting him in a position where he could generate ideas Reid hoped to tap Luke's amazing potential.

"So, what's going to happen to our team?" I wondered aloud.

"We'll put out a request for a new VP of marketing," Luke explained. "It's going to take a while. It will have to be someone really good, though, someone who can build the brand and help take the company public." He smiled after making that last point, then paused for a minute and looked at me. "Don't worry," he added, "we'll make sure it's a candidate whom you all like."

Judging from what Luke said, our young marketing team stood to be without an executive for some time. And since Luke's mind was evidently already on other matters, it meant we should not be holding our breaths for top-level guidance. I realized I had been handed an opportunity to step up during that interim period and fill the void.

At that moment, however, I didn't foresee just how big the void would be.

◊

Despite my reservations about merging with X.com, the clear benefit of the deal was the acknowledged lead it would give us in the emerging online payments arena. Just as the launches of dotBank, X.com, and PayMe roiled our company in the prior months, the announcement of our merger should have reset the playing field and established our combined company as the clear market leader.

But, while X.com and Confinity prepared to make our plans known to the world, eBay thrust a spoke into our PR machine's wheels. On March 1, eBay announced the launch of its own payment service, Billpoint.

Ten months had passed since eBay had bought the startup for $86 million in stock. EBay had shown foresight with the acquisition—Meg Whitman's team had recognized eBay's need for credit card processing capabilities well before I had targeted auction users with my direct mail campaign or Sacks had discovered the homemade PayPal banner. Creating a viable credit card processing service for its sellers stood to improve eBay's core business. Auction turnover, the source of fees that accounted for the vast majority of eBay's revenue, could be increased by instant payments that cut down on transaction fulfillment, allowing sellers to spend more time selling and less time waiting for checks to clear.

Although Whitman's idea was right, the same could not be said about eBay's execution. The outside world had heard nothing of Billpoint for nearly a year. The internal upheaval in eBay's engineering department that led to Mike Wilson's ouster was one reason. Another was the state of the acquired company itself. At the time of the purchase, Billpoint was, in the words of Whitman, "a very nascent company." In fact, Billpoint was not even eBay's first choice of credit card processing companies; eBay had entered into negotiations to buy a startup named Accept, only to be outmaneuvered by Amazon.com, which itself had just entered the online auction business.[3]

As a result, Billpoint languished through a lengthy development process and beta test. Toward the end of 1999, as PayPal was launching its service, eBay invited 5,000 sellers to test Billpoint at the hefty cost of 4.75% per transaction. Few took them up on the offer; scans using eBay's own search tool indicated that far less than 1% of eBay's listings offered Billpoint as of February 2000. We knew Billpoint would roll out at some point, but the March 1 announcement still jolted us. Whitman's previous statements had suggested a second quarter launch, but now it appeared the service was finally ready to go online ahead of predictions.[4]

That wasn't all. Equally troublesome was the fact that eBay had brought in a new equity partner with credibility and payments experience. Under the terms of the deal, Wells Fargo purchased a 35% stake in Billpoint and agreed to provide Billpoint with its back-end payment processing and customer service support. [5] In essence, eBay would only be responsible for Billpoint's front-end actions on its Web site, leaving Wells Fargo to do the heavy lifting for transaction processing and fraud control, areas outside of eBay's expertise. This division of labor would play to the relative strength of two industry leaders and provide Billpoint with a huge amount of resources to draw upon.

The Billpoint announcement ushered a somber mood into X.com's offices. Peter, who at the time had been traveling throughout Asia and the Middle East to line up investors, called Luke's cell to get an assessment of the deal. From my desk by the window overlooking the back entrance I watched Luke pace back and forth in the alley, one hand holding his cell while the other gesticulated passionately.

Judging from the online news articles that portrayed the Billpoint deal as a piece of business genius, the marriage of X.com and Confinity would have a difficult time competing for media attention. The eBay-Wells Fargo agreement, symbolizing a combination of the new and old economies, attracted coverage in numerous outlets. When our own announcement went out the following day, every article referenced Billpoint. *Forbes* called our merger a sign that "radical change" was coming to the banking sector, but then added that we could expect fierce competition from eBay. AuctionWatch's daily news report on the online auction industry implied that Billpoint's infrastructure would be more reliable than X.com's in scaling to meet customer demand.[6]

Our customers took notice of our merger, though. On the day of the announcement, Bill Harris had Jamie Templeton update the PayPal Web site to feature a PayPal spinning dollar sign morphing into the X.com logo along with a hyperlink that read "Newsflash: PayPal is merging with X.com!" Customers began posting their reactions on eBay message boards and their sentiments were all over the map. While most were pleased with the promise that PayPal and X.com accounts would eventually be able to transact together, some fretted about the lack of competition and the possibility that all bonuses would be taken away.

As the days went by, it began to look like Billpoint's heralded launch was nothing more than a false start. Although the press release from eBay and Wells Fargo hinted otherwise, eBay did not make Billpoint registration immediately available to the masses; subsequent articles revealed that eBay had decided to put its payment service through one more beta phase before making it available site-wide.

While still not ready for prime time, Billpoint had earned an upgrade from its first test phase. EBay added the service as an option in the payments section on the Sell Your Item (SYI) form, the page sellers complete to create an auction posting. When selected on SYI, Billpoint appeared in the auction's header, giving its link and clickable logos prominent placement toward the top of the listing—an advantage unavailable to PayPal. To let buyers know that they accepted PayPal, sellers had to check off the "See Item Description" option on SYI and include either a PayPal logo or text instructions in the body of their listing.

This integration advantage promised to make Billpoint all the more formidable. Fortunately for X.com, eBay's inability to make Billpoint available to all its sellers gave PayPal additional time to gain traction before being forced to go head-to-head with this new competitor. We knew that a clash would soon come, but in the meantime we were determined to take advantage of Billpoint's absence.

◊

Online payments became a bona fide industry in March 2000. As Confinity and X.com came together and eBay sealed its partnership with Wells Fargo, a slew of giant corporations and tiny startups joined dotBank and PayMe in entering the nascent market created by PayPal. Other entrepreneurs and businessmen sought to get a piece of the potentially lucrative action—the gales of "creative destruction" were beginning to blow at full force.

Watching from the sidelines as other players made their moves, Tim Koogle, CEO of the mega Internet portal Yahoo, was frustrated. For several years Yahoo had been eyeing online auctions as a means to diversify its advertising-heavy revenue stream, but its ability to challenge eBay's dominance had proven limited. Despite growing to more than 1 million live auctions, about one-fourth the number of listings on eBay, Yahoo found it difficult to turn its millions of visitors into auction buyers. Koogle hoped that an online payment service, increasing the convenience of trading on Yahoo's site, might do the trick. His staff entered into separate acquisition discussions with both Confinity and X.com only to have Peter and Elon reject him in favor of merging their two companies together.

Still seeking to jumpstart its e-commerce efforts, Yahoo then tried to put its $90 billion market capitalization to good use by offering to acquire eBay outright. It wasn't the first time. Two years before Yahoo had tendered an offer for the still-private auction Web site, but Meg Whitman and Pierre Omidyar had opted to follow through with their IPO plans instead. This time, with eBay's valuation clearly determined by the market, Koogle figured he would have better luck. Stressing that Yahoo's overseas presence could help accelerate eBay's international expansion, Koogle found Whitman receptive to his advances. But the talks broke down when Koogle insisted that Whitman report to his president rather than directly to him. Concerned that this structure would make it impossible for eBay to maintain any degree of independence, Whitman's team balked. Whitman seemed to have no regrets, later telling author Adam Cohen that the cultures of the two companies clashed: "You would, based on the nature of the companies and the age of the officers, assume the cultures would be similar, but the cultures were not similar at all."[7]

After losing out on its bids for Confinity, X.com, and eBay in a month's time, Yahoo finally found a firm to acquire. In late March it agreed to purchase dotBank for an undisclosed amount.[8] The announcement didn't exactly strike fear in our hearts, given that DotBank had stopped innovating soon after its December launch and even failed to follow Confinity and X.com into the auctions market; in this sense it was ironic that Yahoo would now want dotBank to be the official payment service for its auctions. Within a few days of the deal Yahoo shuttered dotBank's Web site, posting a message thanking dotBank's users and promising that the service would soon re-launch under the name Yahoo PayDirect.

Shortly before Yahoo's acquisition was announced, Chicago-based Bank One threw its hat into the online payments ring with the launch of a division named eMoneyMail. The media jumped all over the news of a staid and respected bank entering the online payments fray. I was at a Starbucks near my San Francisco apartment, getting a coffee for the drive down to Palo Alto, when Beatrice called to tell me she'd read about a new competitor in the paper. I picked up a copy of *The San Francisco Chronicle* and found a profile of eMoneyMail on the front page of the business section.

Dubbing itself the first "national financial services company" to introduce "an e-mail capability for sending money," Bank One positioned eMoneyMail as a standalone service.[9] Though the company could have integrated eMoneyMail's functionality into its existing online banking accounts, it chose instead to host eMoneyMail on a different Web site and charge the sender a $1 convenience fee. Billpoint's various beta programs assessed payment recipients a fee, but up until this point no online payment company had collected a fee from money-senders.

Cash-rich companies like Yahoo and Bank One weren't the only firms jumping into online payments—a steady stream of new startups continued to enter the field. Mambo.com, an online invitation service competing with Evite, had just added credit card processing capabilities to its site as a way of settling event expenses when Yahoo announced it would start providing free event planning software. A panicked Mambo sought to diversify and spun off its payment processing into a separate division amusingly named PayPlace. Meanwhile, a startup focusing on group payments called gMoney debuted with a bizarre publicity stunt of donating 220 bicycles for students at the University of California at Berkeley to share.[10] With all this going on, estranged Confinity investor Bill Gross married off PayMe to another Idealab hatchling. PayMyBills.com, an online bill payment company, had just closed a $30 million venture round. Gross's team convinced PayMyBills to merge with the cash-starved PayMe so the company could add e-mail payment functionality to its service.[11]

In the course of just a few weeks, a sector that did not exist six months earlier had become crowded with four startups (the merged X.com, PayMe, PayPlace, and gMoney), one portal (Yahoo PayDirect), one giant bank (Bank One's eMoneyMail), and the eBay-Wells Fargo partnership (Billpoint) all vying for supremacy. PayPal's road to "world domination" was suddenly well traveled, indeed.

◊

Despite the appearance of so many other competitors on the payments scene, Billpoint and its home court advantage on eBay concerned

X.com the most. And even though Billpoint still languished in beta mode, eBay was about to show us that it would not meekly stand by as PayPal encroached on its Web site.

EBay fired its warning shot on a bright day toward the end of March. The couple of weeks following Billpoint's announcement had been relatively quiet up until my phone rang and Reid's voice huffed on the other end. With an obvious sense of urgency, he simply said, "Could you come over? We've got an eBay emergency."

I grabbed a note pad and headed for the door. Unlike most of the executive team, Reid Hoffman still had his office at 165 University, Confinity's old building on the other end of the street. In the weeks following our merger it was a common site to see X.com employees trudging back and forth on University Avenue to meet colleagues at one office or the other. Ever since Luke had left his role as the head of marketing, our tiny team technically reported directly to Reid. Yet because he was running X.com's entire payments division we seldom saw him.

Reid rose to greet me as I entered his office, shaking off his obvious preoccupation with the matter at hand. As he settled back behind his cluttered desk, his eyes narrowed and he launched into a quick summary of the situation: "We've got a big problem brewing."

Reid went on to explain that eBay had posted an official notice on its Web site's announcement board informing users of a new logo policy. Citing a need to keep its site clean and limit distracting ads on sellers' listings, eBay decreed that effective immediately all "third party credits" could be no larger than thirty-three by eighty-eight pixels. Any auction listings violating this policy could be shut down by eBay's staff and removed from the Web site without warning.

This posed a massive problem for PayPal. The thirty-three by eighty-eight pixels maximum translated into a small amount of screen space—roughly the size of half a stick of chewing gum. PayPal's logos, which typically featured the company's name, the Visa & MasterCard symbols, and a reference to our $5 bonus, were about four times that size.

Since the launch of our AutoLink logo-insertion tool a month and a half earlier, the number of PayPal logos on eBay had soared. Scans using eBay's search tool showed that PayPal was now accepted as a payment option on nearly 20% of eBay's listings—up from 10% at the start of March and a number far greater than any other third party auction service—and most of these auctions featured a PayPal logo somewhere in the listing's description. All of these auctions violated eBay's new policy, meaning that our sellers would have to remove the offending PayPal logos immediately or risk having their listings closed.

"But eBay has another policy that prevents sellers from altering a listing that has received a bid," I pointed out. "If they have one of our logos on it already, there's no way for sellers to remove it." I paused for a minute while Reid nodded. "That means hundreds or even thousands of PayPal users could have no way to prevent eBay from shutting down their auctions and they'd be told it was because they used PayPal logos. That would be a nightmare! Many of them might never want to use PayPal again."

I realized just how high the stakes were. If this situation spiraled to the point where eBay started shutting down auctions with our logos, at the very least it would scare many customers away from advertising PayPal in their auctions. At worst, it could force thousands of users to turn off AutoLink or stop using PayPal on eBay altogether.

"So what's our response going to be?" I asked.

"I've got a call in to an acquaintance of mine in the legal department over there," Reid replied, revealing that he had already been operating in crisis mode for several hours. "Hopefully he will agree to not shut down the listings of all the sellers who already have our logos in them. Meanwhile, Jamie is working with our engineers to make AutoLink's logo size-compliant."

"Which we'll need to tell our users about," I added, acknowledging the reason Reid had pulled me into the fray. "We should get word out to them quickly so they don't panic."

Reid nodded. "Of course, there's also the matter of being limited to microscopic auction logos from now on, which is going to make it harder for buyers to learn about PayPal. In any case, let me call up my contact at eBay again to see what the odds are of exempting our live auctions from being shut down."

Reid's point highlighted the threat to X.com posed by eBay's move. This new logo policy not only made PayPal run the risk of losing its current listings, small logos would hamper our efforts to reel in non-users and convince them to register for PayPal. It didn't seem coincidental to us that this policy change came as Billpoint moved into its final beta phase.

Soon after I left, Reid managed to reach Rob Chesnut in eBay's legal department. Chesnut, who as a U.S. Attorney prosecuted CIA mole Aldrich Ames, ardently denied that the logo policy was targeted at

PayPal. He stood by its stated purpose of removing ads from eBay's cluttered site, but he did concede that eBay should not shut down the listings of sellers who used the large PayPal logos before the policy went into effect. After twisting some arms behind the scenes, the lawyer called Reid back and delivered the news.

That evening the new version of the PayPal auction logo went live on our Web site and an e-mail with instructions on complying with eBay's logo policy was sent off to our sellers. While some users groused on discussion boards that they were worried that despite our reassurances eBay would take down existing listings containing the old logo, there was no mass movement on the part of sellers to strip PayPal logos from their auctions. Our quick response on both the engineering and marketing fronts had kept the situation under control and averted a potential crisis.

What we couldn't prevent was eBay changing the rules in mid-game. The timing of the announcement hinted that eBay might purposefully alter the configuration of its marketplace to discourage the use of PayPal in favor of Billpoint, yet there was no way to prove that the move targeted our company. This left X.com without a real option for recourse except to brace and prepare for similar challenges in the future. We were playing with fire. We had committed to building our payment network on top of eBay's online community, and it was clear that eBay would no longer turn a blind eye.

◊

EBay's aggression came at a time when X.com had become increasingly difficult for the auction giant to ignore. In addition to securing a presence on one-fifth of eBay's auctions, by late March an average of 18,000 customers registered for PayPal each day. We had just crossed the 1 millionth user milestone and our servers were processing more than $1 million in daily payments, double the February average.[12] In the month since the merger agreement was struck and the original X.com banking service was deemphasized, auction usage continued to accelerate PayPal's growth even though we lowered user bonuses from $10 to $5.

But as the PayPal network scaled up, the company burned through money at an escalating clip. With PayPal transactions still free to our users and very little revenue coming in from either the float or X.com's financial services, we depleted our cash supply every time customers earned a bonus or charged a payment to their credit cards. For the entire quarter the merged company booked only $1.2 million in revenue against a staggering $23.5 million in operational expenses, an imbalance that drove our cash on hand down to just a few million dollars.

With this as a backdrop, Peter Thiel set out to close X.com's $100 million financing round as quickly as possible. Opting for expediency instead of haggling over the company's valuation, Peter and his team traveled the globe and lined up investors in record time. By the end of March Madison Dearborn Partners of Chicago agreed to contribute $30 million, and was joined by J.P. Morgan, Japanese Internet investment company Hikari Tsushin, and many former investors of both X.com and Confinity.[13] The terms and pricing had been accepted in principle; all that remained was to get the parties to sign on the dotted line and transfer their portion of the $100 million.

On the surface, it appeared that X.com could not have picked a better time to raise capital. Silicon Valley remained flush with cash and hope, and startups had no trouble attracting funds for almost any business idea. For example, Jim Clark, the founder of Netscape, raised $20 million in venture capital for his startup Healtheon with only a sketch of a diamond that purported to show how he'd use the Internet to transform the health care industry.[14] The world's public and private equity markets had a nearly insatiable appetite for technology companies, especially for dot-com startups like ours.

On Friday, March 10, the tech-heavy NASDAQ composite closed at an all-time high of 5,039, an increase of 1,500 points just since I had joined Confinity. Over the following week it briefly dipped before climbing back to just under 5,000 on March 24. It hovered near this record level for another couple of days before starting to freefall.

On March 28, the composite closed at 4,833. The next day it hit 4,644. Then 4,457.

Many financial pundits showed no alarm over this precarious slump in tech prices. "First quarter earnings are really going to stabilize this market," an asset manager from SunAmerica told CNET. An analyst from Prudential agreed, commenting that "there's potential for some upside this earnings season... The NASDAQ has pulled back from its highs, so there's room for it to move (up)."[15]

Their optimism was understandable. Equity prices had enjoyed an unprecedented bull market during the late nineties as a nearly inflation-free economy grew at a brisk pace. The Federal Reserve helped accelerate that run-up when it slashed the federal funds target interest rate by seventy-five basis points to 4.75% during late 1998. Hoping that the lower rates would increase the money supply and protect the U.S. economy from the Russian currency crisis, the Fed effectively churned out new dollars into the pockets of American consumers. Many of these dollars worked their way into the stock market, pushing lofty valuations still higher. It seemed as if stocks could keep on climbing forever.

But when the Russian threat subsided, the Fed reversed course and hiked the federal funds rate multiple times in a bid to head off inflation. The rate climbed by 125 basis points in just nine months, reaching 6.0% on March 21, 2000, and the Fed would raise it by another 50 points just two months later.[16] This policy change caused the money supply to ebb just as stock prices reached their peak and the economy began to slow down. The majority of investors may not have recognized what was happening at the time, but thanks in part to Mr. Greenspan the party he had helped create abruptly ended.

Overseas, Peter correctly read what was happening as soon as the NASDAQ started to teeter. Even though public capital markets were the ones crashing, he realized that the cash available for private equity would soon become scarce, as well. Calling upon Kenny Howery, Jack Selby, and the other members of his finance team, Peter told them to work the phones non-stop until every penny of the promised $100 million was deposited into the company's bank accounts. Mark Woolway, one of Peter's top lieutenants, created a physical indicator of the situation's intensity as a pile of discarded Red Bull energy drink cans accumulated on his desk over several tense days.

Peter's desperate tactics worked—the round promptly closed with none of the investors dropping out. The final wire settled just after the beginning of April. On April 3, the NASDAQ slumped to 4,223, and by mid-April it had given back the entire 1,500 point run-up it enjoyed following my arrival at Confinity.

Had Peter waited even a few days, the stock market's collapse would have taken X.com's agreed-upon valuation with it. In turn, the financing round might have stalled as investors began to second guess the equity stakes they were receiving in return for their money. Had Peter been forced to go back to square one and start the investment process over, it's unlikely he could have secured such a large infusion of funds. As the year wore on, the stock market slide made venture capital in Silicon Valley much harder to obtain; after peaking at $9.7 billion in investments during the second quarter, the regional total fell 12% in the third and another 16% in the fourth.[17] Peter's foresight brought in millions of extra dollars for a company in dire need of them.

With $100 million in the bank, our newly merged and rapidly growing company had survived a close call and now seemed ready for anything. External and internal challenges would soon put this readiness to the test.

CHAPTER FOUR

GROWING PAINS

APRIL—MAY 2000

"OH MY GOSH! Did you see this?!"
By now I had grown used to such exclamations from Luke. Often excitable, my former boss still sat near his old team's bullpen, so it was not uncommon to hear him let out an occasional cry when something attracted his curiosity.

"What's going on?" I asked, lackadaisically spinning my chair 180 degrees toward the direction of X.com's vice president of strategy. Four months removed from the old economy, I was becoming accustomed to out-of-the-blue conversations interrupting my work, especially from my colleagues hailing from the Confinity side of the company. While this cultural openness sometimes made it difficult to manage workflow, it also gave employees a chance to learn about and discuss a host of new ideas. And almost any piece of information coming from Luke, whether or not it was practicable, was guaranteed to be interesting.

"Did you see this headline on News.com? 'eBay, Visa Partner in Bill-Pay Deal,'" Luke replied, already in the process of grabbing his cell phone to call Reid Hoffman. "EBay convinced Visa to work with them on Billpoint! This is bad!"

I shuddered as I turned back around toward my monitor and pulled up the Web site Luke mentioned. Somehow eBay seemed capable of seizing headlines whenever it wanted—and not just seizing but one-upping its performance of the last time around. The Wells Fargo announcement at the beginning of March already had us worried, but now eBay had just brought another player into its camp with even more manpower and money than the auction service itself.

The article stated that the credit card oligopolist had agreed to market Billpoint through a combination of print and television ads in exchange for eBay promoting Visa on its Web site.[1] But as worrisome as this marketing support for our payments competitor sounded, it wasn't even the worst news in the piece. The companies had decided to waive all seller fees to receive payments funded by a Visa credit or debit card until the end of May. Since Visa accounted for more credit card payments than MasterCard and all other brands combined,[2] this would dramatically lower Billpoint's fees for all sellers who opened accounts.

I sat there stunned, thinking over this latest development. Even though eBay seemed to have had a devil of a time ironing out the technical aspects of Billpoint, within a single month it had forged business alliances and drawn up marketing plans that positioned its subsidiary as the top contender to PayPal while it still remained in beta testing. Whenever Billpoint officially launched—and this announcement suggested that day would come soon—it would have integration into eBay's Web site, back-end support from Wells Fargo, and promotional exposure from Visa. How was our tiny marketing group of three people with no official budget supposed to stand up to this?

Growth would have to be the source of our salvation. PayPal's breakout performance in March gave us a nice lead over Billpoint, and our expansion showed no sign of abating. Sellers continued to use AutoLink to insert PayPal banners even after the logo dust-up with eBay, and total payment volume climbed every week. Whatever we lacked in marketing firepower, I thought, hopefully we'll make up for with our young but growing network, easy-to-use product, and $5 user bonuses.

We soon had a chance to find out. After monitoring eBay's site every day for weeks on end for any signs of activity, we saw that Billpoint opened its registration process to all users in early April. The sign-up procedures seemed similar to PayPal's. Users had to click on one of the many Billpoint banners that populated eBay's site to go to the Billpoint Web site and complete an account registration module by supplying their name, e-mail address, credit card number, and eBay login information. After creating an account, a seller posting an item on eBay could select the Billpoint payment checkbox on the "Sell Your Item" form to have eBay display a Billpoint logo at the top of his auction. This integration promised to make it much easier for sellers to advertise Billpoint rather than PayPal to their winning bidders. If an auction offered both services, our tiny AutoLink logo, buried at the bottom of the description section, would have a difficult time competing for the buyer's attention.

In connection with Billpoint's launch, eBay decided to turn to a proven method for generating immediate interest in its new service. The auction site announced a free listing day for all sellers who included Billpoint as a payment option in their listings. In the past, eBay had periodically held free listing events during which it waived the fees charged to sellers for posting an auction on its site, an amount that typically ranged between 25¢ and 50¢ per item.

The prospect of saving money attracted a fair amount of seller attention. Within the course of a day Billpoint's penetration of all eBay listings rose from under 1% to 10% of eBay's 4 million auctions. To put this gain into perspective, this free listing day propelled Billpoint to a listing share level that took PayPal a month to reach after we began focusing our efforts on eBay. It was utterly demoralizing.

Shocked by this development, we held an intense round of strategy sessions to determine how to respond. At Reid's request I started working on a marketing campaign to our customers reminding them of PayPal's benefits in an effort to keep them from abandoning our service. But as the dust settled and a couple of days passed, we realized that maybe the apocalypse wasn't upon us just yet.

Billpoint began to give back its gains. Slowly but surely, the service's listing share ticked down each day for the next week until it settled at around 6%.

The explanation for Billpoint's sharp rise and gradual decline came from the average lifespan of online auction listings. EBay's site allowed sellers to choose between three, seven, and ten days for their listings, a choice that essentially let the seller decide on the tradeoff between attracting more bids through longer listings versus turning over more product with shorter ones. The average listing time worked out to be just under one week. While Billpoint's free listing day did convince some sellers to sign up for the service, the subsidy also encouraged these same individuals to add extra inventory on eBay's site in order to avoid paying a fee. These two effects combined to cause a spike in Billpoint's listing share that partially subsided as the auctions closed over the following three to ten days. Sellers with Billpoint accounts allowed their listed inventory to return to normal levels as eBay's listing fees resumed, bringing Billpoint's listing share down from 10% to 6%.

Even though our office breathed a sigh of relief as Billpoint's numbers dropped, we saw eBay's big-name partnerships and free listing day as clear signs that the auction giant intended to pursue the payments sector aggressively. Beating them in the race to build a payments network would require all of the ingenuity, tricks, and moxie X.com could muster. Unfortunately an entirely different set of problems was about to confront our young company.

◊

Aside from receiving a periodic call from Reid when a crisis began to brew, the marketing group had otherwise fallen off the radar of X.com's post-merger regime. While talented, our little team was also young and inexperienced. Jennifer Chwang had started at Confinity just a week before me and had a similar background in finance. Twenty year old Paul Martin had dropped out of Stanford only one month earlier. Between the three of us, we had a grand total of about ten months of experience in marketing roles.

Contrary to Luke's initial reassurance that hiring a new vice president of marketing would be a top priority, no candidate for the position had yet been interviewed. And without a head our department received minimal day-to-day guidance. Reid, in charge of the entire payments division, seldom had the time to check in with us on routine matters, and the other executives such as Sacks who interacted with our group before the merger were now tasked with other goals, depriving us of their informal counsel, as well.

To make matters even more bewildering for our team, many of the advertising campaigns we pursued prior to the merger were discontinued. In an effort to save cash, the company phased out all direct mail and banner ad campaigns as X.com moved away from advertising toward a combination of viral growth, eBay auctions, and corporate partnerships to acquire new customers. Even the charity robot project was scrapped following the merger, a victim of the expensive buying binge it would have required just as much as the minor problem that it never functioned exactly as Max had intended.

Marketing's neglect was not shared by our colleagues in business development. The ranks of their group had grown to nearly a dozen people, and their vice president, Matt Bogumill, an easy-going classmate of Peter's, frequently accompanied Bill Harris on high profile trips to negotiate user-swapping promotions with other Internet companies. Somewhat symbolic of their post-merger importance, on Friday afternoons at five o'clock Matt and the rest of his team did an end-of-the-week boogey by their desks to the tune of Britney Spears's "Baby One More Time."

Although business development may have been Harris's favored division, PayPal's scorching growth soon forced customer service onto center stage. Our record-setting increase from 10,000 accounts at the beginning of the year to over 1 million in March helped Peter convince investors to part with their cash but it also began to overwhelm the company's fledgling operations department.

In contrast to my first day at Confinity, when a customer service director could leisurely spend thirty minutes on the phone with a user who wanted to synch our Palm software, X.com now had thousands of e-mail queries pouring in daily. While most customers used PayPal's service without a problem, user error as well as quirks with the credit card and bank account systems made it impossible to eliminate the chance of a customer having a problem. And since we had nearly 20,000 people signing up every day, this meant the number of daily inquiries quickly became very large. X.com's customer service staff in Palo Alto, even with the assistance of contractors in Burbank, could not keep up with the influx. Frustrated users awaiting a reply often sent a second or third message to follow up. The situation began to snowball and by the end of March our queue of unanswered customer service e-mails topped 100,000.[3]

To be fair, X.com wasn't the only young Internet company to experience customer service woes. Leanly staffed startups, minted to bring an online product to market, seldom have the infrastructure in place to deal with an escalation in customer service needs; a research firm reported that half of all online retailers took more than three days to respond to e-mails.[4] And in some ways, X.com found itself facing a unique set of customer demands. A provider of an online service such as e-mail or resume-hosting knows that its users can generally wait several days for a reply, and an online retailer who cannot generate a timely answer to a potential customer's question only has one sale to lose. But PayPal proved to be different.

We found out that both senders and receivers who are concerned about the status of a payment take more than a passing interest. And for good reason—it's their money! When the status of a transaction was in doubt or funds were inaccessible, our customers needed quick answers and understandably were not willing to wait days for assistance. Some, as I had seen firsthand from my seat at the old Confinity office, were willing to take matters into their own hands, even if that meant driving from nearby states to reclaim their funds.

EBay sellers who used PayPal to receive payments for their auctions were especially upset over growing delays in the amount of time it took them to receive withdrawal checks from X.com. While sellers had the option to transfer funds electronically from their PayPal account to their bank, most periodically chose to request a check for the full amount of their balance. One seller with the username "Pianotoone" described to a reporter what had become an all too common experience: "It took over three weeks to get my money and four calls to their 800 number (waiting an average of twenty-five minutes each on hold) and five e-mails (of which three were answered one week later)."[5]

Unfortunately this seller wasn't alone. Customers posting on Web site message boards became increasingly critical of the company's handling of the customer service crisis. Many board posters seemed almost nostalgic for the PayPal of just a couple of months before. A fictional history of PayPal was being created—many users claimed that PayPal had been a great little startup until a bank named X.com took it over, reduced the bonuses from $10 to $5, and cut back on customer service personnel to save a few bucks.

In truth, the causes of the customer service problem were less devious. While the dramatic increase in the e-mail backlog took everyone by surprise, neither the post-merger X.com nor its two predecessor companies had been guilty of ignoring customer needs. Soon after I arrived, Confinity began to reorient its customer response strategy to revolve around e-mail. Inbound phone calls were costly and labor-intensive, making them difficult for any startup to scale up as its total number of users increased, especially if it planned to grow its users as fast as Confinity envisioned. To that end, the online help section of PayPal's Web site had been changed to encourage e-mail inquiries and the company's customer service phone number was placed on an obscure site page. Dave Wallace had taken the lead on a project to implement an e-mail management system from Kana to handle account holders' inquiries, a process that continued after the merger.

Yet even though the company took early measures to put a customer service program into place, the tidal wave of new users overwhelmed our infrastructure's capacity and the solutions we were relying on proved incapable of scaling up. Customer service needed additional manpower, but with the Silicon Valley unemployment rate still hovering near 1% in early-2000, local labor was scarce and expensive. While perhaps more cost effective, outsourcing had not produced high quality results; it was rumored that many of our contractors in Burbank had never opened their own PayPal account. Facing these constraints, Elon Musk tasked Julie Anderson, one of his first hires at X.com, with finding a quick way to increase the size of our customer service department. Realizing that local expansion and outsourcing were out of the question,

Julie set out on a multi-city tour across the country to find a location for a new customer service center.

In addition to Julie, other members of the company sought ways to help alleviate the crisis. David Sacks emerged from a month of near-exile with a proposal he contended would address the customer service dilemma—adding message boards to PayPal's site. By allowing customers to communicate with one another they could solve each other's problems, he argued, stemming the flood of inbound e-mails. Sacks hired an intern to talk to third-party providers to determine the fastest way to get a PayPal message board live.

Management even called on the hitherto forgotten marketing team to join the fray. Reid put the word out that my writing skills should be utilized on canned e-mail responses for our service representatives to use with the Kana response system. Paul was tapped to compile much-needed training manuals for our Burbank contractors.

But without additional customer service staff to work the queue, the backlog remained. With nearly half a million new accounts opened in the month of April alone and our payment volume averaging close to $2 million a day, PayPal continued to bring in new users faster than our customer service team could handle it. Rather than surfing along on the crest of our wave of growth, it increasingly looked like that same wave was about to pull us under.

◊

"Hey! Are you running a query?" Jamie Templeton rumbled from halfway across the room.

I looked over my shoulder as the tall, Polo shirt-clad project manager approached. "I'm putting together the daily user report," I replied. Maintaining this report was a project the marketing group took over from Jamie soon after I joined the company. Over the subsequent months I had expanded its scope to include key metrics such as payment volume and the percentage of accounts with linked credit cards, making our analyses more valuable but also more complicated to compile.

"You've got to turn it off now," he insisted, leaning over my desk. "I think it's causing the live site to crash!"

As April progressed, the PayPal Web site had become slower and less stable. Pages took longer to download and users would frequently be confronted by error messages while trying to log in to their accounts. Max and Jamie had already killed off the World Domination Index, the user counter that employees could run on their desktops, out of concern over the load it placed on our over-burdened live database. Now, for the first time, a query that had been written by an engineer for my report was putting too much strain on the database and actually caused the site to go down.

I pulled up my UNIX session and canceled the query. After that I was successfully able to log in to my PayPal account.

"Well, I guess we can't run that any more during the day!" Jamie quipped, his attitude shifting from serious to playful as soon as the threat had ended.

"So what does that mean for the future of this little report?" I sighed, contemplating all the complaints I was sure to receive over its absence. At Confinity Peter had encouraged the broadest possible dissemination of data so all employees could understand how the business was tracking and have the data necessary to discuss high level strategy. The tradition of sending the report to everyone had continued following the merger, and by now the entire company looked forward to its midday distribution.

"We're working on putting together a reporting database. Basically it will be a backup of the live database that gets replicated every evening. We'll be able to run queries on it without compromising the live site."

"So when will that be ready?"

"I don't know," he groaned, answering a question that evidently he'd been asked more than once before. "Hopefully in the next couple of weeks."

Although the two companies had been wed for six weeks, Jamie and Max still found themselves struggling to integrate two very different engineering teams. The majority of Confinity's engineers knew UNIX, while X.com's engineers used Windows NT—a schism that proved difficult to reconcile. The two engineering teams were also culturally different. Many of Confinity's engineers were friends of Max from the University of Illinois and, like him, were young, outgoing, and inquisitive. This contrasted to X.com's team, which on the whole struck me as more introverted and less entrepreneurial. These technological and cultural rifts were exacerbated when X.com's former CTO, after losing his position to Max in the merger, departed following the close of the deal.

Since that time, very little development had gone on and as a result no changes went live on the PayPal Web site. X.com's original service had been re-branded as "X-Finance" and its bonus program had been ended, but none of its financial products had been grafted onto PayPal, nor had any steps been taken to merge the PayPal and X.com databases as Bill Harris had promised. The PayPal and X-Finance Web sites continued to run as completely separate services. Even our corporate e-mail systems took two months to integrate; most e-mails that Confinity employees thought they were sending to their X.com colleagues never arrived.

Given the tumult in engineering and customer service, marketing's isolation seemed almost insignificant. In my self-appointed role as the tiny group's head, my frequent status inquiries to Reid signaled our need for executive guidance. Toward the end of April, citing the obvious importance for marketing to have an outlet to management, Reid placed our group under Vince Sollitto, the company's recently hired PR director, in what he described as an interim move.

Vince came to Confinity soon after the Scotty affair exposed the company's need for in-house public relations. He had worked with Sacks in D.C. on the staff of Congressman Chris Cox, a high ranking Republican from Orange County. The two later parted ways when Sacks went to law school and Vince became the spokesman for Arizona Senator John Kyl (whom he dubbed "the *other* senator from Arizona" to distinguish him from the headline-grabbing John McCain). The pair stayed in touch, and Vince even served as a reader for Sacks on *The Diversity Myth* before later rejoining him at Confinity.

I instinctively liked this hard-boiled, smooth-talking PR man. Although his arrival relieved me of my role as the quasi-head of marketing, I was happy to have a director at the helm of our group to elevate its status and provide us with some high level direction. Little did I know that it would turn out to be a very brief arrangement.

◊

With the customer service crisis mounting, the engineering team divided, the Web site's performance faltering, and Billpoint looming on the horizon, Bill Harris turned his attention to negotiating even more business development deals—this time with companies in the so-called "group space."

In late 1999 a host of Web sites popped up to provide friends, clubs, and teams a place to congregate in cyberspace. The logic was that people who met regularly in the real world would need an online venue to communicate and plan their activities. EGroups, the largest group service, boasted of having 15 million users, and its competitor eCircles claimed to have several million itself. Both companies offered their services free to their customers, collecting money from advertisers who paid for banners on their sites.

Reasoning that many of these online communities would need to send money to pay for club dues and joint activities, Harris inked deals with both eGroups and eCircles. In exchange for promoting PayPal on their sites, X.com agreed to pay them a generous bounty for every customer they referred to us.

In the media, the executive team began to trumpet X.com's position as market leader for group payments. The press release announcing the close of the $100 million financing round tried to make our market penetration sound more diverse than it really was, lumping the group sites into the same class as eBay: "X's PayPal service is the preferred payment service on eBay and other online auction sites, and the payments provider of choice for the Internet's leading virtual community sites eGroups and eCircles."

The group sites weren't the only Internet sector Harris was targeting for business development deals. The company also began courting AllAdvantage, a pay-to-surf Web site that flashed banner ads in a large toolbar while its subscribers accessed the Internet. AllAdvantage's business model was simple—advertisers would pay the company to serve up online ads, and the company would pass on to its subscribers a portion of those fees to look at the ads. Net surfers, as well as those rumored Asian Web farms, downloaded the company's toolbar and went about their business, periodically collecting checks.

With hindsight, the potential benefits of partnering with group space and pay-to-surf companies were at best dubious. None of these three companies had sustainable business models, and all would be gone within a year.[6] The energy Harris expended in marathon meetings with his executive team discussing costly customer acquisition deals could have gone into addressing the scalability problems exposed by our rapid growth. If PayPal's customer service, Web site performance, and money-losing business model could not be fixed to support our ever-increasing number of users, then eventually our viral growth would be choked off and our cash bled dry. Conversely, if we focused too much on infrastructure at the expense of growth, Billpoint or another competitor might overtake our lead and reach some level of critical mass before us. In this way growth and scalability resembled the proverbial chicken and egg problem—we needed to find ways to improve PayPal's scalability without interrupting its torrid viral growth.

Even from my position in the organization, I wondered at the time how costly customer acquisition deals with flavor-of-the-month dotcoms fit into that equation.

If there was a silver lining to our rapidly deteriorating situation, it was that Billpoint failed to capitalize. After its initial boost from the free listing day subsided, Billpoint hovered around 6% listing acceptance for most of April. Meanwhile, during that time PayPal continued its upward march, growing from 25% to 30% listing share in only a few weeks. EBay, watching our uninvited startup blow past its own subsidiary, reacted by declaring another free listing day for all sellers with Billpoint accounts. This time Billpoint's listing share surged up to about 14% of all auctions overnight, but once again the gains were short lived. It tumbled back to around 7% within a week.

Like the Federal Reserve's earlier decision to slash interest rates in hope of reviving a sluggish economy, a week later eBay took the unprecedented step of declaring a third free listing day for Billpoint.[7] The results followed course. Billpoint acquired some new accounts and its existing users listed more auctions on the site, but after a few days this inventory surge cycled through the system and Billpoint's listing share retreated. By the time this flurry of promotions concluded, about 9% of eBay's listings accepted Billpoint. This was an impressive relative increase in just a month's time but in an absolute sense it had to be a disappointment for eBay. During the same period, PayPal's listing share continued to rise, taking us to 35% of all auctions by the middle of May. Even with eBay's promotions, the gap between our two services actually grew from 20% in mid-April to 26% in mid-May.

Several factors contributed to Billpoint's inability to gain significant ground in spite of our infrastructure woes. The lack of any fees in addition to our $5 referral bonuses gave sellers a strong financial motivation to choose PayPal despite Billpoint's free Visa offer. PayPal also had a first-mover advantage in its favor, meaning that many of the more sophisticated sellers looking to use one of the new online payments services had already discovered PayPal before Billpoint launched. And, finally, it stood to reason that we were beginning to see the creation of a nascent network since both buyers and sellers who signed up for PayPal during one transaction insisted on continuing to use it for future payments.

Of course, PayPal's ability to fend off Billpoint while on cruise-control came as small consolation. EBay's apparent dogged willingness to promote and integrate its payment service with its auction site signaled future skirmishes ahead. X.com needed to get its own house in order or the next clash might prove more fateful than the free listing days.

◊

With our management team spending time cutting deals, the rest of the company struggled to address the customer service crisis. Following a cross-country tour that took her through Reno, Boise, and Denver, Julie Anderson selected Omaha, Nebraska, as the location for X.com's new customer service center. With a large, educated workforce and lower costs than Silicon Valley, the decision to set up the 500-person call center in Omaha made financial sense. It also elicited a fair amount of attention. Word of a California-based firm opening a division in the heartland attracted headlines in local papers and prompted Nebraska Governor Mike Johanns to attend the press conference announcing the decision.[8]

The media coverage paid immediate dividends; a recruiting session at the Holiday Inn in early April was flooded by job-seekers. Given our company's desperation to get the new center up and running, almost every applicant was hired on the spot.

As Omaha prepared to come online, debates over several customer service initiatives raged in Palo Alto. Sacks's idea to place message boards on our site ground to a halt as solutions proposed by third party providers required several months to integrate into PayPal's Web site. That was time we didn't have. Paul suggested an alternative scheme of hiring customers to answer e-mails as a temporary solution to the crisis, but a method of carrying out the logistics proved elusive. There was just no way to supervise the quality of the service we'd be offering.

In contrast to the message board and outsourcing proposals, the company did manage to find an approach that helped resolve some customer problems. Paul and several other employees began to monitor and respond to the message boards on other companies' Web sites. Two community sites, AuctionWatch and the Online Traders Web Alliance (OTWA), attracted many of eBay's regulars who enjoyed the conversation topics and dynamics that they found there. Posting replies under the pseudonym "PayPal Paul," Paul Martin quickly became a welcomed fixture on these sites. This tactic allowed us to interact directly with the auction community, and both AuctionWatch and OTWA agreed to permit X.com employees to post official messages on their sites. EBay, whose message boards attracted more traffic than either AuctionWatch or OTWA, extended no such invitation.

Having employees answer questions on third party message boards did not turn around the customer service nightmare overnight, but it did lay the groundwork for a communications strategy that would prove critical in the coming months. And with our Omaha center still hiring in preparation of opening its doors, this gave us an outlet to reassure our customers that better times lay ahead.

◊

Peter Thiel's e-mail on Friday, May 5, arrived just after noon. I had been talking with Paul about going down the street to pick up some lunch when I saw a subject line that robbed me of my appetite: "Resignation as Executive Vice President."

I blinked and did a double-take. There must be some mistake, I thought. But when I clicked on the message to read its contents, I knew it was not.

"Effective today, I am resigning as Executive Vice President of X.com," the message began. "[After] seventeen months of working literally day and night, I am simply exhausted. In the process, we've gone from the early planning stages to a business that's implementing our plans for world domination... I'm more of a visionary and less of a manager [so] it has become all the more critical to transition to a team that will manage and scale X.com's operations. The recent $100 million financing round... seemed like a natural point of closure for my day-to-day involvement and like a good point to transition to those who will lead X.com's IPO." He concluded by stating that he hoped to stay in contact with the tremendous individuals he had met at X.com and wished everyone well.

Something smelled rotten.

While my interaction with Peter declined after the merger, I knew him well enough to know that he wasn't the type to walk away from implementing the vision he spoke of during my first Confinity meeting. His e-mail offered multiple reasons for his departure—perhaps too many—and none of them sounded convincing, especially the point about transitioning to a team that "would manage and scale X.com's operations." Since he ran our finance department, how was his presence impeding our operations? From what I could tell, his group was the only one that was functioning correctly. Clearly the reasons for his departure ran deeper than what the e-mail publicly stated.

This realization was unsettling. Not only was some unspoken factor driving a talented leader out of the company, it revealed significant divisions in the executive team at a time when X.com desperately needed a unified front. Two months had passed since the merger and we had made no progress on what Bill Harris had identified as the major benefit of the deal—the ability to offer X.com's supermarket of financial products to PayPal's account holders.

Acting on my suspicions, I made some discreet inquiries and learned that Peter and Harris had indeed locked horns. In an attempt to address X.com's soaring red ink, Harris floated an idea to charge customers a fee to send money. Peter opposed the suggestion, calling it both ineffective at fixing our business model and at odds with PayPal's sender-friendly service. Bank One had done the same thing with eMoneyMail, Peter countered, and it led to a dead end—no one used their service. The pair clashed again when an outraged Peter learned that Harris had used company funds to make a $25,000 donation to the Democratic party.[9] Tension between the executives boiled over and it became clear that X.com had grown too small for the "Big Three." Peter was the odd man out. Whether he technically quit or was asked to leave was unclear but also irrelevant. By this point Peter blamed Harris for the company's woes and Harris resented his insubordination; a parting was inevitable.

As much as this turn of events dismayed me, following Peter out the door was not an option. After just six months on the job, I—like most of the other young Confinity recruits—had nowhere to go. My only choice was to stand and fight against the scalability challenges threatening to overwhelm the company, even if one of our best and brightest would not be there to fight them with us. I didn't realize it as I reconciled myself to staying with a company that no longer held quite the same meaning, but this management struggle had already set into motion a series of events that would change X.com's destiny.

◊

Over the previous weeks, David Sacks, who had not fared well in Harris's org chart, often found himself spending time with Elon Musk, X.com's flashy chairman, to discuss branding issues for PayPal's Web site. Elon was a major advocate of X.com's brand and maintained a hands-on approach for a chairman. Realizing this, Sacks often sought out his opinion in trying to strike the right balance between the PayPal product name and the overall X.com umbrella brand. As they reviewed dozens of logo mockups from the design team, the two formed a close working bond.

At the time I paid their collaborations little attention. Interaction with our chairman wasn't limited to VP-level officers—almost everyone had worked with X.com's founder at some point or another. Elon kept long hours, occupied a desk in the same office as Harris and Peter, and often involved himself in day-to-day management decisions and meetings. In fact, as I got to know him I realized Elon was nothing like the brash playboy the press made him out to be. Not that this was entirely the media's fault—a more image-savvy executive probably wouldn't have asked a reporter from *Upside* to photograph him seated in his black 1967 Jaguar E-type convertible with his girlfriend and dog.[10] But public image notwithstanding, Elon worked incredibly hard and cared a tremendous deal about his company.

It was from his active vantage point that Elon witnessed the company's growing pains firsthand while listening to grumblings from members of the executive team upset with Harris's direction and the company's inability to execute tasks under his stewardship. Faced with an uncertain situation, Elon did not shy away from the spotlight—to the contrary, as tension mounted over the company's malaise, he moved to reclaim it.

Elon called an emergency board meeting on Thursday, May 11, to oust the man he had hired as CEO just six months before. Harris caught word of Elon's plans prior to the meeting, and in the hours leading up to the event both sides furiously lobbied the independent directors, barraging them with cell phone calls in an attempt to curry favor. Harris prepared a lengthy PowerPoint presentation to make the case that the company needed him to stay on as chief executive and instead replace certain "unscalable" members of the management team—most likely the personnel he had inherited from Confinity. But when the meeting commenced it became evident that his pleas were falling on deaf ears; a fellow director cut off his slideshow with a resolute declaration: "Bill, it's over." Elon's claim that Harris had failed to get the company to execute in the face of mounting obstacles carried the day.

With the board closing ranks behind the chairman, Harris had no choice but to tender his resignation. Elon took over control of operations by assuming the position of CEO and—in a conciliatory move to Confinity's stakeholders—turned over his position as chairman to Peter. Harris resolutely pledged to help with the transition but then sat in stony silence for the remainder of the meeting.

Employees learned of the news through another bombshell e-mail that afternoon. Elon did his best to frame it as a positive development; after facing the challenges of a startup under their co-leadership, the company now stood at a point where it only needed one man at the helm. Elon would be that man, allowing Harris the opportunity to spend some much needed time with his family.

In spite of the semi-public clash between Harris and Peter, the news came as a surprise to those of us who were unaware of the tense board meeting. Whatever the quality of his decisions, the loss of Harris's star-power could certainly hurt the company's prospects if we needed to raise more money. At the very least, the continued infighting forced me to rethink the wisdom of my purchase of a new Ford just the day before.

The vanquished Harris, in a final public display of charm, stopped by each employee's desk that afternoon to wish the staff farewell prior to his departure. "Thanks for all your hard work," he said to me, clasping my hand. "Those reports you put together were very helpful. Best wishes in everything; I know you're going to do just great." Even in the face of defeat, Harris still exuded the natural grace and charisma I observed the first time I heard him speak. His charm evidently knew limits, though. According to one eyewitness, as soon as Harris finished making the rounds, the former CEO filled a box with the contents of his desk and exited the building for the final time. (So much for the transition process.)

It wasn't long before the media caught word of the boardroom rebellion. The Internet-focused publication *The Industry Standard* broke the story. Painting it as a clash of egos, the article quoted an anonymous source as saying, "From what I understand, there were personality conflicts at the top… Some people threatened to leave if [Harris] didn't, and the board asked him to step down."[11]

"We were sharing the CEO role," Elon told the same reporter, "and the board thought it made sense to have one hand on the steering wheel. They thought that should be me."

With the benefit of hindsight, Harris's departure seemed inevitable. The company ground to an operational halt in the two months following the merger, and a long list of challenges threatened its future. The centralized reporting structure, with the entire payments division reporting to Reid, isolated much of the company's operations away from the CEO while asking one executive with little support staff to take on too many tasks. Combined with the endless stream of business development deals and never-ending meetings that kept the CEO's attention elsewhere, the situation allowed some very real problems to emerge. This contributed to the operational risks, such as the customer service crisis, the Web site's increasing unreliability, and the failure to develop revenue-creating features, that jeopardized the company.

To be fair to Harris, managing the post-merger company would have presented a tough challenge to most chief executives. The trials that accompany either merging two companies or growing a business were worsened by having both needs present at the same time. He faced a daunting task and he did score a few successes, including negotiating the merger itself and garnering some positive media accolades—such as the inclusion of X.com on the tech magazine *Red Herring's* "100 Most Important Companies in the World" list.[12] But in the end his old-economy management style clashed with those around him and prevented the company from moving to address its mounting challenges.

The irony to this saga is that the very same rampant customer growth that caused X.com's scalability problems also preserved the firm's competitive position during this post-merger drift. PayPal's viral model had a life of its own, holding off Billpoint at a time when our company would not have been able to deploy an effective engineering or marketing response to a direct assault. Even if Bill Harris did not survive the turmoil following the merger, PayPal made sure that its parent company, X.com, did.

◊

"Hey, buddy, we need to talk," Vince called out to me. The dark haired, bespectacled PR director wore an unusual scowl just above his square chin as he motioned for me to follow him to a nearby conference room.

Something big was happening. Just a few minutes earlier Paul had come by my desk and mumbled in a hushed tone that he was being transferred to a new department. Sacks, who had stopped by the prior evening to speak with him, told Paul that Elon had tasked him with the formation of a new product group. This team was to manage the design of new features for the Web site, and Paul was Sacks's choice to oversee the construction of new auction tools.

"Look, I wanted to give you the heads up on this," Vince said hastily as we sat down. "Sacks is going to come over in a minute. He's starting a new product group and you're being transferred over to it."

I was taken aback learning that I was to share in Paul's mysterious fate. "Do you know why? What about marketing?"

Vince shook his head. "There won't be a marketing group left after this," he sighed, removing his glasses and rubbing the area between his eyes. Judging from his demeanor I suspected that the shake-up had come as a surprise to him, too. "I guess you've heard Paul is also going. I'm not sure what the purpose is, but Sacks has a mandate to pull anyone he wants into this new team. There's nothing I can do about it."

The thought of reporting to the intense Sacks did not thrill me. While I respected his keen intellect, I worried about his reaction to several clashes he and I had had over the company's message board strategy. And, more importantly, I liked marketing. I had learned a great deal on the job over the prior half year and took pride in having helped to stabilize the marketing team at a time when it needed it the most. Abandoning the team that I had worked to keep together in favor of building features for the Web site sounded unappealing, but I had little time to worry about it.

At this point Sacks marched in, a triumphant spring in his step. After dispensing with the briefest of greetings he bluntly cut to the chase. "We're forming a new product group to work directly with engineering to create features for the site," he said. "A lot of successful Silicon Valley companies have structures similar to this. It's going to eliminate bureaucracy and get our Web site development finally moving again."

"So what role do you see for me?" I asked.

"Product marketing," he answered. "Promoting new features, doing analysis of product adoption—that's all going to belong to you. You're going to be our one man marketing team!"

My PayPal career had just taken off.

CHAPTER FIVE

THE PRODUCERS

JUNE—JULY 2000

"OK, LET'S GET THIS STARTED!" David Sacks barked as he strode into X.com's main conference room.

The waiting employees fell silent as the vice president occupied a seat at the table's head. The narrow room he had chosen for this gathering was the largest of the company's three meeting rooms and nearly impossible to book on short notice. That Sacks had reserved it the day of the meeting said something about his newfound influence. Late morning sunlight from a large window overlooking University Avenue fell on the backs of the half-dozen members of the product team now turned to face their new boss.

"I suppose you all know why we're here," Sacks began, his mouth hinting at a smile. Exuding an air of confidence seldom seen in the weeks immediately following the merger, he added, "Our job is to fix the company, and we've got a lot of work to do!"

Just then the slim figure of the company's new CEO glided through the door. "Hello, everyone," Elon Musk said as he unassumingly took a seat off to Sacks's side.

After briefly glancing over at Elon, Sacks returned his gaze to my colleagues and me and continued: "Welcome to the product team. In figuring out who should be here, Elon and I considered everyone in the company. We tapped the best to be product managers, or—as I like to say—'producers,' since you're going to be responsible for producing results.

"The goal of forming this new team is to decentralize decision-making as much as possible. For the past couple of months everyone has talked about doing things but nothing has actually gotten done. As producers you are going to be working directly with your counterparts in engineering to build products for our Web site. I'll be involved with charting strategy at a high level and setting priorities, but each of you will be responsible for determining the optimal way to implement your specific features."

Sacks's tone made it clear that he wanted his producers to feel empowered. X.com's internal chaos in the wake of the merger had paralyzed most of the company. By contrast, Confinity's freewheeling atmosphere had allowed minimal supervision to be counterbalanced by shared goals, clear priorities, and encouragement from management that the staff suggest new ideas. I did not fully comprehend this on my tumultuous first day on the job, but Confinity had struck a balance that fostered both employee individuality and corporate flexibility. This winning formula enabled us to stop on a dime and implement new ideas quickly, to the point where we overhauled our business model to focus on eBay in less than a week. The disorganization following the merger had robbed the company of its ability to execute, and Sacks wanted to drive the point home that he saw the product team as the remedy.

Pausing to let everyone reflect on his message, Sacks looked up at the faces sitting around the table and resumed, "Now for some quick introductions so everyone knows what roles people have.

"Since the design team will still be reporting to me, Julie Anderson is going to help me in organizing and running this group." On the heels of establishing the Omaha customer service center, Julie had secured a promotion to director and with it earned the title of Sacks's second-in-command.

Sacks continued to go around the table to introduce each producer. "Amy Rowe will be responsible for building our business features... Denise Aptekar is going to be in charge of anti-fraud features... Patrick Breitenbach will handle products for our partners..."

The young Arkansan sitting to my right was next. "Paul Martin is going to build all of our auction-related products." Finally he got to me. "And Eric Jackson will be responsible for all of our product marketing."

Looking around the table, I noted my fellow producers' youthfulness. With an average age of just two and a half decades, our team was similar in age and experience to the rest of the company. Nevertheless, our vice president of product didn't view this as a negative. Displaying a steely self-confidence, on a subsequent occasion I heard Sacks dismiss our collective lack of experience: "That just means we haven't had the chance to learn how to do things wrong."

As Sacks alluded to in the kick-off meeting, my role as a producer was unique. Instead of working with engineers to develop new Web site features, Sacks wanted me to be product's liaison with our customers. I would be the channel of information from customers to product using surveys and metrics to help shape our offering to the marketplace. Likewise, I was tasked with communicating our services to users to drive adoption of new features and encourage profitable behavior.

Sacks had not been joking when he said I was to be the one man marketing team. With the transfer of Paul and me to the product group, the old marketing team disbanded. Jennifer Chwang stayed with Vince in a public relations capacity, meaning that no one else in the organization was focused on day-to-day marketing. Despite my having just six months' experience, Sacks and Elon had entrusted me with the responsibility of being PayPal's solitary marketer.

Within a matter of days following the product team's first meeting, Sacks relocated his squad down the street to 165 University, Confinity's former building, to be under his watchful eye. Thanks to the continued inflow of new employees, the old office had little space left for additional personnel; the design team had taken over the ping pong room, and almost every corner already housed a desk. Along with Paul, Amy Rowe, and the company's Web site content manager, I found myself assigned to the office's lone conference room. Nicknamed the "fish bowl" because of its glass wall, the twelve-by-twelve-foot room had only one phone line. Space was so limited that Paul and I shared a folding table that sagged under our monitors' combined weight.

Since only a month remained until the entire company would be moving to its new one-story building in the office park on the outskirts of Palo Alto, our spirits were lifted by knowing that our time in the overflowing office was temporary. And, given all that Sacks expected us to produce in such a short time, the cozy dorm-like environment—complete with dodge ball fights and water gun ambushes—that sprouted up between the producers and the engineers helped the two groups to bond. Our workspace was tight, but we knew we were there because we had a mission.

◊

X.com's business model needed help. While neither Elon nor Sacks said so in those terms, our woes went beyond the customer service meltdown and Web site crashes. The sea of red ink produced by the company's operations rose in tandem with the thousands of new users signing up for PayPal. Our burn rate averaged $10 million a month in the second quarter and continued to increase. Without a revenue-generating supermarket of financial products to upsell PayPal's users to, the company lacked any positive cashflow from operations to offset our bonus payments to our customers and processing fees to the credit card associations. Each new sign-up and credit card-funded transaction meant X.com parted with another chunk of the $100 million raised two months earlier by Peter.

While still a believer of his original vision of building a full-fledged financial mega-store, Elon acknowledged that we couldn't develop one overnight. None of the handful of X-Finance funds or services, which ran on different platforms, could be accessed through the PayPal system, and fee-generating offerings would take time to set up and gain subscribers.

The plan also posed a regulatory risk that forced us to move deliberately. Unlike X.com's original online service—which was set up under a commercial banking charter with clear rules to abide by—PayPal was not classified as a bank. This was fine by us. Since banks pay interest and extend loans they have a host of regulatory and capital requirements that cost a lot to comply with; keeping our flexible customer acquisition service from being categorized as a bank was therefore certainly desirable. Management knew that PayPal would eventually have to be classified as *something* and had instructed our lawyers to begin contacting the individual states that regulated money transmitters to obtain their interpretation of PayPal's status.[1] In the meantime, this meant that we couldn't just start throwing bank-like features on top of PayPal; the financial supermarket would have to wait until the regulated X-Finance system could be accessed by PayPal account holders.

Instead, Elon and Sacks concentrated on decreasing our burn rate by finding a way to generate revenue from PayPal transactions while at the same time lowering the cost of payment funding. Although this stopped short of scrapping the business model that Bill Harris adopted in the wake of the merger, this newfound focus on the marginal profitability of the "loss leader" PayPal service still marked a significant strategic shift.

But finding a way to book revenue on transactions would be tricky given how prominently the PayPal Web site promised to be "Always Free." The marketing problems posed by this pledge notwithstanding, charging senders a fee to use PayPal was not a viable option for the reasons that Peter cited in opposing Harris's suggestion along these lines. This left us with no option except to ask the recipients of funds to pay up, especially the auction sellers using PayPal to power their online businesses. But our collections could only go so far—demanding payments from all customers who received money could scare off the fee-sensitive occasional users and shatter our nascent network. We would have to find a solution that would only charge frequent sellers while leaving the service free for personal use.

Complementing the push to charge transaction fees was an effort to lower costs by reducing the percentage of payments funded by credit cards. Until only a few months back, Confinity's expectation had been that the ability to send money to anyone with an e-mail address would convince most users to leave money in their accounts. But with the ease of using a credit card to fund future payments, users instead opted to withdraw their balances immediately by asking for a check. This high turnover not only prevented us from booking revenue on the float, it also meant that customers funded the vast majority of their payments with costly credit cards. This forced X.com to pay a fee of about 2% to Visa or MasterCard almost every time a user sent money with PayPal.

Lacking a compelling suite of financial products that would induce users to keep more money in their PayPal accounts, the company instead focused on finding a cheaper alternative source of funding payments. At a cost of just several cents each, automatic clearing house (ACH) transfers from bank accounts seemed like an attractive option. An ACH acts like a paperless check by transferring funds from one bank account to a designated beneficiary, which in this case would be X.com. But ACHs also have drawbacks; unlike expensive bank wires that are instantaneous and guaranteed, an ACH can take several days to clear and runs the risk of bouncing.

The ACH time delay was a hurdle. PayPal users wanted to initiate instant transactions that didn't take days to complete. We realized that ACH-funded payments would seem instant to the customers if X.com itself advanced the money to the intended recipient until the sender's ACH cleared. But this would mean X.com would be essentially extending a line of credit to every buyer who linked a bank account, a maneuver fraught with risk since a user could have insufficient funds in his bank to cover the ACH. While the original X.com banking service did grant its users $500 in overdraft protection, there was no easy way to expand this to PayPal users given the delicate regulatory situation.

Ironically, credit cards provided the solution to our ACH problem. While costly as a funding source, credit cards could serve as collateral in case an ACH bounced. By using credit cards as a back-up funding source, we were able to front the cash ourselves on ACH-funded payments until the bank transfer settled. This decrease in risk made "instant ACH" a viable funding alternative for PayPal, enabling us to offer a bank account-funded payment option to all of our customers.

Introducing fees for sellers and encouraging buyers to use low-cost funding methods required some major changes to PayPal's Web site. Jamie Templeton and the engineers had made progress on the instant ACH feature prior to the creation of the product team. With producers now assuming the role of working directly with engineers, Sacks focused his group on creating a system of transaction fees while continuing to revisit the funding mix problem.

The product team's first feature release centered around the creation of new types of optional fee-bearing accounts. These business accounts, which included options for both corporations and sole proprietors, charged a rate of 1.9% as a fee on incoming payments. In return, customers choosing these accounts would receive enhanced services, including twenty-four hour customer support and special invoicing tools. We renamed PayPal's existing free accounts as personal accounts, an implicit suggestion to sellers to upgrade to a business account. Choosing to register for a fee-bearing account remained optional, although PayPal's user agreement had always said that we reserved the right to charge fees for "business use" of the service, effectively providing the company with wiggle room to mandate that sellers upgrade at some point in the future.

Amy Rowe took the lead on designing the business accounts, collaborating with me to launch the Web site content introducing our customers to this new service. Paul worked on improved auction logo insertion tools, and the rest of the producers focused on their areas of responsibility. For the first time since the merger, the company was addressing many of the risks threatening our business.

◊

Within just a few weeks the members of the energized product group had largely mastered their new jobs. Meeting daily with their counterparts in engineering and Web site design, the producers wrote specifications for the proposed features, tested their functionality, and planned out their appearance on PayPal's Web site. By mid-June the new features stood almost ready to go as Sacks's team rallied the company from two months of lethargy.

In some ways this surge of productivity struck me as less the result of the reorganization and more a resumption of the traits I first encountered at Confinity. Agility of thought and nimbleness of execution had provided Peter and Max's startup with a competitive advantage, and the producers' swift tinkering with X.com's business model hinted that these characteristics might become strengths of our post-merger company, as well. But this pair of qualities could also be a double-edged sword. If a bad idea hastily circumvented the vetting process, it had a greater potential to be implemented than in a company relying on more methodical procedures. Consider the case of Scotty.

With only one day until the new business account features launched, we fell into this trap. I was sitting in the fish bowl putting the finishing touches on our marketing campaign to announce the new services when Paul Martin walked in at eleven o'clock. I glanced up and thought about commenting on his bloodshot eyes—the byproduct of yet another late night of staring at a monitor—when he tipped me off to a new development.

"Have you heard that we made a change to the push?" he asked nonchalantly.

I shook my head to indicate I had not. "It's for funding expenses," he continued. "Sacks and Elon decided to introduce a $1,000 lifetime credit card spending limit on each account."

"A $1,000 lifetime limit!" I parroted. "When did this come about?"

"Last night," Paul answered. "Sacks and Elon were talking about it in Sacks's office when I stopped by around three, and we spent some time hashing it out and agreed it was the best thing to do. That way, after customers send $1,000 through PayPal with their credit card, they'll have to use a bank account to fund all future payments."

Something about the proposal caused my marketing instincts to recoil. Feeling as though I had increasingly become Peter Thiel's disciple of the network effect, this spending limit's potential to hinder growth concerned me. I feared this move would be unpopular with our users, especially eBay sellers concerned that many buyers would lack the option to pay them with credit cards. To stanch our flow of red ink, we needed to convince these same sellers to upgrade into fee-bearing accounts. As incomplete as our financial supermarket still was, at least PayPal enjoyed continued momentum from account registrations and a rising eBay listing share while we refined our business model. This proposal seemed to threaten that growth while offering no silver bullet for the business model in return; decreasing our funding expenses would bring little consolation if this meant driving sellers to Billpoint with its unlimited credit card policy.

Sensing high stakes, I decided to take a stand against this policy change. Fortunately the rough and tumble intellectual openness that Peter and Max imbued in their startup was not lost on Sacks. His ascent up the managerial ranks had not changed his willingness to tolerate dissent. As blunt as he could be in dealing with colleagues, he welcomed that same level of directness from his own staff. I realized soon after transferring to his team that my new boss cared more about results than glory. He accepted challenges on strategic issues so long as a rigorous analysis accompanied the opposition.

Sacks heard me out, but this time he didn't budge. He explained that the board gave Elon, and in turn, himself, control with the under-standing they would make quick progress on the company's cashflow, and they both saw this measure as a way of doing something about the problem. During the second quarter the margins on PayPal transactions plunged to a jaw-dropping -3.5%. The company paid about $2.50 in credit card processing fees and lost another $1.04 to fraud on every $100 in payments that flowed through our system. Changing our user policies to encourage the use of inexpensive ACH payments, Sacks said, was the best way to attack one of our largest expenses. I left knowing that I'd lost that round. Our executives' motivations made sense, but the potential unintended consequences of this decision worried me.

Late the following night, after I had headed home for the evening, our engineers pushed the new features and content to the Web site, including the amended text in the terms of use about the new lifetime credit card spending limit. Hundreds of users, still surfing the Web in the wee hours of the morning, flocked to our site after reading about the changes on eBay's message boards. All hell promptly broke loose.

Angered over the stringent new buyer spending limit, our sellers were also fearful that they'd be forced to upgrade to a business account. Violently claiming they were not really a "business" and that X.com had reneged on Confinity's "Always Free" promise for PayPal, sellers linked the spending limit policy change to the new fee-bearing ac-counts. "They want me to pay expensive fees while my buyers can't even use a credit card to pay me?" screamed the typical message board objection, "Then I'm just going back to checks and money orders only! Goodbye, PayPal!!!"

Our users' response was not lost on management. Sacks often made a point to lurk on message boards after a feature launch, and together with Paul he read the posts as they poured in. Sensing that a monumental backlash was brewing, not just against the new fee-bearing accounts but also against our brand, he called Elon to join them.

After a swift early morning meeting to regroup, Sacks and Elon sent PayPal Paul to do damage control on the message boards. Paul posted a "clarification" that the $1,000 lifetime credit card spending limit was a typo, it was supposed to be a $2,000 per six-month-period limit. He also explicitly stated a promise from management that would later prove fateful—X.com would never force sellers to upgrade to fee-bearing accounts.

After posting his message several times on the OTWA and Auction-Watch message boards, Paul went to eBay. Without an official discussion area for PayPal in eBay's community section of the site, Paul tracked down the random threads discussing PayPal in order to post the clarification. Management's speedy about-face worked; it soothed our angry customers and assured them that X.com would respond to their feedback.

This was the first time PayPal had explicitly used eBay's message boards to communicate with our users. EBay itself was not amused. EBay's community board watchdogs—nicknamed "Pinks" because of the pink line that appears at the top of the messages they post on the boards—observed PayPal Paul's messages and quickly scrambled to shut down his account on the grounds that X.com was abusing the boards by posting commercial messages.[2] Despite Reid Hoffman's subsequent protest to its legal team, eBay used the event to justify officially banning PayPal from its community boards. Fortunately this scuffle came after Paul succeeded in putting out most of the fires caused by our ill-conceived policy.

As the dust settled our young company learned a valuable lesson on the need for customer research, especially for changes that could impact the thousands of sellers now depending on PayPal for their livelihood. What was an item on the income statement for us could be a life-or-death business issue for our users. Although we would need to make tough choices in the weeks ahead to reverse the company's growing losses, the spending limit fiasco served as a reminder to all of us that those decisions could not be made in a vacuum—or, for that matter, at three in the morning.

◊

If Confinity's unofficial rallying cry had been "world domination," the post-merger company's was "X rocks!"

Elon's fondness for the X.com brand was physically evident throughout our offices. Ten boxes of "X rocks!" T-shirts sat in one corner. Employees wore four different versions of X.com polo shirts, drank coffee from X.com thermal mugs, and tossed around X.com Frisbees to relieve stress. Occasionally an engineer would lob an X.com foam rubber ball over his neighbor's cube wall, hoping to hit his unsuspecting victim on the top of the head. The entire company even took an afternoon off to go see a private screening of the movie *X-Men* at a local theater.

Not that this was out of the ordinary. Most startups, including Confinity, indulge in some corporate-branded paraphernalia. But Elon's designs for the "X" name went beyond tchotchke; he envisioned it as the all-encompassing brand for our business, PayPal included. Elon characterized X.com as a simple and memorable URL, symbolic of the company's mission to make financial management easy for everyone. X would be approachable and straightforward, a contrast to multinational, impersonal off-line competitors like Citibank. An unlimited number of product offerings such as X-Finance and X-PayPal could then be placed under the trusted X umbrella brand.

While that was Elon's branding vision, he seemed reluctant to acknowledge that his letter of choice came with baggage. Anyone who's walked through the red light section of a big city knows that X has connotations that have nothing to do with easy-to-use financial services. *Playboy* and *Penthouse* aside, the letter X can also hint a sense of mystery, such as "X marks the spot" or the TV show *The X Files*. In recent years, the term Generation X has also entered the vernacular, allowing X to lend itself to a number of edgy and youthful uses, such as "X-Games," a San Francisco competition for alternative sports like skateboarding and off-road biking.

Since the letter X was already branded with several distinct and vivid associations—pornography, mystery, edginess—well before X.com came into existence, these undertones weren't merely a distraction from the simple and straightforward image our company sought to foster. Each of them directly clashed with it. As the company's solitary marketer, I felt obligated to raise questions about the matter. Consumer familiarity with PayPal's brand was on the rise. By the end of June, more than 2.1 million PayPal accounts existed. We noticed that PayPal was increasingly used as a verb in eBay auction descriptions and message board posts, as in "you can PayPal me the money." But besides its nascent brand equity, PayPal's self-explanatory name also helped introduce the service to non-customers. Subjugating PayPal under the X umbrella, or phasing it out altogether in favor of X.com—a move I feared was the unspoken plan—seemed to be discarding a brand that boasted considerable promise for one with significant baggage.

And yet it was happening. Following the merger, while still in the capacity of chairman, Elon personally took an interest in Web site design and worked with Sacks to change the logo on the PayPal site. It went from a simple "X.com's PayPal" to a stylized X in a circle adjacent to the PayPal logo. Elon verbally referred to this as "X-PayPal," although most customers seemed uncertain what to make of it and continued to refer to the service simply as PayPal in their e-mails and auctions. Elon also modified the AutoLink auction logos to display the word X.com in large fonts and relocated the PayPal Web site to an X.com sub-domain (www.paypal.x.com).

While I had reservations about the branding strategy, dissenting with Elon was a different process from taking on Sacks. Questioning the CEO required a bit more diplomacy. On one instance, while setting up the agenda for a consultant's presentation to summarize findings from her customer research, I told her to devote a few minutes at the end to discuss user feedback on the PayPal and X.com brands. When she came to the slides with users' comments, Elon roared, "Why are we discussing this?! This issue has already been settled!" With that, the subject was awkwardly tabled.

As much as I supported PayPal's brand over X, I wasn't ready to lose my head over it. Nor was Sacks. He seemed eager to ignore the X-PayPal matter, content to label it a "dual brand." Luke Nosek, who earlier had declined Sacks's invitation to join the producers, put forward an amusing alternative to this plan. He proposed that we adopt a "disposable brand" strategy where we would rely on one brand while we weathered the customer service and Web site stability crises, and after resolving them we could jettison it with its negative connotation in favor of the unspoiled alternative. Luke's proposal never enjoyed any real traction, though, and by June internal debate over the company's branding essentially ceased.

Despite X's baggage and the lack of a company-wide consensus, Elon supported the X.com brand in the face of all objections. His unwillingness to even revisit this topic seemed particularly difficult to explain since Elon was a smart businessman and an accomplished individual. While I never confirmed it, employees from the pre-merger X.com side of the company repeated as common knowledge that Elon paid $1 million for the rights to the X.com Internet domain. If this was the case, it's easy to understand his passion for the brand given the high price of his investment—a price driven up no doubt by bids from purveyors of assorted online "entertainment" services.

If that fact sheds some light on the CEO's stance, a subsequent discovery clarified it further. While compiling research to support the continued use of the PayPal name, I tracked down a videotape of several focus groups held by an X.com researcher hired the prior summer. The participants in the groups unsurprisingly disparaged the X brand. Women complained that it seemed pornographic, and middle-aged men remarked that it sounded too much like Generation X, comments similar to what we'd heard during several focus groups held by Confinity. The tapes provided no rationale whatsoever for the use of the X brand, raising the question of how the original decision to adopt the troubled letter could have been reached in the first place.

The official write-up from the research answered the question. In almost Orwellian fashion, the summary claimed that the participants liked the X.com name and identified it with "brand X," which supposedly stood for the underdog or the sympathetic little guy. While acknowledging some associations between X and pornography, this summary reported an overall positive reaction to the proposed brand.

The gap between the comments made in the focus groups and the conclusions of the official report was astonishing. Whether the summary's author set out to regurgitate what management wanted to hear or the feedback was legitimately misinterpreted was unclear, but the fact still remained that the company's brand strategy rested on very shaky premises.

Although my research turned up this interesting discovery, I had no way to put it to use. Elon's outburst directed at the marketing consultant effectively ended all internal debate on branding. With Sacks's reluctance to step into the middle of the issue again, I decided not to throw away my rising career on a matter I could not influence.

At least not yet.

◊

As our brand-challenged young company struggled to decrease its burn rate while continuing to grow market share, we constantly glanced over our shoulders at eBay. Our ever increasing dependence on the auction giant for customers and payment volume forced us to keep a concerned eye on eBay's activities, and for good reason. In the weeks following Elon's reorg, eBay was up to more than just exiling PayPal Paul from its community boards.

At the beginning of the year an upstart e-commerce Web site caused a media stir with a publicity stunt more memorable than Scotty beaming $1 million with a Palm Pilot. Half.com attracted worldwide attention when it cut a deal with the town of Halfway, Oregon, to rename the municipality after the Web site. The media latched onto the story as headlines hailed the decision by Halfway's city council while Half.com founder Josh Kopelman landed an appearance on NBC's *Today Show*.[3]

More worrisome to eBay than Half.com's media circus was its business model. When browsing for a bestseller novel on eBay, Kopelman noticed that many commodity items such as mass-produced books failed to attract bids. While eBay's success proved that auctions work well both for unique items with unknown values and for goods that buyers can wait for the listing to close before receiving, he theorized that the format was ill-suited for widely available items with established prices. Sensing a weakness in eBay's business model, Kopelman created a site that easily allowed individual sellers to list mass-produced items such as books, CDs, and videos at fixed prices. Posting a listing on Half.com was even simpler than listing on eBay—all a seller had to do was enter in his item's ISBN or UPC number from its bar code and Half.com would provide an image and description from existing databases.

Recognizing that Kopelman was onto something, Meg Whitman deployed her analysts to run a "build or buy" study. When word came back that it would take eBay's methodical development department up to nine months to complete a duplicate of Half.com, Meg—wary of giving Half.com the chance to scale up its network beyond the quarter-million users it had already—decided to do the deal. EBay acquired Half.com on June 13, 2000, for around $350 million in stock.[4]

The Half.com acquisition sent ripples through X.com. Besides once again demonstrating eBay's ability to flex its muscles whenever a competitor threatened its dominance, it also marked the first time that eBay controlled a trading platform that limited a seller's payment options. Half.com collected a credit card payment directly from the buyer and told the seller to ship the item with the knowledge that the seller would later receive a check from Half. This disintermediation of the buyer and seller froze PayPal out of the process. If it wanted, eBay could make Billpoint the mandatory payment processor for Half.com, compelling all of Half's buyers and sellers to open Billpoint accounts while giving PayPal no chance to compete.

Fortunately for us, the same slow development cycle that prevented eBay from building its own version of Half.com also impeded Billpoint. Our rivals had failed to introduce any innovations since Billpoint's launch in early April. This lethargy, coupled with PayPal's tenacious growth, kept Billpoint hovering around 8%-9% listing share, exactly where it stood following eBay's series of free listing days. Meanwhile PayPal approached the 40% mark, up from 35% the month before.

Toward the end of June Billpoint finally unveiled a new feature. EBay began to insert "Instant Purchase" buttons into the headers of closed auctions that accepted Billpoint. These buttons provided a one-click option to generate a Billpoint payment form for buyers, who previously had to wait for sellers to send an electronic invoice. Although Billpoint's product still stopped short of perfection, this demonstrated eBay's commitment to narrowing the quality gap between Billpoint and PayPal. But this competitive thrust would not go unanswered—our producers were set to respond with another volley of innovations.

◊

The brouhaha caused by our retracted credit card spending limit policy notwithstanding, our feature release in early June was a watershed event for the product team and an important stepping stone for our company.

For the producers, the launch of the business accounts marked our first major deliverable as a new team and our last milestone in the old office. Our departure to the new building had been delayed while the finishing touches were put on the features. Every group except product, design, and engineering started moving out of the University Avenue offices in May. Turning off the lights at 165 University became an excuse for a party. Caterers brought food to our second story interior courtyard, and an all-day water gun fight was interrupted just long enough for Sacks to do a keg stand. After the energy and long hours that went into the team's first development cycle, we all shared an understandable desire to celebrate.

Unfortunately, in terms of the new features' immediate impact on X.com's burn rate, the results proved mixed. Even after Paul's quick action quieted down the message boards, uptake of our new fee-bearing business accounts remained slow. Only a small percentage of our sellers decided to upgrade, which, given the accounts' meager list of benefits, was not surprising despite my best marketing spin. In an effort to increase adoption, Paul and Sacks stole a page from Billpoint's playbook with our own free listing day. Paul set up a scan tool to count the number of listings posted on eBay by our business account users for a given day, and I publicized the event to our sellers as a reason to upgrade. The uptake remained modest and the percentage of our payment volume generating revenue stayed in the single digits. Our fee-sensitive sellers would not be easily persuaded to upgrade even though the future of our company hinged on this outcome.

Given our lack of revenue-generating progress, the next round of features aimed to address the problem by increasing the value proposition of our business accounts. In preparation for a continued scaling up of product development, several new members joined the team. Chris Gregory, another Stanford classmate of mine, transferred from business development to design a multi-payments tool so merchants could send rebates or promotional payments to hundreds of recipients at once. Lee Hower, recruited by Elon out of the University of Pennsylvania, came aboard to build a wireless product and international accounts. And JoAnne Rockower, a longtime eBay seller with a feedback score of 500, transferred from our customer service group to work with Paul on auction products.

The influx of talent to the producers reflected our growing status within the company as much as our busy development schedule. Sacks billed our group as an elite team during his initial pep talk and in some regards that was what we had become. With Bill Harris's departure the emphasis on business development waned, and given the break-up of the marketing group, product's influence began to grow immediately following its creation. With the producers' ability to influence PayPal's Web site directly and our vice president acting as the CEO's right hand man, the impression spread that product was the place to be. Our ranks soon reached double-digits and we turned into one of the larger teams in the growing venture.

Armed with new recruits, the producers continued to overhaul PayPal. The most significant feature launched in July was a one-click checkout button for e-commerce Web sites. Using our Web site, a seller with a business account could generate customized HTML payment buttons and paste them onto his site. Then his buyer simply had to click a payment button to be taken to a pre-populated payment form where he could enter his PayPal password and authorize the transaction, eliminating the need to log in to fill out the send money form. Web site payments, coupled with the multi-payments tool, added substantive benefits to our fee-bearing business accounts. The improvements caused the upgrade rate to begin a slow climb, increasing the percentage of payments generating fees to the double-digit mark.

Meanwhile, Sacks and Elon settled on a new approach to reduce our daily outflow of cash. After back-tracking on the lifetime credit card sending limit, they decided to require bank account registration in order for users to receive a $5 bonus. This change promised to reduce our total bonus payments by mandating additional steps, and these optional requirements would also encourage additional customers to begin using their bank accounts to fund payments. While the added bonus complexity did cost us a few referrals, this new policy kept the popular bonus program in place while not limiting the ability of our customers to use the system. Sellers didn't care about getting fewer bonuses so long as we kept our hands off the features that impacted their core business.

The bonus change turned out to be just one step in our evolving strategy to encourage bank account-funded payments. During those frantic summer months, multiple rounds of brainstorming hatched a new user status called "verified." We opted to provide customers who confirmed ownership of a linked bank account with this trust-inducing credential in exchange for proving to PayPal that they had been screened and identified by a financial institution. This move allowed us to piggy-back off the mandatory background checks done by banks, reducing our fraud risks while rewarding users with a status they could use to gain credibility in eBay's online community. Similar to eBay's feedback system, we positioned the verified status as a way to reassure potential buyers or sellers that PayPal vouched for the other party in the transaction.

Verification provided a springboard to address another growing problem that Vince Sollitto had started to encounter in the media. As our user base continued to increase, journalists more frequently began to hear from disgruntled customers who had fallen victim to scams after using PayPal. Although people would not expect their bank to refund them if they had given cash to a con-artist, many customers thought that PayPal should guarantee transactions under all circumstances.

Several reporters noted the absence of a customer protection program, as well as a clause in our user agreement that required account holders to promise not to initiate a credit card reversal, known as a chargeback, against PayPal.

From our perspective, PayPal was just providing users with a funds transfer service; once the payment was done they would need to rely on the dispute resolution methods provided by eBay or whatever marketplace they were using, just as they would if they had mailed a cashier's check. But increasing numbers of honest customers, taught that their credit cards always provided fraud protection, did not see it that way. "I'm not an expert," one customer who fell victim to a con job later declared to a journalist, "but if you ask me, they're acting like a bank and they should be held to the same standards as a bank."[5]

Facing understandable public pressure to find a solution, Elon, Sacks and Julie Anderson hammered out a plan to offer buyers and sellers a transaction guarantee tied to verification status. Payments sent to a verified recipient would be protected against fraud, allowing the sender to get his funds returned to him even if the fraudster managed to smuggle them out of the system. The company was making a calculated gamble that the cost savings of encouraging additional customers to verify by linking a bank account to PayPal would exceed the fraud losses we would have to pay out.

The design team created a special "X.com Verified" logo in the shape of a gold lock for sellers to display on their auctions, and within days thousands of them appeared across eBay. Our users embraced verification and helped market it for us, often coming up with their own phrases like "I'm PayPal verified, so bid with confidence!" to include in their listings. It was a display that likely caused concern for our friends at the auction behemoth—our customers had begun using PayPal for a purpose other than transmitting payments. PayPal had started to play an ever-increasing role in our sellers' business processes and even their online identities. The growing bond between PayPal and its users was strengthening by the day.

◊

In the course of just two months, the product team unleashed a flurry of new features to collect transaction fees while driving down the cost of funds entering the system. While the job was not finished by any stretch, X.com's business model had undergone a substantial realignment and the producers had made progress on implementing the new strategy. Just as important, after product development stalled following the merger, Elon and Sacks's reorganization got X.com moving again.

The company also made reasonable gains on the customer service front. While our Omaha center still faced a backlog of e-mail inquiries, the queue stood at just a fraction of its earlier total. Increased site stability also contributed to an improved customer sentiment; Max and his engineers had moved forward in dealing with the database's scalability following the outages in April and May. Damon Billian, a former customer service manager who transferred to Vince's PR group, adopted the online persona of "PayPal Damon" and picked up where Paul left off, proactively addressing customer concerns on other Web sites' message boards. The change in tone on the boards as well as Damon's deft handling of inquiries convinced many of us of the desirability of adding message boards to our own site, but the lengthy implementation time required to accomplish this feat kept it off the engineering docket.

This surge of productivity, positive customer feedback, and our widening lead over Billpoint gave a boost to the company's morale and our employees' confidence. To celebrate the July feature launch, the product, design, and engineering teams planned an offsite event at Angel Island, an undeveloped isle located just a few miles north of San Francisco and run by the state park service. During the short kayaking trip from the mainland to the island several producers and engineers started chanting "Sacks in the water! Sacks in the water!" The VP of product was not eager to oblige. The outing's beleaguered guides were upset, having misunderstood "Sacks" as "sex" —an easy mistake when chaperoning employees from a company named X.com.

I played hooky from the festivities on Angel Island, instead taking Beatrice away for a weekend at the quaint seaside town of Carmel. A surprise diamond ring and her answer of "yes" turned the getaway into the beginning of a much longer journey.

I didn't know it at the time, but my feeling of life falling into place would be short-lived. X was about to get rocked.

CHAPTER SIX

REVOLUTION—PAYPAL 2.0

JULY—OCTOBER 2000

T HE FIRST TIME I heard of V2, I was sitting in a park eating lunch on a wooden bench with Paul Martin. "I had dinner with Yu Pan and some of the other engineers last night," Paul said, mentioning his lead auction engineer. Paul's late night schedule helped him connect with the company's engineering team, many of whom lived lives that could be called nothing short of nocturnal. "These guys are really worried about something."

I glanced quizzically at my friend to encourage him to continue. Although I had known Paul casually before I helped convince him to drop out of Stanford, our shared experiences over the past months had turned us into fast friends. When the infrequent opportunity arose for both of us to get away from the office on a lunch break, we made a point to take advantage of it.

"Have you heard about V2?" he asked. I shook my head. "It stands for version two of the PayPal Web site. It's a project to move PayPal over to a new platform."

Sensing my interest, he went on. "When Max and the original engineers first built PayPal, the database really wasn't designed to scale up past several million accounts. They focused on getting a working version out the door as fast as possible. That's one reason we had those site stability issues a few months ago."

I grimaced at the recollection. The event triggered a volley of media inquiries that called PayPal's scalability into question.[1] The crisis reached its high point during Elon's first week after reclaiming the CEO role, and no doubt dealing with the PR fallout burned the importance of Web site reliability into his mind.

"Anyway, engineering was able to get things under control then, but they've pretty much always known that eventually they would need to overhaul the database to increase our capacity."

"OK, I'm with you so far," I replied. Even though marketers are stereotypically dense when it comes to technical issues, I prided myself with grasping the high level concepts involved with PayPal's engineering. But after serving as our lead auction producer for the past two months, Paul's technical understanding of the PayPal system far exceeded my own.

"The problem is the way they're planning to build it," he explained. "Max and the engineers set up PayPal on an Oracle platform, but V2 is set to be on a Windows NT platform." Sensing the significance of this revelation to be lost on me, he continued. "None of the Confinity engineers really know NT, and what they do know about it is a problem. They say it's not as stable as Oracle, and the way they're being asked to build it has a greater risk of not being recoverable if there were a major crash."

At this point I had to stop him. "Wait a minute. So our engineers have just started a new architectural project that could crash and wipe out the entire system? That makes no sense." Paul nodded his head as if to reiterate his conviction. "Look, there's got to be more to it than that," I added. "Jokes aside, Microsoft doesn't try to make its products implode on you, and Max isn't going to decide to use a service that's that unstable."

"Max didn't make this decision," Paul shot back. "Elon did. Some of the engineers that came from the X.com side supported it. They say it will be faster to develop new features on NT since there are more tools for Windows. But Max doesn't agree—he thinks it's a mistake and wants us to stick with the same platform we're currently using."

Thank goodness, I found myself thinking, it's just the Oracle/Microsoft engineering schism again—a programmer's equivalent to arguing over the number of angels that could fit on the head of a pin. "Paul, the engineers gripe about this kind of stuff every other day," I told him.

"No, it's different this time," he replied, his earnest face displaying an unnatural frown. Paul was one of the most easy-going people I'd ever met, so whenever he showed concern it had to be because he believed something was serious.

"Max feels really strongly about this. Some of the guys think he's going to leave after this is done." I suddenly understood Paul's apprehension. As much as Peter and Sacks supported the open culture on the business side of the company, the hard-working but informal attitude of the engineering department came from Max. Given his involvement in recruiting many of Confinity's engineers, it was no wonder that personnel from all parts of the company widely admired him.

Whatever the alleged technical risks involved with switching to an NT platform, Max's departure would devastate the brittle morale of the engineering team, again putting our company's ability to innovate in jeopardy. What I didn't realize at the time was that V2 would trigger that same outcome with or without Max Levchin.

◊

The entire V2 initiative remained in the background for several weeks before Julie Anderson began an otherwise routine product staff meeting with a bang: "We're putting the development of all new features on hold."

The producers, seated around a table in "Dollar," our new office's largest conference room, exchanged glances. The flurry of product improvements implemented after the reorganization had left the company in a position to fix the flaws in its business model, but our status was still far from secure.

David Sacks's lead producer continued. "All of you know that Elon wants us to move PayPal onto a new, scaleable platform," she said. "Some of you have already been working with the engineers on coding V2 products. As you might guess, every time we build something new on the live site, it adds another feature that has to be replicated for V2.

"Since Elon feels that it's important to implement V2 soon," she went on, "we need to freeze development on the live site and shift all resources to finishing V2. This will speed up the transition, which is good since the sooner we finish V2, the sooner we can scale up the business and merge the PayPal and X-Finance user bases."

While delaying the building of new features was a surprise, this proposal came across as reasonable. If the PayPal service had to be moved to a more scaleable platform, the project would never get finished if product continued with feature development. The timeframe Julie went on to describe suggested that V2 could be fully coded and tested within a few weeks. If V2's completion was right around the corner, then delaying the roll-out of features to grow revenue and shrink costs seemed acceptable. Plus, since there had been no apparent further rumblings about Max departing, it looked as if some of our pro-Oracle engineers had exaggerated their concerns to sway the product managers to their side.

As I looked around, my fellow producers nodded in agreement after hearing our team leader's justification of the new plan. Everyone, that is, except for Paul, who brooded silently while staring down at the table in front of him.

◊

The following weeks proved that our Cassandra from Arkansas had reason to worry. Events undermined the reasoning behind the decision to move the producers away from creating new features. Despite the efforts of all members of product, engineering, and design, the duplication of the PayPal service progressed slowly. The first build handed off to our quality assurance team came back DOA when the basic "send money" functionality did not work.

The background of the company's engineering team hindered the project. Although the Oracle versus Windows debate seemed academic to a non-engineer, the reality was that more than half of our programmers weren't familiar with NT and had to get acquainted with it while writing code. Conversely, the engineers from the X.com side who knew NT were not comfortable with the architecture that Max and his colleagues had used to build PayPal and often deviated from the chartered course. The resulting chaos led to bitter disputes in a department already strained in the wake of the merger.

EBay also did its part to slow down development. As PayPal continued to acquire additional sellers, our automatic logo tools placed an ever-growing burden on eBay's servers. After suffering several days of downtime the prior year, eBay was not eager to allow a third party—especially X.com—to put strain on its site. Several times that summer eBay blocked PayPal's access, preventing us from inserting our auction logos until Paul could find a way to reduce the load and Reid Hoffman could lodge the latest round of complaints with Rob Chesnut. This recurring drama grew so frequent that Paul received an emergency call on the matter during the wedding reception for our X.com colleague Jennifer Chwang and my venture capitalist friend Steve Kuo, and Max later had to leave a friend's bachelor party at two in the morning for the same reason.

As August rolled by with limited progress, Elon and Sacks desperately looked for ways to streamline V2. To decrease the number of features that needed replicating, Sacks signed off on terminating the now insignificant Palm application. The focal point of Confinity's initial business plan—and in some sense the cornerstone for PayPal itself—had a negligible following compared to our Web site service. Only 10,000 customers had ever downloaded the Palm software but by this point nearly 3 million had created PayPal accounts. When we announced the Palm application's demise only a few grumblings from Palm user groups marked its passing.

Seeking to "spice things up," Elon announced that every employee in product, design, and engineering would receive a $10,000 bonus if we could meet a September 15 deadline to finish V2. The bonus would decrease by $1,000 for each subsequent day before completely disappearing on September 25. This came on the heels of a generous round of salary raises approved by the CEO for the producers. Elon hoped this large carrot would motivate his staff and move V2 along faster.

The company's continued flow of red ink explained his haste. While we now had some transaction revenue thanks to the limited user adoption of business accounts, our rising costs overwhelmed what little we collected in fees. PayPal's margins improved slightly to -3.28% for the third quarter, due to a drop in credit card processing costs as more customers began to use bank accounts to fund payments. But growth in payments caused our gross losses to increase despite this small improvement in margins. With our average daily payment volume reaching $4.6 million, up 70% from the prior period, it meant we were losing $150,000 every day just from ordinary business operations. As Peter's $100 million in venture capital began to dissipate, Elon realized that X.com was living on borrowed time.

The company's losses could not be blamed solely on the incomplete product implementation of the business model. As word of our service spread around the Internet, PayPal became an increasingly attractive target for fraud.

PayPal looked like a gold mine for crime rings as well as sophisticated independent crooks trafficking in stolen credit cards. Unlike online retailers who ship physical goods in exchange for a credit card payment, PayPal converted those transactions into cash. With a CD-ROM full of stolen numbers and a robotic script designed to open PayPal accounts, Internet-savvy criminals could easily automate the creation of hundreds of dummy users. These feeder accounts could then use the stolen credit cards to send payments through a layer or two of additional fraudulent accounts before the criminal initiated an ACH to transfer the balance out of the system. Instead of fleecing a thousand copies of *Harry Potter* from Amazon, the fraudster would have tens of thousands of dollars from PayPal to show for his efforts.

In this case the criminal's gain was X.com's loss. The credit card associations allow cardholders victimized by fraud to charge the questioned payment back to the merchant who processed it. In these cases of "unauthorized use," X.com was that merchant. When the Russian and Nigerian mafias rung up online charges, they ultimately plundered PayPal, not the cardholder. While our customer base continued its explosive growth, these brazen criminals walked in through our front door and carried on their activities largely unmolested. In what we would later refer to as "a significant fraud episode," one such fraud ring cost the company $5.7 million over a four month period in mid-2000.[2]

X.com also faced other forms of fraud risk besides unauthorized credit card use. Even though our terms of use contained an unenforceable section restricting customers from initiating chargebacks, official credit card regulations allowed cardholders to reverse a charge when a merchant failed to deliver promised goods. Intended as a mechanism to protect cardholders from unscrupulous merchants and to encourage buyers to use plastic, this provision exposed PayPal to two additional types of losses. X.com was liable not just for seller fraud—which happens when a seller doesn't ship an item as promised after receiving payment—but also buyer fraud, when a consumer with "buyer's remorse" lies about not receiving an item or initiating a charge.

As if all of these existing risks weren't enough, X.com actually increased its fraud exposure when we created the buyer and seller protection policies earlier in the summer. While successful in shielding us from some media flak, this blanket immunity for our verified buyers and sellers created a moral hazard by introducing negative incentives to our users. Buyers had no reason to shun the too-good-to-be-true offers they found while poking around on eBay, and previously well-behaved sellers had no need to go the extra mile to satisfy a disgruntled customer, knowing PayPal would foot the bill. Though the bank account-based verification process helped reduce losses on ACH transactions, it failed to offer a predictor of how risky a verified user would become after he received full protection.

This deadly brew of scheming criminals, shifty merchants, remorseful buyers, and unintended consequences caused our fraud costs to go through the roof. After posting transaction losses of $2.57 million in the second quarter, the fraud bill for Q3 soared to $5.13 million, or roughly 1.2% of all of PayPal's payment volume. Or, to put it another way, X.com incurred $2,300 in fraud losses each hour.

The two major credit card associations, Visa and MasterCard, rumored to be concerned that PayPal's gains at training consumers to use bank accounts to fund online payments could undermine their cartel, reprimanded us for our fraud rate. MasterCard took an especially strong stance and threatened to cut off our ability to receive payments from its cards unless we made swift progress bringing PayPal into compliance with its regulations.[3]

With the continued climb in our loss rates, Elon had no choice but to return to the private equity markets for additional financing. By the end of the third quarter our cash on hand would have dwindled to dangerously low levels without another influx of capital. A consortium led by the French retail bank Credit Agricole contributed $30 million; our company publicly spun the investment as money to fund overseas expansion.[4] Although we knew that we would ultimately have to find a way to deal with the fraudsters and Mafioso intent on bleeding our company dry, this infusion of cash ensured that we could at least afford to keep the lights on for a little while longer as we plotted our retaliation.

◊

"All of these sellers using X to receive credit card payments are costing us a lot of money," Elon said with near indignation. "We've got to make them upgrade to a business account *now*." The emphasis on his last word was impossible to miss.

With V2 implementation dragging and the company's burn rate increasing, Elon charged Sacks and me with transitioning more sellers from free accounts into fee-bearing ones. Meeting in his double-sized cube, I had the impression that Elon was showing the strain of the company's dire situation.

"Yeah, well, these guys just don't want to do it," Sacks grumbled. "Eventually we're going to need some sort of feature that takes care of it for them." With a growing number of the business's operations under his supervision, the perpetually direct Sacks really did not have time to beat around the bush. When a problem came up, he instinctively sought a specific product-driven solution that he could delegate to someone on his team.

"We can't subsidize these users forever!" Elon shot back, the stress caused by the daily worsening of the company's financial situation apparent in his voice. Since the V2 feature freeze meant no product could be built to address this problem anytime soon, the wary CEO was looking for other answers. "We have the *right* to require them to upgrade. When we updated the terms of use in June we clearly stated that business users need to have business accounts now that they're available."

"Don't forget our promise after the uproar over the lifetime spending limit," I reminded them, speaking as calmly as possible given the mounting tension. "We specifically said we'd never force anyone to upgrade. If we go and upgrade users without their permission we're going to have a huge backlash on our hands." All three of us paused for a moment to reflect on this point. Our public pledge meant we needed to find a way to coax our sellers into voluntarily upgrading; the same customer fury that had prompted that promise in the first place left us no room to backtrack.

"How about some sort of shareware-style pop-up? The kind they harass you with on free software until you pay," Elon ventured, his voice subdued again. "We could show it to them every time they log in until they upgrade."

"Let's just give them a clickthrough page with the user agreement when they log in," Sacks responded. "We'll have one button at the bottom that says 'upgrade me,' and another that says 'I'm not a seller.' That way we'll let the user choose between being honest and complying with the agreement or otherwise lying."

Although our user agreement stated that all customers engaging in "business use" through PayPal needed to do so with a fee-bearing account, we had not defined what "business use" meant. Damon Billian, in his discussion board alter ego of PayPal Damon, frequently heard from customers asking for clarification. "Did business use mean one payment a day?" "I just sell a few items a week from my house—I'm not a 'business,' am I?" Many of our customers evidently were willing to play by the rules but were also unsure as to what those rules were. Sacks's tactic avoided giving them the definition they wanted and instead put the burden of that definition on each user.

Following Elon and Sacks's instructions, I pulled together a page that we presented to our 70,000 most frequent transaction recipients. The text invoked the user's sense of fair play, and also explained that since Visa and MasterCard charged PayPal a fee every time we processed a credit card transaction we could not indefinitely afford to provide a free service to our sellers.

Customer reaction was intense. Just three hours after the midnight launch of the page, Damon counted more than 130 posts on the AuctionWatch and OTWA discussion boards. While a few sympathetic customers pointed out that PayPal still cost less than traditional merchant accounts for credit card processing, many users charged PayPal with a bait and switch. An AuctionWatch article quoted one strident customer as saying, "What they have done is dirty and sneaky. They pulled everyone in with promises of free accounts—'Don't worry folks, we get our money from the float time.'"[5]

Despite some customer backlash, about one-fifth of our targeted sellers voluntarily upgraded while only 0.1% closed their accounts. While the ratio of account upgrades to closures was encouraging, it still meant that 80% of our sellers would not opt to pay fees so long as X.com's vague rules gave them a choice. If our company was ever going to stem the tide of red ink we needed a policy that made our rules both clear and enforceable. Sacks tasked me with the job.

◊

I had been handed the assignment of a lifetime, one that could make or break not just my career but also the company's future. We needed to find a way to get revenue from our reluctant sellers without driving them to Billpoint; it meant we'd have to transform PayPal from a free Internet service into a successful fee-based one, something that few dot-coms had accomplished.

I realized early on that a pair of factors would complicate any attempt to resolve the "business use" problem. First, any definition would have to be consistent with the information captured in PayPal's database. PayPal's easy-to-use processes were streamlined, so as a result we collected very little information on either our users or their transactions. An auction payment looked the same as repayment for a dinner bill, so even if we came up with a clear definition of "business use" there was no foolproof way of identifying business transactions within the database.

The second challenge consisted of actually getting our sellers to comply with whatever definition we settled on. Our June pledge meant that even with a clear policy our business users would ultimately have to choose whether to upgrade or not. I knew that this campaign would certainly damage the budding relationship between X.com and its customers, and as the solitary custodian of PayPal's brand I refused to make the fallout worse by breaking our promise.

Given these constraints, the only alternative was to select a reasonable activity level that would denote whether a customer was operating as a business user or not. Several competing ideas along these lines had circulated within the organization for months; the most popular was limiting free accounts to receiving thirty payments per month, or one free payment per day. I rejected this proposal, fearing that the number was ultimately arbitrary and conversion for this method seemed in doubt since total payments could easily be tracked by anyone intent on avoiding the cap.

Instead I opted to base the upgrade trigger on the company's biggest expense, credit card processing fees. While users couldn't be expected to sympathize about paying their pro-rated share of our overhead costs or fraud losses, the direct cost of their credit card payments was clear and understandable. Plus it had a useful analogy in the offline world, where only businesses accept credit card transactions. This conveniently implied that PayPal's high volume credit card recipients were justifiably categorized as "business users."

I turned to my trusted friend for help in designing a mechanical process that would accomplish these objectives. Paul and I locked ourselves away in a windowless conference room to hammer out some conclusions. We agreed it was critical not to block credit card payments to sellers who surpassed the receiving limit—this would disrupt their operations before they even had a chance to choose whether or not to upgrade. Instead buyers should be able to continue sending payments to sellers who had passed the limit with those payments classified as pending and the funds held in limbo until the seller opted either to accept or to reject them. Accepting the payments would upgrade the seller's account, while rejecting them would refund the money and send a notice to the buyers that the seller needed to be paid a different way.

This plan was our only option. It would benefit our company by leveraging the growing network of PayPal buyers to keep our sellers from fleeing, but it would also aid our sellers by neither blocking payments nor automatically upgrading them when they hit the "business use" limit. And, equally important, it meant we could keep our promise to let our users decide whether or not to upgrade without fear of reprisal from PayPal.

Since the company still didn't have a formal reporting group, I sought the help of our head database administrator, Paul Tuckfield, in querying the system to determine the optimal credit card receiving limit. His results suggested that a $500 limit per six month period would account for the 100,000 sellers who received three-quarters of all of

PayPal's payment volume. Besides being a clean, round number, $500 in credit card payments felt sufficiently large to imply "business use." Since consumers wouldn't likely need to receive such a high level of credit card payments, I felt we at last had an adequate policy to present to an understandably anxious user community. After vetting the proposal with Sacks and other executives we were given a green light.

Unfortunately it turned out that there was nowhere for the project to go. The days of September continued to roll by and V2 slid further and further behind schedule. Paul and I argued the case for pausing production to allow us to implement the upgrade campaign. When that tactic failed, we pushed for including the upgrade mechanism into V2 itself, a request that was also rejected. Julie Anderson said her marching orders from Elon were to streamline V2 as much as possible and no additional features that would hinder this process were being considered. Revenue would just have to wait. Paul and I approached Sacks and asked him to intervene, but he pointedly said he couldn't do anything about it because Elon himself was now personally overseeing all decisions on V2.

What on earth is happening? I asked myself. The company finally had a plan to tackle our growing losses head on but this controversial engineering scheme threatened to delay it for months. Elon's employee bonus challenge failed to make V2's launch date materialize even as the morale on the product and engineering teams began to falter. The grumbling that Paul had first alerted me to two months earlier returned, and rumors of Max's potential departure started to circulate once more.

For the first time I doubted our company's future. Our explosive growth and marketplace leadership were not going to solve the problems we now faced, and our company would never achieve "world domination"—much less survival—without fixing our business model soon.

A few days later I returned to Paul Tuckfield's desk to thank him for running my queries. The database administrator inquired about the status of implementing the credit card receiving limit. I glumly shook my head and described how V2 prevented it from being built, possibly for several months. Tuckfield remarked that this was unfortunate, especially since he had already figured out how to make a few modifications over the course of a weekend that would allow the existing database to expand from its current level of 3.5 million accounts up to at least 10 million. The response he had received from on high was not to bother.

I shook my head again, this time in disbelief. As the soft-spoken engineer went on to describe the specific changes he wanted to make, I dwelled on the implications of what he had told me. Regardless of the merits of NT versus UNIX, this platform change wasn't even critical at this point! We had burned two months of development time when a simple upgrade could have seen us through another year while allowing us to launch the "business use" process, attack fraud, and address any of the other challenges to our business model. V2 wasn't murder, it was suicide.

◊

The 2000 summer Olympics in Sydney started later in the year than normal. After selecting a Southern Hemisphere city for just the second time in the history of the summer games, the Olympic committee scheduled the event during the mild weeks of September, as opposed to Australia's winter months of June or July. This scheduling fluke proved fateful.

Before leaving to attend the games, Elon sentenced the PayPal brand to death. The CEO instructed my fellow producer Amy Rowe to phase out all references to PayPal on the company's Web site. It seemed like an odd breach of protocol for the chief executive to bypass both Sacks, his direct report, and me, his marketing specialist, to implement a branding decision. But since Sacks and I both came from Confinity and were more likely to be loyal to the PayPal brand, his reasoning seemed obvious.

Spurred into action by this unexpected event, I discreetly approached Amy about the timing of the decision in light of the tumultuous upgrade campaign that would soon need to go out to our sellers. Since our users liked the PayPal brand, I argued, now did not seem like the ideal time to force this change. Amy saw no fault in Elon's rigidity, and reiterated the statement about moving to the more flexible X brand. If anything, this logic implied, user preference for the PayPal name only meant we should move faster to phase it out before customers became too attached!

Once again I had nowhere to turn but to Sacks. It was the first conversation in months that the two of us had engaged in on the subject of branding. This time I found him receptive. Sacks fired off a combative e-mail across the Pacific to Elon that included some quotes from disgruntled message board writers. Calling it an example of the tension that existed between the company and its sellers, he repeated my remark that eliminating the PayPal brand now would only further antagonize our anxious users.

At about the same time Luke Nosek burst back onto the scene. Despite being the company's VP of strategy, Luke only sporadically involved himself in strategy discussions with the producers. But the re-emergence of the branding issue was one of those occasions.

Luke had Vivien Go, a recent hire to his team, distribute an online survey designed to learn more about user perceptions of our two brands to several thousand randomly selected users. Early responses suggested what we anticipated—the PayPal brand enjoyed stronger loyalty than X, which many still related to pornography and edginess. What was not foreseen was that our vacationing CEO would be one of the users randomly selected to receive the survey. The odds of Elon being picked were less than 1 in 1,000, but somehow his name wound up unobserved on the distribution list.

A furious Elon fired off a midnight round of e-mails and calls until he tracked down the source of the survey and ordered Vivien to shut it down. Sacks, whom I had seen less and less around the office over the prior several days, seemed nonchalant when I told him of the mishap. The survey didn't matter, he insisted. What mattered was the PayPal branding on the Web site, and he had made up his mind that he wasn't going to let that be jeopardized.

"What about Elon's instructions?" I asked.

"I'm not going to change the Web site," he coolly replied. "If he insists on doing that, he'll just have to fire me."

A line in the sand had been drawn, and it was time to choose a side.

◊

The following day I was sitting at my desk when Sacks abruptly appeared. "I need to talk to you for a minute," he declared, before adding, "Where's Paul?"

"He just left," I answered.

"We'll call him."

Sacks motioned for me to follow, turned on his heels and started walking. I matched his brisk pace as he shot past the long row of cubicles belonging to the accounting department and headed toward a vacant conference room on the far corner of the building. Glancing over at my boss, who had recently turned twenty-eight, I noted a touch of gray on his previously jet-black temples. The stress associated with his leadership role had evidently taken its toll, but the young executive wore his new gray hairs with the same increasing confidence with which he wore his title.

We entered the "Yen" conference room and Sacks shut the door. Without speaking, he punched in the digits of Paul's cell on the speakerphone. After Paul answered, Sacks looked over at me, took a deep breath, and at last spoke.

"We're demanding that the board remove Elon." I leaned forward in my chair, open-mouthed, shaken to hear those words. I could only return Sacks's quizzical glance with silence. While this demand made sense given the events of the past two months, the shock I felt as my mind raced through the implications of this decision kept me from speaking.

Sacks cleared his throat and continued. Knowing he was addressing the two producers most likely to be sympathetic to his point of view, he asserted that Elon's dedication to V2 and determination to eliminate the PayPal brand endangered the company. Besides the technological risk of moving to a new platform and the peril of customer-backlash over removing PayPal, these efforts diverted the organization's energy away from the real priority at hand, fixing our company's business model so we'd stop bleeding cash.

To force the board's hand, Sacks and several other executives would threaten to quit unless board members removed Elon and named Peter Thiel the interim CEO. In order to make a more powerful statement, Sacks asked us if we'd be willing to sign a petition stating we would also leave the company if the board refused to acquiesce.

Sacks painted the choice as obvious. The status quo trajectory would destroy the company, and the departure of key personnel would only hasten but not cause that same outcome. His demand of the board offered stakeholders a different scenario, a "PayPal renaissance" as he termed it, a chance to return to an emphasis on developing new products in an attempt to mend our business model.

After Sacks finished this dress rehearsal of the speech he intended to deliver to PayPal's board, he fell silent, waiting to hear how we would respond.

I sat dazed, my left-brain processing what he had told me and envisioning the tumult to come. Elon was not a bad person—far from it! His work ethic was outstanding and he had supported Sacks's decision to bestow a great deal of responsibility on me, so I could hardly speak poorly of him. He had also made many positive changes to the company, and his reorganization had gotten the post-merger entity functioning as an integrated whole for the first time. Would supporting his removal make me a traitor? Could we somehow convince him to change course on V2 and the PayPal brand? My mind silently wrestled with these questions when Paul at last broke the silence: "Tell me what I need to do."

The moral clarity in Paul's voice refocused my thoughts onto the unpleasant realities of the present. Regardless of Elon's personal qualities and past contributions, the company was headed on the wrong path and more than two months of discussions had done nothing to change that. I had presented logical arguments against the X branding decision and in favor of building our upsell mechanisms before V2, only to fail on both counts. Unlike the decentralized intellectual marketplace from our Confinity days where ideas were always given a hearing, the post-merger company increasingly looked like a centralized management system with the CEO calling all the shots.

I nodded my head toward Sacks and voiced my support. He breathed a short sigh of relief and promised to have copies of the petition for us to sign later in the day. Before we dispersed, he asked me to track down a pair of my fellow producers to see if they'd be willing to lend their support to the plan. And with that Sacks headed out of the office, leaving me to lobby my peers for more signatures. They readily agreed.

I left the office that Thursday night knowing that one-half of the product team now backed its vice president in his effort to oust the CEO, while the other half had no idea of the gathering storm. During my forty-five minute car ride north to San Francisco I called Beatrice as I did every night to give us a few extra minutes to talk during the hectic work week. My preoccupied mind tried to focus on her words while simultaneously acting out multiple boardroom scenarios. If Peter and Sacks had most of the executive officers in tow, along with the product and design teams, then I reasoned they probably had enough leverage to force the board's hand. But any significant defections could hurt their case and make the outcome anything other than certain.

Tallies of executive officers still danced in my head as I walked through the door of Beatrice's apartment. She sensed something was wrong and I hastily repeated an abridged version of Sacks's speech. After finishing the overview, I collected enough courage to tell her that, in spite of the wedding we were saving money for, I had just put my job on the line.

I asked her if I had done the right thing, unsure of how she would respond. The average wedding costs $20,000—more money than we had between us—and we lived in one of the country's most expensive cities. While taking a stand for PayPal's future was the right decision for the company, we could not afford for me to spend any time unemployed.

Without missing a beat, she calmly agreed that this was what I had to do.

◊

I didn't know it at the time, but neither Sacks nor Peter—the man seeking to reclaim Elon's job—were the impetus behind this thrust for leadership change. If anything, the decision to take this stance was an especially difficult one for Sacks given his close personal bond with Elon, and Peter's role as a non-executive chairman provided him with little insight into many of the issues now causing day-to-day upheaval within the company. The movement had instead bubbled up simultaneously from several different sources within the company, ultimately forcing the executive staff to collude during Elon's absence to determine what exactly to do about it.

Max, already exasperated over the V2 decision, had become increasingly concerned over the company's course as he began to track fraudulent activity in the PayPal and X-Finance databases. This moved him to draft a terse e-mail to Elon to argue that the fraud problem was close to getting out of hand. Elon's reply, which Max later characterized as dismissive, prompted the engineering whiz-kid to lobby his fellow executives for change. Shortly after this exchange Luke crafted the branding survey that provoked Elon's wrath, a response which inadvertently helped further convince the executives that a new course was needed. Even Sacks now conceded that it was time to separate the needs of the company from his personal fondness for Elon—the company needed Peter Thiel back at the helm. Peter consented to their entreaty, and the rebellion began in earnest.

Max met with Sacks and Reid in a corner conference room to scour an org chart to determine the number of employees that would likely agree with their call for regime change. After tallying up the numbers, the executives drafted a petition to the board and fanned out to collect signatures. While Sacks presented his case to Paul and me, Max secured the signatures from nearly all of the engineering team. The following day the trio, joined by the CFO, marched into the office of board member Mike Moritz to present him with a stuffed red folder containing the signed petitions.

As the uprising began to unfold, Elon's loyalists—including one employee who hid outside the conference room while Max and his co-conspirators drafted the petition—alerted him to the fermenting revolt. The beleaguered CEO cut short his Olympic vacation and returned to Silicon Valley to face the pending challenge to his leadership. Elon seemed to harbor no willingness to back down; if anything, the typically unwavering confidence that he so often displayed suggested that he would staunchly defend both his past decisions and his position as chief executive.

How the ensuing corporate struggle would unfold remained to be seen. The board members' alliances were not obvious, but the rebels appeared to have the upper hand. Since Max, the only officer on the board besides Elon, would vote with Peter, Elon needed support from at least two of the three independent directors: Moritz from Sequoia Capital, John Malloy from Nokia Ventures, and Tim Hurd from Madison Dearborn.

Malloy would likely cast his vote with Peter—he had led Confinity's initial funding round and later served on its board before the merger. Moritz, however, was the second largest investor behind Elon of the pre-merger X.com, suggesting he might be sympathetic to the CEO. If this was the case, it made Hurd the wildcard. Unlike Malloy and Moritz, the clean cut Chicagoan had not invested in the company until after the merger, making his loyalties less clear. If Hurd sided with Peter, Elon would lose the vote, but if Elon could sway him, the board would be split, leaving the outcome in doubt.

I slept fitful sleep on Friday night. I dreamt of a ringing phone and on the other end was someone calling with news of the board meeting. No matter how hard I tried to reach it, though, the receiver was always just beyond my grasp.

The next morning Beatrice took me out in search of some diversion, or at least some distraction. We wound up browsing at the Stanford Shopping Center in Palo Alto, a favorite hang out from our college days. Anchored by upscale department stores like Nordstrom and Neiman Marcus, every weekend this mall welcomed hundreds of Silicon Valley's increasingly luxurious citizens to its breezy, flower-lined archways. But my attention was not on the relaxing surroundings or even the Palo Alto housewives wearing giant sunglasses and walking their miniature dogs; instead I clung to my cell phone as I anxiously waited to hear word from Sacks.

If my wait seemed long and anguishing, it was because the board meeting was, too. Peter and Max fielded the conference call from Max's apartment in Palo Alto, periodically shooing away Reid and Luke who paced nervously in Luke's neighboring apartment down the hall. The directors acknowledged many of the problems cited by the dissident officers, but some of them hedged on giving the Confinity side of the company effective control by returning Peter to power. Max and Peter held fast to their position, though, and after breaking for lunch the duo traveled to the Sand Hill Road offices of Peter's hedge fund to resume the call. Upon arriving, though, they realized that the office lacked a speakerphone, prompting Max to rig Peter's fax machine to serve as a makeshift substitute. The fax-speakerphone somehow worked, and when the call resumed Confinity's founders continued to press their demands.

The word finally came in the early afternoon while Beatrice and I stood next to the Macy's sunglasses counter—PayPal was saved! Sacks relayed the news that the board had agreed to a compromise solution that placed Peter in charge of day-to-day activities pending a full-scale executive search for a new CEO. I hugged Beatrice and amused several nearby clerks by letting out a muted whoop. My own job was intact and our company had a new lease on life. The rebellion had carried PayPal to the brink of disaster, but Peter and Max ultimately pulled it off.

After the rush of adrenaline gave way to simple relief, it occurred to me that this latest development was in some ways only a beginning. "World domination" was still a long way from reality, especially given the disastrous state of our business model. And despite my satisfaction with the board's vote, I knew that not everyone working at X.com would feel the same way. The ouster of Elon risked shattering the company's unity at a point when we still had much to accomplish.

◊

Monday came and much of the company was in shock. The news went out Saturday evening with the customary bombshell e-mail, this time from the company's chairman. Peter spun the announcement to say that Elon, after filling in as interim-CEO following Bill Harris's departure, was stepping down from the position so that an executive search for a permanent replacement could begin.

Elon later followed with a gracious company-wide message of his own. Using terms similar to Peter's "resignation" e-mail from five months earlier, he explained that startups were his forte and that now was the time to look for an executive who could take the company to the next level. He thanked everyone for their hard work and promised that we would all still frequently see him around the office. While I doubt that Elon authored that e-mail himself, to his credit he resisted the obvious temptation to throw any bombs and instead quietly faded from view. Of course he had a strong financial incentive to promote a peaceful transfer—he owned 13% of the company[6]—but the private poise he showed after his defeat and his subsequent willingness to remain active on the board hinted at a humbleness I had not previously detected. As much as I disagreed with his business strategies, I respected Elon's grace and continued dedication to the company.

Peter realized that Elon's departure left him with a delicate situation. He needed to heal any wounds caused by the change while rallying the company to a new set of priorities. It promised to be a challenge. Since Peter had not been involved in the company's day-to-day affairs since his falling out with Harris at the beginning of May, many of the employees hired over the past half year did not even know who he was. And those from the X.com side of the pre-merger company were sure to offer him a frosty reception.

Peter called a company-wide meeting, appropriately enough, in the "Arctic Circle," our large conference room known for its faulty thermostat. The stakes couldn't have been higher. Many employees loyal to Elon wore scowls as they peered at Peter through puffy eyes, while nonpartisans worried about their own jobs after seeing the company's second chief executive sacked in just under six months. Sitting in the middle of the group, I sensed tension in the air all around me.

Striking a conciliatory tone, Peter began the session by praising the former CEO for his past work and ensuring everyone that Elon would remain an active influence. Pointing to this harmony, he tried to calm jittery nerves by assuring the crowd that the board was unified on the company's direction. Then he moved on to detail two changes in strategy. V2 coding was being suspended to enable development to begin again on the live site after a two month absence. At this point, several X.com employees sitting near me bristled. After briefly explaining the dire state of our cash-hemorrhaging business model, Peter tried to sooth any hurt egos by leaving open the question of resuming V2 coding a few months in the future after our cashflow stabilized.

Branding was the other strategy change. Peter informed everyone that over the following weeks we would begin to shift the Web site away from X and return to the PayPal brand. "I think PayPal is now the second most well known private service on the Internet after Napster," he said, citing the infamous music-sharing company. "While we've been acquiring nearly 4 million customers we've also built a tremendous amount of brand equity behind the PayPal name. PayPal's turned into more than just a way to pay your pal—it's evolved into an online payment service that *is* your pal." As a conciliatory gesture, he said there was no plan to change the corporation's name from X.com to PayPal at the present time (although this change would eventually be made several months later).

Peter's compassionate tone, coupled with his logical defense of the strategy realignments, soothed many rattled nerves. His willingness to field hostile questions while stressing the interim nature of his own role calmed Elon's supporters' fear of reprisal and encouraged employees to be frank about their feelings. Over the following days the number of hushed conversations in the hallways diminished and the mood in the building gradually returned to something close to normal.

The producers suffered some fallout as two of our members, including the team leader, requested transfers to other groups after learning of Sacks's involvement in the process. The rest of the group embraced the opportunity to put V2 behind them, and Sacks tapped Skye Lee, the head of the design department, to also oversee product.

Other parts of the company responded in similar fashion. Design, business development, and operations suffered no personnel losses. And while several NT-devoted engineers chose to leave, the majority of the company's programmers happily bid farewell to building an NT platform.

With Confinity employees now occupying almost every executive position, the fact that so few of our colleagues from the X.com side quit following what could be called a "Confinity coup" is a compliment to Peter. Mending fences with upset employees and preserving a company's spirit de corps while overhauling its business model is no small feat, even for the man who built Confinity, negotiated the merger, and closed the $100 million financing round.

But compared to the competitive onslaught yet to come, all of this was just a warm-up exercise.

CHAPTER SEVEN

THE MONOPOLIST STRIKES

OCTOBER 2000 — FEBRUARY 2001

PETER THIEL'S RETURN to the helm set in motion a frantic effort to finish implementing PayPal's business model and reverse our staggering cash outflows. With the V2 initiative mothballed, Peter tasked Sacks and the rest of the executive team with ending our banking operations, reducing the company's fraud and credit card expenses, and completing the process of upgrading our sellers to fee-bearing accounts.

With this new set of priorities the debate over the company's macrostrategy ended — PayPal, Inc., would be a payments company and not a financial supermarket. The original X.com database, which had never been merged with PayPal's despite the long-standing intention to do so, was modified to prevent the creation of new accounts.

As the finance team learned more about the X-Finance customer base, its discoveries, interestingly, validated some of my initial skepticism about the merger. By handing out bank accounts, debit cards, and $500 overdraft credit lines without even running credit checks, the X.com system had racked up its fair share of bogus accounts and bad debt in its race to build a network before Confinity.

Based on their findings, Peter and the board opted to close down the entire commercial banking operation. It was an expensive decision — the company shelled out a $1 million termination fee to back away from X.com's November 1999 agreement to purchase First Western National Bank. The price tag also included an additional $1 million reimbursement to First Western's parent company for operational losses.[1]

The company's exit from online banking meant that PayPal's ambiguous regulatory status needed clarification. Peter instructed the legal team to engage regulators to seek a classification before one could be thrust upon us. He sought to avoid having the company labeled as a commercial bank but also feared that compliance with state-by-state laws governing money transmission companies would prove excessively burdensome. In search of a third option, our team made inquiries to determine if PayPal could be classified as a federally chartered trust bank.[2] Since trust banks exist primarily to manage the funds of their investors as opposed to making loans, they also enjoy less stringent regulations and capitalization requirements than commercial banks. This would obviously benefit a startup such as PayPal that was no longer in the business of extending lines of credit or issuing checking accounts. Trust bank status would also simplify the company's operations by allowing us to deal with the federal banking regulator, the Office of the Comptroller of the Currency (OCC), instead of the miscellaneous regulatory agencies in the several dozen states with money transmitter laws.

Jettisoning the online commercial banking operation was only one of the ways Peter attacked our expenses. Roelof Botha, a twenty-seven year old actuary whom Peter later elevated to CFO, identified our generous buyer and seller protection programs as a major cause of our rising fraud losses. Underwriting all of the risk for our verified buyers and sellers was a costly proposition, especially when we didn't demand any risk-reducing behavior in return.

Roelof concluded that the seller protection policy could be kept alive, but users would have to follow strict guidelines to qualify. Sellers would receive protection on transactions only when they could produce proof of shipment to a buyer's credit card billing address (which PayPal provided them). These conditions reduced the likelihood of a transaction resulting in a buyer complaint, allowing PayPal to continue protecting our sellers from much of the chargeback risk in exchange for following our optional guidelines.

The prospects for buyer protection were not as good. Since sellers tend to transact frequently with multiple buyers and their shipments can be tracked, it's easy to monitor the repeated behavior of individual sellers to assess their trustworthiness. Buyers, on the other hand, are likely to be much more sporadic with their online activities. Without the capacity to profile any but the worst shopaholics, we had less ability to anticipate the risk on the buying side of the equation. And with our protection program making it easy to indulge in buyer's remorse, Roelof concluded that this costly policy needed to go. Pierre Omidyar may have claimed that "people are basically good," but evidently not all of the people shopping on his Web site acted that way.

Vince Sollitto protested that media backlash would inevitably follow the program's rollback, a point which prompted the always-creative Luke Nosek to suggest a clever spin: PayPal would create a new policy that doubled eBay's own buyer insurance program. While eBay didn't detail buyer insurance expenses in its financials, we suspected that its costs were low. The process of submitting a claim took time and numerous forms accompanied by a $50 deductible and a $200 cap. Since the average cost of an eBay item was $10 less than the deductible, eBay obviously designed this largely symbolic program to shield itself from being called indifferent to consumers. Luke's idea to match eBay's coverage dollar-per-dollar would lower our costs while still providing buyers with some protection.

In addition to overhauling the buyer and seller protection programs, the rest of the company searched for other ways to drive down costs. Max Levchin took the lead in developing an anti-fraud system to track down suspicious account activity that looked like stolen credit card transactions. Sacks sought to reduce our credit card processing expenses and to encourage ACH payments by lowering the total amount a user could send with his credit card before completing the verification process from $2,000 down to just $250. While stopping short of repeating the lifetime credit card spending limit blunder from June, this policy change—coupled with the other cost-cutting measures—understandably caused some of our users to grumble. But the flak from these initiatives proved mild compared to what Paul and I were preparing to unleash.

◊

With a green light from Sacks, Paul unofficially began the upgrade campaign on a positive note by switching the image in our auction logos from X.com back to PayPal. Sellers, reacting on message boards and in e-mails to our Omaha center, enthusiastically supported the surprise move. Tired of fielding questions from their buyers about X.com's questionable connotations, they'd long been asking us to bring back the PayPal icon. Since the outside world remained unaware of Peter's return, some skeptical users mused that giving them back their favored logos was simply a way of buttering them up for something to come. They were right.

My iron fist followed Paul's velvet glove. As Paul and his engineers put the finishing touches on the mechanism to enforce our $500 credit card receiving limit, I launched a Web site page to a targeted group of 50,000 sellers announcing the new policy. The entire eBay community had been waiting for it with baited breath, so I cut to the chase and outlined the changes:

> In order to reduce the cost of processing expensive credit card transactions associated with accounts that do not pay fees, PayPal will introduce a new limit on Personal Accounts: a $500 limit on receiving credit card payments every six months… Recipients exceeding the $500 limit will no longer be able to accept credit card payments unless they choose to upgrade. Credit card payments sent to a Personal Account in excess of the limit will be held as 'pending' until the recipient chooses to accept the payment by upgrading or to return it to the sender by refusing the payment. [3]

A deluge of complaints triggered by the announcement poured into our customer service center and onto every auction message board. The bait-and-switch allegation that we had heard when we first hinted at a forthcoming policy resurfaced. CNET even quoted one AuctionWatch user who compared PayPal to a drug dealer—"(PayPal) gave it away for free until they got us hooked and then started charging."[4] Other customers suggested alternative ways for PayPal to increase its revenue, with a few taking a page from Confinity's original business plan by advocating we limit our users' monthly number of withdrawals so we could earn interest from the float.

While many sellers voiced loud objections, the initial furor gave way to grudging acceptance. Obviously none of these small business owners were enthusiastic about paying for a previously free service, but they understood that PayPal needed to book revenue to survive. Since many of their buyers demanded PayPal, they resolved to pay the fees as a cost of doing business. As one seller on a message board phrased it, "Yes, the new fees are crummy, but it is true that bids are higher [when I accept PayPal]. I figure they more than offset the fees. I will continue with PayPal and will continue to suggest it to fellow auctioneers."

As the results from the campaign began to trickle in, the data told the same story as the message boards. In the week following the policy's announcement, one-tenth of the high volume sellers voluntarily upgraded before encountering any limits. When Paul activated the enforcement of the new policy later in October, the rest steadily began to upgrade and, within a month's time, 95% of the targeted personal accounts had switched to business status.

After all the exhaustive debate and planning that went into it, our predictions were right—in fact, the outcome surpassed even what we had hoped for. No significant customer defections occurred and PayPal's listing share of eBay auctions held steady. As the campaign's team lead, co-architect, and head cheerleader I certainly had professional reasons to celebrate. My reputation had been on the line, but that seemed inconsequential compared to the company's business model. Failure would have sent us all packing.

Beyond the enforcement of the "business use" policy and our communication strategy, our fledgling network drove the campaign's success. The flood of sign-ups that had staggered our Web site, caught our customer service flat-footed, and caused cash to fly out the door—this same unbridled growth that had nearly overwhelmed our company only a few months earlier was now our biggest asset. Peter's initial obsession with building PayPal's network had succeeded; faced with its first major challenge, the network held together.

Unfortunately the upgrade rates and account retention statistics don't tell the entire story. As anyone who's had trouble with the phone company will testify, the fact that people use a network doesn't mean they always like it. Charging our customers to receive credit card payments when many of them believed PayPal would always remain free could not fail to place a strain on our brand. Sellers who felt betrayed might have continued to accept PayPal on their auctions or Web site, but their earlier trust in our company was shaken. We did our best to minimize any brand damage by promising to launch an international version of PayPal by Halloween and having Damon Billian engage our users directly on the message boards, but it was inevitable that some customers grew increasingly wary.

◊

Watching their competitor trim costs while forcing sellers into fee-bearing accounts, Billpoint CEO Jane Crane and her staff experienced an emotion she would later describe to a journalist as "great delight."[5] Half a year had passed since her company's official launch yet none of her group's efforts had made much impact on the payments market. Despite the free listing days, integration into eBay's search tool and SYI form, and a recent round of fee cuts, only about 10% of all sellers accepted Billpoint compared to 45% for PayPal.

"The market is shifting," Crane told the same reporter. "People understand they have to pay for this service," a development she claimed would drive them away from an "unknown startup" to an alternative backed by the trusted names of eBay and Wells Fargo. While her claim seemed odd since it suggested that auction customers care more about name brands than value when looking at service providers, Billpoint's subsequent actions showed Crane wasn't going to bet solely on her backers' names to dethrone PayPal.

Leveraging its marketing agreement with Visa, eBay announced in October that it would once again waive all Billpoint fees on Visa-funded payments. Though similar to what eBay had tried after Billpoint's April launch, the timing of this two month promotion meant our competitor would effectively be cheaper than PayPal for the entire holiday season.

The free Visa promotion didn't radically alter the payments land-scape overnight. A week later PayPal still held its commanding lead over Billpoint, though our competitor had managed to grow its listing acceptance by a couple of percentage points. Our own share held constant—most of the customers Billpoint picked up used PayPal already and continued to do so after also adopting our rival.

Free Visa wasn't the only October surprise eBay had in store. Earlier in the year Janet Crane signed off on a strategy to overhaul Billpoint's brand in order to further cash in on its eBay relationship. Billpoint's Web site and e-mails gradually began to refer to the service as "eBay Payments," an explicit attempt to draw a closer connection between the trusted auction house and its unknown payment provider. This phase-out of the Billpoint brand continued over the course of the fall as the "eBay Payments" name began appearing throughout eBay's site, often accompanied by a mascot—a cartoon dollar bill with arms and legs that zipped around on roller skates. It was exactly the sort of whimsical character you'd expect to find in eBay's virtual kingdom of primary colors, a stark contrast to PayPal's icon-free, "banker in a blue suit" Web site.

But eBay wasn't leaving Billpoint's fate in the hands of a skating dollar bill. The salvo that followed Billpoint's free Visa promotion and re-branding effort demonstrated the real leverage that comes along with ownership of the marketplace. As was typical, we learned about it in late fall not from a description of their tactics in the press but from Paul making a discovery on eBay's Web site.

Five months had passed since eBay had squelched the threat posed by Josh Koppelman's fixed price model by acquiring Half.com. Now eBay had finally introduced a version of fixed price transactions on its own site. Under the name "Buy It Now," or BIN, eBay gave sellers the option to name a price for which they'd be willing to skip the auction bidding process and immediately sell the item to a buyer. If a seller activated BIN for an individual listing, the Buy It Now option and price would be visible to potential buyers until someone submitted a bid in excess of the item's reserve price. BIN would then be deactivated and the standard auction process would take over.

In and of itself, Buy It Now didn't threaten PayPal. If it succeeded in convincing auction-averse buyers to shop on eBay's site, it would mean a growing audience of potential PayPal users. BIN also promised to increase eBay's auction velocity by shortening the average length of time before a listing closed. This, too, could be good for PayPal, since increased inventory turnover meant more potential items in need of payment. But what Paul had found overshadowed those potential benefits.

"Look at this," Paul said, handing me several printouts of screenshots. "I just did a Buy It Now for an auction that accepts Billpoint. Look at how they built this."

"Good grief," I blurted out, before adding, "Those rats!" In reality I chose a slightly stronger word to express my anger, but my outburst didn't faze my Southern Baptist friend—he was focused on eBay's perfidy.

While BIN itself stood to benefit PayPal by boosting the number of eBay transactions, eBay was using it to funnel buyers into Billpoint by giving them the impression that this was the only way they were allowed to pay for their items. Previously, when a buyer wanted to bid on an auction, he first entered his name, password, and bid amount. After bidding, buyers waited for the auction to close, typically leaving eBay in the interim. Winning bidders were later notified by e-mail and given instructions for completing the transaction with the seller. At this point, if the buyer had a PayPal account, he could go to our Web site and send a payment for the final amount. The buyer's extended absence from eBay's Web site gave PayPal a chance to insert itself into the process.

Buy It Now altered this dynamic. When a buyer chose to use the BIN option to close out a listing, the auction immediately ended with the buyer still on eBay's Web site. This allowed eBay an opportunity to influence the buyer's next steps through messaging on its site before the buyer would ever have a chance to come to PayPal.

Under the new Buy It Now format, buyers entered their log in information on eBay's site to authorize the purchase. They were then presented with a "continue" button that took them to a Billpoint payment form, implying that Billpoint was mandatory to complete the process. While the buyer could actually select to click on a smaller link on the page or even close the browser, the flow clearly suggested that the use of Billpoint was required. It was easily the boldest move pulled by eBay up until that point.

Taken together, Billpoint's branding change and BIN integration meant one thing—if Billpoint couldn't dislodge PayPal from eBay, then eBay would turn Billpoint into eBay.

◊

While eBay pressed on with its autumnal offensive, the world's largest commercial bank joined the online payments arena. In July, Citigroup announced a strategic alliance with America Online that would provide its forthcoming payment service "prime placement throughout the AOL network." With 100 million Citigroup account holders and 23 million AOL users, the duo's media machine waxed poetic about becoming the Internet's payments standard.[6]

If the hype was about the visionary Citi-AOL partnership, in reality it was a simple pay-for-placement contract. AOL had approached X.com earlier in the year to see how much of our venture financing we'd be willing to part with for run-of-site advertisements. When Reid Hoffman and the business development team balked at a long and costly contract, AOL sought out Citigroup's deep pockets. Selling ad inventory to the highest bidder isn't exactly revolutionary.

As it turned out, neither was Citigroup's payment service. Citi delayed its launch until the end of October, when it finally debuted under the name C2it. A phonetic play on the phrase "see to it," the company's site billed itself as a tool to get errands done and avoid wasting time writing checks. Citi's emphasis was similar to PayPal's at launch nearly a year before—it targeted person-to-person payments with little focus on auctions. In addition to overlooking the fastest growing online payments market, C2it also repeated a mistake made by Bank One's eMoneyMail, charging senders a fee to use the service. Though free for the first three months, C2it transactions would cost $2 each thereafter.[7]

Despite shelling out money for AOL ad placement, Citi's executives apparently expected C2it to operate gross margin positive from the start. If Citi's announced intention to enter into our space had been a source of concern for us earlier in the year, now its stumble out of the gate came as a relief. Chairman Sandy Weill and his lieutenants weren't interested in pursuing market share to build a payments network. I can only surmise that the mandate they gave the C2it team was to build a marginally profitable online site that could also shill for the company's core banking services.

If PayPal's payments leadership was going to be challenged, this muddled approach suggested Citigroup wouldn't be the one to do it. Neither would many of our earlier competitors—startups PayMe and PayPlace.com both shuttered their doors around this time for lack of cash, and Bank One's eMoneyMail soon followed for lack of users. But that didn't deter the press from jumping on the C2it bandwagon. *ComputerWorld* lauded it as the 800 pound gorilla of payments. An analyst in *Business Week* hailed C2it as less prone to fraud than its competitors. And *Business 2.0* said C2it would push electronic cash into "prime time."[8] The business media lapped up Citi's spin, seemingly oblivious to the real payments battle between PayPal and eBay playing out in public under their noses.

The press proved not to be blind in all matters, though. In early October, several weeks after the fact, the news finally broke that Elon had stepped down as CEO. Elon managed to keep the PR damage to a minimum by framing his departure as a career choice: "One has to recognize where one's strengths lie. It's more interesting for me in the early stages of running a company, where all the concentration is on developing the product... I guess you can say I'm a serial entrepreneur."[9] He added that he was leading the search committee to find a world class replacement. Peter Thiel's name—or the executive team's revolt—mercifully didn't come up.

I'll stop short of claiming that the puff pieces on C2it and the uncovering of Elon's departure demonstrated any systematic media bias against PayPal. Quite the contrary, the attention we had received up until that point was almost exclusively positive. After *The Red Herring* proclaimed us one of the world's one hundred most important companies in June, *Forbes* placed PayPal on its "Best of the Web" list and we took home a Webby award for favorite financial site.[10] But then again, we weren't the only startup receiving this kind of press. As with the supposedly revolutionary Japanese *keiretsu* in the eighties, during the late nineties the heralding of the dot-com movement was a popular fad in business reporting.

It's easy to understand why the topic fascinated journalists. For one thing, dot-coms' high-flying IPOs, irreverent advertising, and creative business plans made for good copy. In a broader sense, though, the seemingly endless supply of venture capital financing suggested that investors believed the U.S. really was on the verge of developing a new economy. For a journalist, it just didn't make sense to risk missing the boat, especially when all of his peers were on board. How else can one explain why columnists and talking-head gurus never blinked when Accenture CEO George Shaheen—proclaimed the "digital messiah" by *Forbes*[11]—left his position with the $9 billion consultancy to become the head of home grocer Webvan? In 1999 and early-2000 the Internet was in vogue and a myopic view prevailed, meaning that dot-coms like PayPal could do no wrong.

With PayPal getting the kid glove treatment during the business media's enthusiastic embrace of the startup phenomena, it stood to reason we wouldn't be immune if the general sentiment ever soured. And in the half year following the NASDAQ's April crash, that's what happened. As the Webvans of the world struggled and in some cases closed their virtual doors, the press turned vicious. If the perception of success generated accolades for dot-coms, it's no surprise the perception of the industry's failure produced media scorn. That conclusion seems all the more credible considering that many business journalists must have privately felt betrayed by a movement they had publicly endorsed.

So, while still eager to dole out praise when an old economy behemoth like Citigroup journeyed into online ventures, the business media began to heap greater scrutiny on young companies like PayPal. CNET's News.com service—a popular site devoted to high tech business news—in particular showed signs that it had PayPal in its crosshairs. In just over a month it published a string of articles highlighting Elon's departure, complaints from upset customers reacting to the forced upsell,[12] and a notice that our Web site suffered a brief outage following Thanksgiving weekend.[13]

CNET had plenty of company. Rafe Needleman from *The Red Herring* had earlier named Confinity his "catch of the day." Now, in an article titled "Baby, You Can Crash My Car," he mused about the delicious irony of an incident from March.[14] Elon was giving Peter a ride to a meeting with Mike Moritz at Sequoia Capital's office on Sand Hill Road in his now-famous McLaren F1. When he attempted to take a freeway off-ramp at a fast speed, his Formula One-caliber car launched into an airborne spin. It thudded to the earth adjacent to the ramp with both occupants dazed but miraculously unhurt, prompting Elon to exclaim, "Dude, that was intense!" Peter dusted himself off and hitched a ride to the venture capitalists' office, while Elon waited for a flatbed truck to haul away his precious vehicle. In a somber tone, Needleman publicly warned Peter that PayPal's business model was like the flying

McLaren—he needed to find a way to heed the laws of gravity or risk a complete wipe-out.[15]

Disregarding Needleman's melodramatic simile, I'll certainly acknowledge that our company wasn't beyond media dissection. In fact, we deserved it! We had racked up $92 million in operating losses through the first three quarters of the year against revenues of just $6 million. CNET, *The Red Herring*, and other media outlets had every right to sink their teeth into a company with such a dangerous burn rate, especially since 4 million customers depended on our service. But the abrupt change in the press's tone came when we had just gotten our act together. Coupled with the free pass handed to a stumbling C2it, this critical coverage served notice that the business media's herd mentality had switched course and PayPal had fallen out of favor. The press would not be sympathetic in our upcoming struggles.

◊

C2it's shaky launch and the media's grousing were just background noise in David Sacks's department; we kept our focus on the actions of PayPal's primary competitor. Billpoint's integration into Buy It Now and re-branding strategy posed the first real danger to PayPal's lead in the marketplace, especially when coupled with the Free Visa promotion. Our strategic response was threefold—we directly countered eBay on both its BIN and re-branding initiatives, while at the same time moved faster to roll out a new set of product features for PayPal's Web site.

With little leverage but a long list of blustery threats, Reid Hoffman lobbed a formal complaint to Rob Chesnut in eBay's legal department over Billpoint's Buy It Now advantage. Chesnut, by all accounts an even-keeled man who was far removed from the original BIN decision, heard Reid out and reviewed the matter. Following a few exchanges of screenshots and hyperlinks, Chesnut agreed that the "continue" link that led buyers to Billpoint was inappropriate and prevailed on eBay's product team to make the Billpoint link clearly labeled. While the bigger problem of eBay granting preferential treatment to Billpoint remained unresolved, Reid's assertive behind-the-scenes negotiations with eBay nipped this specific manifestation in the bud.

The "eBay Payments" re-branding issue was another matter. Blurring the distinction between eBay and Billpoint promised to give the payments service a competitive boost. But knowing that a goofy, skating dollar bill couldn't pull off a re-branding overnight, I positioned our marketing campaigns to continue referring to our competitor as Billpoint by using unflattering comparisons in our e-mails and Web pages. Since the name that a customer first calls a service is not easily unlearned—as witnessed by the PayPal brand's resilience during the months when we operated under Elon's dual brand strategy—I used our communications to help make sure that the Billpoint name wouldn't fade from view anytime soon.

On the product front, several new features bolstered PayPal's competitive standing. International accounts took PayPal one step closer to Peter's original vision for radical currency liberation. For the first time citizens from thirty countries could open PayPal accounts, and although this initial version only allowed for transactions in U.S. dollars, it still provided many international consumers with their first opportunity to send and receive online payments.

The producers also unveiled a money market feature for our U.S. customers. While nothing like the X.com plans for a financial supermarket, this optional service enabled users to earn interest on the balance in their PayPal accounts. Although called the PayPal Money Market Fund, the fund was owned and managed by Barclays Bank, an arrangement which allowed our company to again steer clear of activities that could land us with a commercial bank classification. Sacks hoped that providing our users with an interest-bearing incentive to keep cash in PayPal would decrease their reliance on expensive credit cards to fund payments.

The one-two punch of international accounts and the money market fund didn't completely repair all the damage that our brand sustained during the upgrade campaign, but it went a long way toward reassuring our customers that we'd continue to innovate and improve our service at a faster rate than Billpoint.

Our competitive responses to Billpoint's advances did the job and we weathered our first holiday season well. Though Billpoint made progress by growing its listing share from 10% to 20% during the fourth quarter, PayPal's acceptance also climbed another 5% to finish at the 50% mark. After extending the program to run through all of December, eBay saw signs that the free Visa program had run its course and allowed it to lapse. But the promotion had accomplished its goal; after losing ground to PayPal in the second and third quarters, Billpoint finally had some modest gains to report.

Billpoint's headway notwithstanding, December brought two significant milestones for our company—PayPal registered its 5 millionth account while also processing $1 billion in cumulative payments. Vince Sollitto's press release proclaimed that "PayPal has confirmed a prediction by Robert Simon, [former] CEO of dotBank... [that] the first company to reach five million users [would] become the clear market leader."[16] Other numbers for Q4 sounded just as good. Our payment volume increased by 29% from the prior quarter despite the upgrade campaign, bringing our average total payments to $6 million per day. Nearly two-thirds of all those transactions went to business accounts and generated $7.4 million in revenue. Though the company was still $25.4 million in the red, this was a considerable improvement over the prior period when we booked a paltry $1.0 million in transaction revenues against $36.7 million in operating losses.[17]

The increase in transaction revenues, coupled with declines in funding costs and fraud losses, caused our payment transaction margins to improve from -3.28% in the third quarter to -0.92% in the fourth. While not yet positive, our rising revenue and shrinking costs suggested our margins would soon swing into the plus column.

After nearly self-destructing from V2 and the X.com branding changes, we'd fended off eBay's competitive moves and succeeded in turning our business model around. We'd proved that customers would be willing to pay us to move payments on their behalf, and that our system could remain easy enough to use while implementing sufficient safeguards to keep fraud losses at acceptable levels. The burn rate was declining—PayPal had a sustainable business model after all.

◊

As PayPal's financial situation turned the corner, so did my own career. Following my successful leadership of the upgrade campaign, in early-2001 Sacks pulled me aside and asked me to join him in a conference room. I grimaced, thinking back to the similar circumstances that heralded Elon's ouster a few months earlier, but this time the news turned out to be far less cataclysmic.

"Congratulations on all your good work," he spoke through a grin that slightly elevated his wire frame glasses. "You've done a great job as our one-man marketing team, and because of this I'm promoting you to director of product marketing."

"Wow," came my startled reply. PayPal's annual review process was taken just about as seriously by most employees as other administrative functions, which is to say not very. The process was held in July, just as V2 was heating up, and most managers and their employees—

struggling to finish what was billed as an urgent site redesign—rushed to complete the paperwork at the last minute. At the time I barely gave the entire process a thought, a fact which made this mid-year promotion all the more unanticipated. "I don't know what to say, but I really appreciate it!" Sacks beamed at me from across the table, clearly happy over my genuine surprise.

"As part of this promotion, I plan for you to head up a small marketing team within the product group," Sacks continued, telling me the names of the two people who would soon be transferred over to report to me. Now I couldn't believe what I was hearing. Besides the satisfaction that came along with the recognition of my efforts, I welcomed the news that the company wanted to commit additional resources to marketing. My days of flying solo were over, and with the chance to form my own team I was eager for the change.

"Alright—just don't think that because you've got a team reporting to you now that you won't have to keep working hard," he barked with mock sternness before clasping my hand with a firm shake and heading back to his desk.

I lingered in the conference room for a moment, dazed by what had unfolded. Seven months earlier I had dreaded the prospect of reporting to the brusque Sacks, but since then the two of us had cemented a strong working relationship. Besides developing an admiration for his uncanny sense for using the product to achieve business objectives, I had grown more comfortable with his leadership style and even came to appreciate his directness. Although he demanded results, knowing that Sacks also meant what he said gave everyone on his staff a chance to work with clearly outlined expectations. Over time I would see him promote many deserving young employees into managerial roles; he empowered his staff to produce results, and in return he strove to make sure their efforts were rewarded.

For his part, Sacks had mellowed in his role as an executive. He was still short on pleasantries when addressing people but he had begun paying increased attention to issues such as morale and culture. He genuinely seemed to welcome feedback on major campaigns and product plans, and he never once held my willingness to stand up to him when we disagreed against me. He had earned my respect many times over.

Sacks's faith in me now meant a major change for my day-to-day duties. While I had served as an unofficial organizer and cheerleader for the now defunct marketing department after the merger, I'd never been asked to supervise personnel before. But the extra resources meant we could finally scale up and refine PayPal's marketing efforts, something I would've been unable to do alone.

◊

Although eBay's competitive thrust in the fourth quarter of 2000 failed to dislodge PayPal from its site, in the beginning of 2001 the auction house did banish one of its other competitors. EBay had long-since established its lead in the online auction world, yet it wasn't the only major online retailer in the sector.

Two other powerful Internet players, Yahoo and Amazon, still maintained auction services on their own sites. But despite its retail clout, Amazon was not a contender in person-to-person auctions. It had largely abdicated the space the prior summer after assessing steep fee hikes and removing a section of its site that provided sellers with online storefronts.[18] While Amazon seldom released updated counts of its auctions, our intelligence suggested it had only a small fraction of eBay's listings. We also knew from Paul and his engineers that sellers were making few requests for us to develop logos or tools that worked with Amazon auctions.

Yahoo auctions, on the other hand, enjoyed something of a following. In fact, by this point Yahoo alone looked like it had the potential to challenge eBay's dominance; its 2.4 million listings were at least within striking distance of eBay's tally of 3.7 million.[19] PayPal had reason to hope that Yahoo would make a run at it. A competitive auction market would give PayPal an edge over Billpoint and Yahoo's PayDirect since our service could be used on both sites. And a strong showing by Yahoo auctions would pressure eBay to focus on its core marketplace, diverting its energies away from payments.

Yahoo had positioned its auction service as a competitor of eBay from the very start. It made a bold statement by launching the service only a few days before eBay's IPO in September 1998. Unlike eBay, Yahoo opted to not charge a listing fee for posting an item for sale on its site. But price competition alone proved insufficient to derail eBay's network, prompting Yahoo to try an aggressive strategy to leverage eBay's success to its advantage. In the spring of 1999, Yahoo allowed sellers to import their eBay feedback ratings into their Yahoo profile.[20] This move was designed to make selling on Yahoo auctions more attractive to eBay's sellers by letting them display their eBay track record on Yahoo. By decreasing the information gap between buyers and sellers on Yahoo's younger auction site, it immediately made the safety of transacting on Yahoo comparable to eBay's. For its part eBay promptly registered a legal protest that convinced Yahoo to reverse course and abandon the feedback-importing service.

After backing away from the feedback plan, Yahoo auctions languished for the next year despite the lack of listing fees. It wasn't until eBay suffered a minor grassroots rebellion in early-2000 that Yahoo began to gain traction. Rosalinda Baldwin, the passionate editor of *The Auction Guild*, a popular auction newsletter, took the lead in organizing a protest against eBay's perceived favoritism toward its corporate clients at the expense of the sole proprietors who'd first made the site successful. Citing eBay's refusal to extend pre-IPO stock to its many supporters in the virtual community, Baldwin called for a "Million Auction March" in which sellers would move listings to alternative sites, punishing eBay while at the same time helping to establish viable alternatives.

This movement apparently aided Yahoo—its daily average number of auction listings grew by about 1 million from March to September 2000 while eBay's held flat.[21] Since eBay's auction business tends to show a large degree of seasonality, increasing in Q1 and Q4 while typically holding flat in Q2 and Q3, this mid-year surge in listings during the "slow" season had to be encouraging for Yahoo.

With its gigantic market capitalization and growing revenue from advertising, keeping its auction service free during the waning days of the dot-com boom seemed logical for Yahoo. Gaining market share by offering a free service was classic Internet strategy, one that PayPal had mastered quite well. I suspect Yahoo also viewed its free pricing as a way to pressure eBay to return to the table for acquisition talks. Given its overtures to eBay in 1998 and early-2000, it's clear that Yahoo wanted to add Meg Whitman's company to its Internet portal.

As Yahoo's advertising revenue began to dry up in the wake of the NASDAQ composite's crash and its share price fell from about $200 to under $30 in just eight months, the mega-portal was forced to initiate a major change in its auction strategy. On January 2, 2001, Yahoo announced it would end its free auction listings and implement fees ranging from $0.20 to $2.25.[22] The pricing was carefully chosen to remain lower than eBay's, and the company talked down expectations, saying it fully anticipated some user attrition.

Attrition turned out to be an understatement—the fees emasculated Yahoo's auction site. In just a month the total number of Yahoo listings fell from 2.6 million to 460,000.[23] Watching Yahoo's auction service collapse, eBay seized the opportunity to increase its own margins and announced its first price hike since 1996. EBay raised listing fees to range between $0.30 and $3.30, a move which spokesman Kevin Pursglove claimed "...will help us keep the eBay business financially healthy."[24] After a brief blip downward, the total number of eBay listings began to climb again despite the higher fees; meanwhile Yahoo entered free fall.

EBay's stranglehold on buyers ultimately doomed Yahoo auctions. The non-transportability of eBay's feedback made switching inconvenient for buyers, so even though Yahoo charged less than eBay this incremental cost was enough to drive away most of the sellers who had previously used the service. They simply could not afford to pay the new fees given that most of their buyers lurked on eBay.

If nothing else, Yahoo's collapse provided some insight into the relative strength of PayPal and eBay's network effects. PayPal's payments network was strong enough to survive the forced upgrade process, although our competitor did make up some ground by undercutting our pricing. EBay's older auctions network, though, was far more powerful. It allowed Whitman to raise prices and still grow following the introduction of a minor fee system from Yahoo. PayPal may have enjoyed a modest network effect, but by banishing Yahoo auctions eBay had gone one step further and established itself as a person-to-person marketplace monopolist.

◊

Whenever Luke Nosek turned up in the product department after a long stretch in seclusion, he tended to have either a sagacious idea with him or, just as likely, a wacky scheme. And sometimes both.

"I figured out a way we can under-price Billpoint!" Luke proclaimed as he stuck his head into my cube unannounced one February morning. "We should give our sellers cashback for using their debit cards."

I turned to face my former boss. The feature, PayPal's debit card, was still in beta testing, but demand for it was already high. Damon Billian routinely forwarded message board requests from customers wanting to use their PayPal account balance to pay for transactions and make withdrawals at ATMs. Co-branded with MasterCard, our card could also be used with any merchant who accepted credit cards.

"That's not going to work, Luke," I cautioned. "We can't start a pricing war while we're still trying to make our margins positive."

"We don't have to give up any payment margins," the vice president answered. "As the debit card provider, we get most of the interchange fee charged to the merchant whenever the cardholder makes a transaction over the MasterCard network. We can just share some of that fee with the cardholder whenever he makes a purchase."

"But what if Billpoint decides to mimic us and does the same thing? There's nothing to stop them from offering cashback," I replied.

"It's not a pricing war since it's something we can do that Billpoint can't," he countered. "Billpoint accounts are structured differently than ours. Their system doesn't let customers keep a balance—it immediately sweeps all payments into the user's bank account. This means Billpoint will never be able to offer debit cards, and without debit card transactions it's not going to have large enough margins to support any kind of generous cashback program."

"That's true," I acknowledged, before adding, "You know, we make about 2% on signature-authorized transactions that use the MasterCard network, so that gives us some pretty significant cash to play around with."

Luke and I smiled at each other as we pondered his stroke of genius. After enduring several months of ferocious competition from eBay, we had a way to fight back.

Sacks, who was out of the office on a business trip at the time, warmed to Luke's idea. He asked me to prepare a specific proposal in time for his return that evening. Luke and I invited the debit card's producer, Premal Shah, a classmate of mine from Stanford and a recent addition to the team, to join us in hammering out the details. What emerged from our discussions turned out to be PayPal's most sweeping promotion since the creation of the $10 referral bonus.

Given that debit card providers received roughly 2% on signature-authorized transactions that used the MasterCard network—but only about a quarter of that for PIN-authorized ones and nothing for ATM withdrawals—we opted to tie our cashback to the high revenue transactions. But the prize would only be available to sellers who spurned Billpoint's advances. They would receive a 1.5% rebate on every signature-authorized debit card purchase in exchange for making PayPal the only online payment service advertised in their auctions. Since our business account fees ranged from 2.2% to 2.9% on incoming payments, this level of cashback would substantially lower our effective fees for any sellers who used their new debit card to purchase inventory or other goods and services.

The proposal, which I dubbed the "PayPal Preferred" rewards program, was admittedly aggressive, but also appropriate given eBay's escalating attacks. While its intent of degrading our competitor's standing in the marketplace was transparent, at least it used benefits rather than slight of hand to do so. And since we were now taking on a monopolist, we needed to utilize every available option.

As enticing as this generous cashback program sounded, it would only strengthen our position against Billpoint if we were able to get debit cards into the hands of our sellers quickly. Premal suggested an audacious solution to this problem. PayPal would proactively mail unsolicited cards to qualified sellers and use Web site content, e-mails, and outbound phone calls to educate our customers on how to use their new plastic. After crunching the numbers with Roelof Botha, the economics validated the proposal, prompting both Sacks and Peter to sign off.

In another repeat of the nimbleness I first encountered at Confinity, we transformed Luke's proposal from idea into action within just a few weeks. Premal and I met daily with our counterparts in fraud and customer service as the company shipped out tens of thousands of debit cards to our top sellers. Even though our customers weren't expecting them, most considered the free cards a very pleasant surprise— recipients activated and used them at a rate that card industry insiders later told me was amazing. And many of our new cardholders opted to join PayPal Preferred and forego the use of Billpoint in their auctions. While Billpoint's recent gains didn't collapse overnight, its gradual upward trend in listing share leveled off and it even gave back a small portion. PayPal was back on the offensive.

◊

We didn't stop with PayPal Preferred. The company's newly restored decentralized approach to generating initiatives, coupled with a healthy appetite for risk and fast product development, served us well during the early months of 2001. After Billpoint hit us with a triple assault of free Visa, BIN integration, and branding changes, Peter sought to improve the company's prospects by strengthening PayPal's young network. Even with the implementation of our business model now complete and our margins improving by the month, Peter often spoke of "the eBay threat" as a systematic risk to our company that needed to be mitigated in order to take PayPal public. But this danger could be vanquished by defeating Billpoint in the marketplace, in effect showing the world that the auction monopolist's own customers would not let them ban PayPal.

Our still uncertain business future dictated which tactics were available to carry out Peter's objective. The company's improving but negative cash flow meant that big advertising buys and a return to liberal referral bonuses were out of the question. Moreover, even though Sacks had created a new product marketing team under my supervision, our rookie company was still a long way from having a marketing-centric culture. Our primary focus remained on developing the product and with good reason—it offered a true competitive advantage over Billpoint. EBay could always outspend us on ad purchases and throw dozens of marketers at sophisticated campaigns, but its ponderous pace over the past twelve months indicated that eBay could not innovate as quickly as we could.

This suggested that gutsy product initiatives, supported by guerilla marketing, remained the primary weapon in our arsenal. As the early months of 2001 rolled by, we fired back with several worthy follow-ups to the PayPal Preferred campaign. PayPal Shops, an opt-in directory that let sellers list their online stores in a site accessible to buyers, encouraged our users to transact off-eBay. Smart Logos, auction buttons that appeared as standard referral logos while the auction was open but turned into bright "pay now" buttons once the bidding ended, made it easy for winning bidders to open a PayPal account and pay for an auction in one step. And Winning Bidder Notification, or WBN, allowed sellers to send an automatic e-mail to buyers that included PayPal instructions and a link to a payment form—a strategy which minimized the odds of the buyer returning to eBay's site, where he might encounter Billpoint.

This frantic rate of product innovation meant that Paul and Yu Pan, his lead engineer, practically moved into the office. In fact, thanks in part to this heavy workload, the PayPal building hosted a special moment. On a weekend evening, after taking his girlfriend out for dinner and a movie, Paul brought her to the office on the pretense that he needed to finish up a project before heading back out. This seemed perfectly normal to his girlfriend, a Stanford student who had gotten used to doing homework assignments sitting next to Paul in his cube for hours every evening. This time, however, Paul was the one who had done his homework and he pulled a sparkling engagement ring out of his desk.

As the grueling pace of product development continued, my marketing team supported the counter-offensive. We used a combination of promotional e-mails and post-login interstitial pages to drive adoption of our new products, as well as to contrast PayPal favorably against Billpoint. My decision to include these head-to-head comparisons thrust my little group into the middle of an internal debate.

One problem with the discipline of marketing is that everyone knows enough about it to make suggestions, but most don't know enough to offer good advice. Some colleagues scolded that the market leader should never mention the competition since this places it on an even playing field—for example, Coca Cola never mentions Pepsi in its advertising. But our situation was the exception that proved the logic of that rule. EBay customers were already aware of the eBay brand name! If anything, it was critical for us not to grant eBay total control in defining Billpoint to its millions of customers.

Other coworkers pushed for us to draw more forceful comparisons. While our communications already used tables and lists to point out PayPal's superior functionality and pricing, they thought we needed to provoke outrage to spur sellers to remove Billpoint from their auctions. This point of view seemed equally problematic. Feedback from customer interviews as well as discussion board comments forwarded by Damon Billian showed that users were increasingly uncomfortable about being caught in the middle of PayPal and Billpoint's conflict. The mounting animosity between our company and eBay was becoming visible to the outside world, and I feared this could ultimately damage PayPal's brand.

So I set PayPal's marketing campaign on a middle course, attempting to engage our competitor head-on without alienating our customers. As I settled into my role as director of product marketing I'd gotten much better at taking criticism in stride. PayPal was a marketplace of ideas that embraced internal debate, and I was guilty myself of offering plenty of unsolicited suggestions to colleagues. This intellectual openness was the source of many of the initiatives that had turned the tide in fixing our business model and in surviving the competition with Billpoint.

Of course, following sixteen months of highs and lows at PayPal I was beginning to appreciate that a turn of tide wasn't the same as victory in war. Our flying McLaren was now safely on the ground, but the race still had many laps to go.

CHAPTER EIGHT

HIGH STAKES

MARCH – SEPTEMBER 2001

CONSIDERING THE POST-MERGER turmoil that roiled the company in 2000, the following year got off to a good start. Our product and marketing responses to eBay's campaigns in late-2000 helped sustain our strong growth through the first quarter. Payment volume increased by 18% to more than $7 million in PayPal transactions each day, and the total number of accounts rose to 7.2 million. While still operating at a loss, we halved our $25.4 million operating deficit from the prior period to $12.1 million in Q1. PayPal rode its wave of viral growth as our financials continued their dramatic turnaround.

Positive margins on our payment volume were the reason for our deficit's decline. After losing 0.92% on every dollar in transaction volume in Q4, payments added a positive 0.20% to PayPal's bottom line in the first quarter. Rising revenue was the primary cause as the upgrade architecture continued to transport sellers into fee-bearing accounts, boosting revenue as a percentage of payments from 1.37% in Q4 to 2.05% in Q1. Transaction revenues totaled $13.2 million for the quarter, more than the amount we booked in the entire previous calendar year. Declining costs also helped our margins. The transaction processing expense rate dropped from -1.67% to -1.36% in Q1 as more users chose bank accounts instead of credit cards to fund their payments, and our fraud losses improved by 13 basis points to -0.48%.

This dramatic about-face in our transaction margins was no puzzle to Peter Thiel. It was a few weeks into his stint as the acting-CEO when I heard him compare our new economy payments network to an abstract old economy machine. PayPal's many policies—such as the fees charged to sellers, spending limits placed on unverified buyers, and our behind-the-scenes fraud algorithms—were like levers, dials, and pulleys. The key was to adjust each of them carefully in unison with the others until the machine hummed along at cruising speed. And Peter had no choice but to tinker. With no documented business precedent similar to PayPal to guide him, he needed his executive team to tweak each variable repeatedly to discover what inputs would optimize the business.

While always courteous to employees, the soft-spoken Peter placed high demands on his officers. Peter kept a running list of critical issues and it was common for him to make impromptu calls for status reports with notepad in hand. Sacks, a close friend of Peter's, was one of his favorite targets. With Peter's cube located adjacent to the product team, we frequently heard "David, get over here!" echo over the gray partitions whenever Peter needed an update. But Peter was by no means a micro-managing executive. Quite the opposite, he began moving the organization back toward the decentralized approach he had employed at Confinity. He gave his officers a long leash provided they checked in regularly and backed up their claims with data. As a former derivatives trader, Peter saw numbers as a language of truth. Anyone entrusted with a major project needed to have key figures at his fingertips in case Peter came calling.

Peter's ability to focus on the company's major problems while leveraging the talents of his friends and colleagues earned him a vote of confidence from the board of directors. In February, five months after Elon's departure and following a brief executive search process, the board asked Peter to become the company's permanent CEO. It was a well-deserved request, and his follow-up act confirmed it was the right decision.

Despite the NASDAQ Composite resuming its free fall in early-2001—the index dropped from 2,800 to 1,800 in just two months—Peter returned to the private equity markets and secured $90 million in additional financing, an amazing accomplishment given the gloomy state of Silicon Valley. This funding from various financial institutions, including Spain's Bankinter and France's Credit Agricole,[1] brought the company's cash on hand at the end of the quarter up to $130 million without devaluing its private share price. With our monthly burn rate down to just $3 million, one-third of what it was in autumn, the threat that PayPal might run out of money was gone.

On the heels of his latest financing miracle, Peter took the ultimate victory lap in the form of a visit to the White House.[2] He later described his encounter with President George W. Bush at a company meeting in PayPal's parking lot. In just over one-half year PayPal was already bursting at the seams in the Embarcadero building, which prompted HR to convert our large conference room into space for yet more cubicles.

Company meetings now had to be held outside with employees seated on folding chairs and Peter standing at a podium equipped with built-in microphone and speaker. It was an odd spectacle, but employees always hurried to be on time ever since Peter had instituted a nominal $1 a minute fine for latecomers to ensure a prompt start to all meetings. After giving an update on the company's finances, our T-shirt and blue jeans-clad chief executive fielded questions from his personnel. "Well, there was a lot of waiting," he responded to a request to describe his day at the White House. "First we waited to go through security. Then we waited in a room for the ceremony to begin. Then after listening to a bunch of aides the president himself finally arrived."

Though downplaying his excitement, Peter clearly enjoyed both the meeting and his chance to recount it. And why not? After struggling for half a year after the merger to fix PayPal's business model and fending off eBay's assault at the end of 2000, we all deserved a moment of levity. PayPal seemed back on the road to "world domination."

Seizing upon the high spirits, an employee asked Peter if he would dye his hair PayPal blue if we met his challenge to make the company cashflow positive by August. After stalling for a moment, the CEO sheepishly accepted the dare.

◊

Peter wasn't the only person responsible for turning around PayPal's financials. Our fraud situation became so critical in the second half of 2000 that MasterCard, seemingly always looking for a chance to come down on our young company, fined PayPal $313,600 for having excessive credit card chargebacks.[3] After his return to the helm, Peter asked Max Levchin to make the construction of anti-fraud measures his primary focus. With his typical quiet intensity, our Ukrainian CTO threw all of his energy into answering this growing threat, plastering his cubicle's walls with graphs showing various fraud metrics.

Max's first objective was to find a way to prevent automated, scaleable fraud from walking right through PayPal's front door. While strong encryption protected our users from having their accounts hacked, the open nature of our service also made our company vulnerable to thieves who already possessed stolen credit cards. As previously mentioned, one such ring opened fraudulent PayPal accounts and used them to siphon nearly $6 million out of the system in mid-2000. Any attempt to contain our fraud losses needed to limit the criminals' ability to create multiple bogus accounts.

Working with David Gausebeck, one of the first engineers to join Confinity, Max developed a mechanism to complicate account creation for fraud rings without hindering legitimate users. The duo placed an image on the sign-up page that contained a random sequence of black letters on top of a yellow background crisscrossed by thin black lines. The person opening the account was asked to read the image and type the letters into a nearby text box. While the human eye could easily interpret the random string of letters contained in the image, the slight distortion caused by the background prevented even the most sophisticated computer from doing the same. Max would later refer to it as a "reverse Turing test," a way to discern a human being opening an account from a computer. Using an automated script to churn out hundreds of fraudulent PayPal accounts linked to stolen credit cards was now effectively impossible.

The Gausebeck-Levchin test, as this addition to the sign-up process became known around the office, proved successful in combating fraud without slowing down sign-ups. And not just for PayPal. Over the following years Max's technique caught on and began to appear on other Web sites concerned with automated account creation.[4] To the best of my knowledge, however, PayPal was the first site to use this technology.

Max's anti-fraud efforts didn't stop with the Gausebeck-Levchin test. While this measure made it more difficult for large fraud rings to get in the system, our operations team needed a reliable way to pinpoint any fraudulent activity that did make it inside. To accomplish this, Max built a program to scan transaction records to look for suspicious patterns. Both the inspiration and the name of the program came from a Russian national who had endeared himself to Max and his fraud team.

Shortly after Max began investigating dubious activity in PayPal's database he closed down a series of murky accounts. No sooner had he completed this than a new round of questionable accounts popped up, this time accompanied by a mocking e-mail addressed to Max. The author, who identified himself only as Igor, taunted the CTO, claiming it would be impossible to keep him out of the system. As his cat-and-mouse game with Igor progressed, so too did Max's knowledge of how criminals tried to manipulate PayPal's open system. The patterns he discerned began to tell a common story.

Criminals like Igor generally tried to wash stolen funds by using feeder accounts to pay an unknown number of middleman accounts before ultimately transferring the money to a bank. The size of the payments, the frequency of account use, and the information stored on file for the fraudulent accounts all shared a common thread. It betrayed a systematic interconnectedness between a finite number of accounts that looked very different from the buying and selling patterns of our normal eBay users and Web site merchants. Or, as Max succinctly told *The Wall Street Journal*: "Fraudsters have different patterns than [legitimate customers] do."[5]

Armed with this first-hand knowledge, Max created a program named after his Russian foe to scan transaction activity for likely fraud. "Igor" froze accounts involved in suspect activities and flagged them for review by a human investigator in our operations department. The investigator, upon examining the account's transaction log and attempting to contact the user, would make the decision whether to unfreeze the account and free up its funds or to close it down and alert the proper authorities.

"Igor," the Gausebeck-Levchin test, and other various anti-fraud measures combined to make a colossal impact. Our fraud loss rate on transactions peaked at 1.21% of payment volume in the third quarter of 2000 before falling to 0.61% in Q4 and the previously mentioned 0.48% in Q1, well under the 2.64% estimated fraud rate for the entire Internet.[6] But despite this amazing progress, Max never set out to eliminate fraud losses outright. Instead he wanted to contain them without stifling growth. Or, as a journalist for *Wired* magazine put it, "Levchin knew that a more intrusive sign-up procedure could hobble online thieves, but he also realized it would discourage potential customers... PayPal came to regard fraud as something akin to an R&D expense."[7]

Our improving ability to track down online crooks earned PayPal national attention when the FBI invited us to present at a press conference on the subject.[8] PayPal also scored some very high profile legal victories. In December 2000, our investigators worked with authorities to bring charges against a California-based company called Gametek. Gametek had collected $1.2 million in payments from unwary consumers for PlayStation 2 video-game consoles in the midst of a nationwide holiday PS2 shortage and allegedly failed to ship any of the promised goods.[9] In May 2001, the FBI arrested two Russian citizens flagged by PayPal's lead fraud investigator—a physically imposing former military intelligence officer named John Kothanek—after luring them into the U.S. with an offer for security jobs at a technology company.[10] And thanks to help from PayPal, federal authorities busted organized crime rings in Chicago, Houston, and Nigeria.[11]

Unfortunately these notable gains didn't come without cost. PayPal's success in fighting back fraud also produced false positives that inconvenienced honest users. For example, Tim Kramer, a plumbing supply salesman from Seattle who sold his wares on eBay, claimed to the media that we unjustifiably froze his account in January 2001 without an explanation. Unable to contact a company representative, he noted his $500 balance sat inaccessible until we restored his account privileges a week later—again without explanation.[12] While I cannot speak to the accuracy of Kramer's complaint, he was not alone. The same article that aired his gripe also mentioned a mounting number of grievances being directed to watchdog agencies like the Better Business Bureau. Similar complaints began to surface on community boards, prompting Damon Billian and the fraud team to spend an increasing amount of time investigating these public claims.

But as bad as the false positives experience for innocent users and resulting negative publicity for the company might have been, it was an acceptable cost. The fact that spiraling fraud losses contributed to many of our competitors like eMoneyMail, PayMe, and PayPlace ceasing operation made this an easy choice[13]—had PayPal not found a way to get fraud under control, it would have destroyed the company. And, just as significantly, our efforts to track down alleged fraudsters like Gametek kept our many honest users from becoming victims. Unchecked fraud would have put all of our legitimate customers and the very existence of our payments network at risk. A few false positives, which our customer service and fraud teams tried immediately to correct, were preferable to the alternative of not vigorously fighting the crooks who exploited our company and users.

In addition to sending criminals to jail, Max's pioneering efforts earned him a remarkable distinction the following year. Specifically citing his work on "Igor," MIT's *Technology Review* named Max its "Innovator of the Year." The real Igor, I'm sorry to report, didn't fare as well. In a coincidence comparable to Elon randomly receiving Luke's branding survey, Peter later realized that Igor had met Peter's own mother through a local chess league! Alas, Igor's chess-playing days were numbered—rumor had it that he was later injured in a suspicious shoot-out at a night club and subsequently dropped off of PayPal's radar.

Max, John Kothanek, and the rest of the fraud team's scrapes with organized crime soon entered into Internet lore. In an interview with PBS's "Nightly Business Report" in February, Peter forcefully summarized their exploits while delivering a warning to other would-be fraudsters:

> **Question:** Have you had problems with security?
>
> **Peter:** [We] started with this incredible obsession with security. [And this] has actually come in very useful because when you are talking about moving hundreds of millions of dollars, you get targeted by everyone from the Russian mafia to the Nigerian mafia to the Indonesian mafia. And we've basically beaten them all back.
>
> **Question:** You've been targeted by mafia?
>
> **Peter:** We have been targeted and we have beaten them all back, which is I think the more important piece to convey... And a number of these people are on their way to jail.[14]

Criminals—organized and otherwise—had met their match in PayPal. But compared to what was about to come out of San Jose, beating back the mafia was a walk in the park.

◊

Toward the middle of the second quarter signs began to appear that eBay, fresh from vanquishing Yahoo, its final marketplace competitor, was ready to do the same with payments. The saber rattling indirectly started during an Associated Press interview with Meg Whitman. The eBay CEO turned heads throughout Silicon Valley when she told the AP that she no longer considered Amazon and Yahoo to be serious opponents. She added that eBay's various anti-fraud measures, including its investigations team and customer support, made eBay an unattractive place for commercial deception: "What we have successfully done, I think, is communicated to the Web community that if you're going to commit fraud, you have to work really hard to do it at eBay. And as a result, I think we've actually exported fraud to Yahoo."[15]

While no eBay executives have ever used the word "monopolist" to describe their company's position as an online person-to-person marketplace, Whitman's frank statements to the AP came amazingly close. Since a common theme in eBay's marketing is to not sound boastful when speaking to the community, this breezy dismissal of competitors and talk of exporting fraud over to another company sounded decisively un-eBaysian. Auction users took notice. The following day the popular *Auction Bytes* news Web site amusingly proclaimed "eBay CEO Disses Yahoo!"[16]

Whitman's public acknowledgement of her company's dominance was accurate, of course, and it signaled growing internal comfort on eBay's part with its market leadership. EBay's early years had been marked by a paranoia that viewed the auction house's position in the market as tenuous. In fact, its management agreed to a costly partnership with America Online largely to keep AOL out of the auctions business.[17] While a healthy level of paranoia is normal and even necessary in young companies striving to survive—PayPal certainly had it—eBay had clearly outgrown this trait in the wake of Yahoo's collapse. EBay's major rivals were vanquished and the acquisition of Half.com and the roll-out of Buy It Now plugged one of the few significant holes in Pierre Omidyar's otherwise amazing business model. EBay had reason to swagger.[18]

If Whitman's comments to the press betrayed a greater private confidence, eBay's subsequent public actions also echoed it. In June the company announced the beta roll-out of its eBay Stores program. Participating sellers obtained an eBay-hosted storefront that linked to items they wanted to sell at a fixed price. This storefront had several customizable features, including the ability for sellers to include their business logo and description, making eBay Stores a distinctive shopping experience from the auction portion of eBay's Web site.

Stores would have been an ideal platform for PayPal. Our "pay now" Smart Logos would have made it simple for buyers to send a payment right after they typed in their eBay password and agreed to purchase the fixed price item. But eBay had other plans. While not outright forbidding the use of PayPal in eBay Stores, the auction giant instead declared that sellers were required either to have a credit card merchant account or to accept Billpoint to be included in Stores. EBay justified this policy by claiming that sellers needed to accept instant payments to ensure a positive buyer experience since fixed price items, unlike auctions, have no natural time lag and hence warrant quick fulfillment.

While eBay offered no explanation as to why PayPal didn't meet the instant payment standard but Billpoint did, the unspoken reason seemed obvious. Only a small percentage of eBay's sellers boasted sufficiently high sales volumes to qualify for credit card merchant accounts. PayPal's ability to service small businesses and fulfill an unmet need was a major cause of our success. Asking sellers to have either a merchant account or a Billpoint account to participate in Stores was tantamount to mandating Billpoint—a bundling strategy similar to the one employed by another monopolist to derail Netscape's leadership in the Internet browser market.

Saying this development threw PayPal's offices into a maelstrom would be understatement. As previously noted, paranoia is an essential ingredient in any successful startup, and this time our fears had a basis. Panicked e-mails flew around the office after the policy was uncovered, and Sacks, Peter, and Reid caucused constantly on the subject. With our product and marketing responses limited, the company had no choice but to fire back with an explicit threat of legal action.

Telegraphing this warning to eBay was in many ways an all or nothing gambit. Back-channel communications between Reid and Rob Chesnut had produced mixed results over the prior year and a half; sometimes eBay conceded, sometimes we backed down. But there wasn't much room for give and take now. If Stores became a popular feature on eBay's site, it would cause a surge in Billpoint's acceptance. And a large increase in its listing share could be disastrous to PayPal's volume, given Billpoint's existing preferential placement in end-of-auction e-mails, searches, and other Web site points. We needed eBay to reverse course and unpackage the two services. Otherwise, if we were going to throw our lots to the legal system the way Netscape did, there was the risk that a remedy would not come fast enough to save PayPal.

Unlike Microsoft, eBay blinked. Sort of. The company agreed to "clarify" its terms of use so PayPal could be accepted as a credit card processor for the purpose of admission to eBay Stores. What eBay failed to do was make this obvious in the Stores sign-up process. The average seller could still reasonably infer that PayPal was insufficient to qualify for Stores and that a Billpoint account was required. To counteract that possibility, I had my marketing team place screenshots and step-by-step instructions on using Stores on PayPal's own site. We even went so far as to recommend they list their eBay Store in our PayPal Shops' Web site directory.

The company breathed a collective sigh of relief. At the time it felt like we had averted a major crisis and forced our competitor to concede on a significant threat.

That relief lasted less than a week.

◊

"Eric, can you come here, please?" asked JoAnne Rockower. The June day was warm and lazy, signaling the approach of summer, but there was a distinct sense of urgency in JoAnne's voice.

"What's going on?" I replied, emerging from behind my desk. JoAnne, who worked on Paul's auction features team, sat gazing at an open spreadsheet on her monitor.

"I want you to take a look at this," she requested. "It's the daily auction report, and something isn't making sense."

Daily scans monitoring both PayPal's and our competitors' acceptance were the cornerstone of our auction intelligence. We had developed a manual method as well as an automated sampling device to gauge our listing share and the total number of listings on several auction sites. Following Yahoo's auction collapse earlier in the year, however, we devoted our energy exclusively to tracking eBay and Billpoint. JoAnne managed the manual report while I worked with our engineers on the automated one and we compared the figures daily to make sure they agreed.

I leisurely walked across to JoAnne's cube and propped my arm on the wall to lean in. But when I glanced at her monitor, what I saw made me instinctively tense up. I blinked and peered at the Excel table a second time. Billpoint's listing share had soared. Our opponent had climbed from less than 25% of eBay listings to 30% overnight.

This apparent 500 basis point jump exceeded our competitor's gains of the past six months. After growing briskly during its free Visa promotion in late-2000, Billpoint's progress leveled off in the first half of 2001 while PayPal's listing share continued to rise, going from 55% to 65%. Somehow in one evening Billpoint had managed to surpass what its prior one-half year of campaigning had achieved.

The discovery set off a mad scramble to determine the cause. A quick check of the automated scan verified JoAnne's discovery, and I immediately called together our product and engineering experts to help me determine the reason for this sudden change before alerting Sacks. The entire group was stumped until I made an accidental discovery while listing a test auction using my own eBay account. When I opened the Sell Your Item form to type in the fields for my auction set-up I saw that the Billpoint payment preferences were selected. The SYI form automatically saved preferences like this every time an auction was added to eBay's site, letting frequent sellers avoid the hassle of entering unchanged information like shipping policies and insurance fees for each listing.

Now, instead of saving my payment preferences, the SYI form had defaulted back to using Billpoint. Had I rushed through this process to post my auction on eBay's site, Billpoint would have appeared as a payment option, triggering all the Billpoint bells and whistles to encourage my winning bidder to use it to pay me. Incredibly, eBay had changed the SYI set-up for sellers with Billpoint accounts without announcing it.

With this realization I concluded that eBay must have defaulted every seller who had ever opened a Billpoint account back into accepting those payments, and I guessed that most sellers were still unaware of this development. Many large sellers used automated tools to list their dozens or even hundreds of daily auctions, meaning they never stopped to view the SYI form, much less their actual listings. This implied that thousands of users were oblivious to the preference change and the subsequent appearance of Billpoint as a payment option in their auctions. And since the default modification was recent, these newly listed auctions had not yet begun to receive Billpoint payments from unsuspecting buyers.

Having obtained an answer, I approached Sacks with a plan in mind. EBay was playing with fire by manipulating its users' preferences to promote Billpoint, and it was time for it to get burned.

◊

The emergency response we sent to our sellers pulled no punches. Believing we desperately needed to roll back Billpoint's gains and attract public criticism to eBay's tactics in the process, I crafted a blunt warning that outlined the potential problem to customers and blamed eBay for changing their preferences. "Unauthorized Billpoint logos can result in confused buyers using Billpoint to pay you, and this in turn can hurt your bottom line," the e-mail cautioned, reminding the sellers of Billpoint's higher fees and lack of chargeback protection. "The only sure way to protect yourself from future unauthorized Billpoint logos is to close your Billpoint account."

This call to action was easier said than done. Unlike PayPal, Billpoint did not provide its users with a way to close their accounts online; customers had to contact the Billpoint offices to do so.[19] But since eBay did not operate phone-based customer service this required users to wade around through eBay's Web site help forms to submit their request. It was a lousy customer experience, but I proposed a novel work-around. I pulled eBay's main phone line from a business directory and navigated through its audio menu until I found the extension for a skeleton customer service telephone support crew. If eBay was going to change sellers' preferences without telling them, I found it only fair to let our mutual customers know eBay's secret toll-free number.

After voicing some initial reservations, both Sacks and Reid signed off on my combative suggestion. Besides aiding sellers in finally closing their Billpoint accounts, I reasoned that flooding the eBay corporate headquarters switchboard would also provide the auction giant's staff with a vocal display of customer discontent.

In addition to the e-mail, Sacks and I enlisted the help of April Kelly to manage an outbound call project to our high volume sellers. April was an entrepreneurial manager from our Omaha office who had supervised the telemarketing campaign in support of our debit card launch earlier in the year. Even though PayPal didn't have a formal outbound call group—we still didn't have enough customer service personnel to answer inbound calls at some peak times—April was a leading proponent of finding ways to turn our Omaha office into a profit center by helping customers learn more about new features. Her first outbound team had helped us increase debit card activation rates substantially, so with Peter's blessing Sacks secured the resources necessary for her to participate in this crucial effort.

The deployment of our e-mail and call campaigns caught eBay off-guard. Sensing an all-out corporate war unfolding, the media piled on. At first eBay denied that the preference change had happened at all, saying it was just a bug confined to the process of re-listing an item that failed to sell the first time.[20] Ann Ruckstuhl, my counterpart at Billpoint, called my e-mail "inflammatory" and added that PayPal was "really misguided in their interpretation of what happened."[21]

While the anti-PayPal media stopped short of giving eBay the lashing we felt it deserved—one dense-headed editor titled an article on the flap "*PayPal* Gets Itself into Hot Water" (emphasis added)—our message got through to the constituency that mattered most: our users. Rosalinda Baldwin, the populist editor of *The Auction Guild*, criticized eBay in her newsletter, saying, "Rather than eBay taking the actions to make [Billpoint] better, they resort to sleaze tactics."[22] April's outbound call team reported tremendous gratitude on the part of most sellers for warning them of the problem, with many asking for directions on canceling their Billpoint accounts. And I'm told from reliable sources that eBay's main switchboard practically melted down with calls from irate users.

In the face of a brewing user revolt, eBay's PR team backtracked. While denying that eBay changed users' preferences and still accusing PayPal of "misleading" our customers, spokesman Kevin Pursglove admitted that eBay actually did change the default setting on the SYI form for sellers with Billpoint accounts. But, he added innocently, "The assumption is that once you register for Billpoint, you want to use Billpoint."[23]

He was wrong. In the wake of our counterstrike Billpoint's listing share sank like a stone. We drove it down from a high of around 33% of eBay's listings to where it sat before the surge, just above 25%. As significant a victory as this campaign turned out to be for PayPal, the reaction of eBay's own virtual community was just as noteworthy. The very same customers who had criticized us during the upgrade campaign this time sided with PayPal in the face of eBay's aggressive move. Even if our earlier growing pains and unpopular decisions weren't completely forgotten, customers showed that they would stand up with us for their right to run their auction businesses as they saw fit.

While eBay's community had certainly rebelled against the company before, it was usually in cases where the goal was to protest a policy or product change driven by eBay's increased corporatism. This was the first instance I'm aware of that eBay's community rallied to the cause of another corporation, and in the process the bond between PayPal and our customers was strengthened. We had demonstrated to them that our company was more than just a group of rapidly moving innovators—we showed our customers that we also possessed a deeper understanding of their needs than our competition.

Our own Damon Billian, with his finger on the pulse of the message boards, witnessed first-hand a shift toward pro-PayPal sentiment. It marked the start of a trend that he would later describe to *Business 2.0* as an increasing tendency for customers to take on the burden of defending and explaining our service.[24] Damon was uniquely qualified to make that observation. As PayPal's status in the community began to rise, the dark and handsome "PayPal Damon" found himself catapulted to near rock-star status. Message board posters clamored for him to post his picture for them to see, and marriage proposals and even a death threat appeared in his inbox.

The marked improvement in our relationship with our customers signaled that users would stand by us in our battle for a level playing field within eBay's marketplace even if the myopic media refused to give us sympathetic coverage. We had a fighting chance, after all.

◊

Though we had largely succeeded in fending off eBay's recent moves, the experiences reinforced in Peter's mind the need to expand PayPal's business away from auctions. Given that eBay's management now seemed determined to drive business to Billpoint, our crisis management, no matter how effective, would not remove this fundamental risk. Peter began to believe it was critical for PayPal to find additional revenue streams while still maintaining its lead in the auction market so that eBay could no longer threaten the company's very existence every time it fired a volley.

A glance at the company's operating metrics highlights the reasons for Peter's concern. In the first two quarters of 2001, auction-related payment volume accounted for a whopping 70% of PayPal's transactions. This wasn't a surprise—we had spent much of the first half of the year building products and running campaigns specifically to bolster our position on eBay. Now Peter felt it was time for PayPal to switch gears and expand into new businesses, a direction he articulated company-wide in no uncertain terms. He even made a point to tell *Wired* magazine that he devoted four out of every five days to growing PayPal's non-auction business.[25]

An obvious way to diversify our payment volume was to encourage our existing users to diversify theirs. While there was no longer a viable person-to-person marketplace competitor to eBay, our Web site payments products, including single item purchase buttons and HTML-based shopping carts, allowed sellers to use PayPal on their own online storefronts. Following Peter's decree, my team began to cross-market these features to auction sellers, frequently pitching them as a way to upsell buyers to additional purchases once the eBay auction closed. Our PayPal Shops directory also provided free visitor traffic to merchants with Web sites, giving users an additional incentive to set up a site to accept PayPal. Since Billpoint's product was poorly equipped for these "gray market" transactions (as eBay refers to deals negotiated by users off of its site), it meant our rival could not compete with us in this arena.

My three-person marketing team wasn't the only group focused on non-eBay transactions; Sacks also shifted the product department lineup to reflect this new priority. He moved several producers into a new merchant services team to work on improving our product offering in an effort to expand our Web site payment reach beyond small eBay sellers. This newly formed group quickly grew to command the largest allocation of engineering resources—even more than Paul's auctions team.

Web site payments were just one diversification option on management's radar. After signing a contract with credit card issuer Providian earlier in the year, we rolled out to our users a PayPal-branded Providian credit card that paid us a bounty for each applicant we referred. We also launched a free BillPay service that allowed customers to settle their monthly bills using their PayPal balance. While a far cry from the X.com financial supermarket vision, we hoped BillPay would serve as a stepping-stone to help us further monetize our customers' accounts.

About this time the board began to debate the merits of pursuing a pair of growing online markets for vice—gambling and pornography. This so-called "Las Vegas strategy" held that PayPal was uniquely positioned to service these two sectors. Our increasing fraud-fighting expertise would provide us with a competitive advantage in these areas with historically high chargeback rates. And, with an economic downturn putting the squeeze on risky accounts, many banks and credit card companies were beginning to exit these high risk fields altogether, especially gambling.[26] PayPal stood to profit handsomely, the logic went, if it could establish itself as a trusted intermediary between consumer and merchant in both of these shady industries.

Online gambling—or gaming, as the industry refers to itself—began to boom as Internet usage soared in the late nineties. Although the 1961 Federal Wire Act, written to combat telephone gambling, prevented these gaming services from setting up shop in the United States, no federal law forbade individual citizens from using online gambling sites. A federal proposal by Representative Jim Leach of Iowa to address this inconsistency repeatedly failed to make it past a House committee. As a result, this form of interstate commerce went largely unregulated and the industry established itself in offshore havens like Antigua and the Bahamas and targeted its services at Americans. The strategy paid off. From these foreign perches the industry's 1,800 Web sites generated an estimated $3.5-$4.1 billion in total annual revenue during 2001 and 2002,[27] with approximately 60% of these funds coming from American bettors.[28]

While consumer interest in online gaming was increasing, payment processing had recently become a major chokepoint for the industry. Risk-averse credit card issuers, tired of being left with the bill when consumers filed for chargebacks after suffering large gambling losses, began to block transactions with gamers. The regulatory environment discouraged issuers from providing these transactions, too. Eliot Spitzer, the fiery attorney general of New York and a rumored future candidate for governor, took pride in publicly scaring banks away from gaming payments. Speaking of his discussions with Citibank, Spitzer recounted having said, "Fellas, we'll get an injunction against you. Do you really want to be in this business?"[29] This offshore industry, a legal source of entertainment under federal law, was at risk of atrophying as its payment providers dried up.

Enter PayPal. Bettors could use our account-based service to fund pre-paid balances with the gambling service of their choice, and since they could use ACH transfers from their bank accounts, credit card providers would no longer need to play a role. While some of the same risks that the credit card providers faced would obviously be present if we were to enter the market, our legal team concluded that no existing laws forbade our payment service from acting as intermediary between gamblers and gaming Web sites.

The prospect of pursuing these billions of dollars in gaming payments could not fail to tempt a startup engaged in daily crisis control. Confident that we were on firm legal ground so long as the Leach bill did not clear Congress, our execs felt this decentralized but growing industry was exactly what PayPal needed—a chance to increase payment volume without becoming beholden to any single large player.

Peter realized that entering the gaming market would require a different approach than the referral bonuses and auction logos that had worked so well on eBay. We would need a sales force to reach out to some of the more well-known virtual casinos and to walk them through the business case for adding PayPal to their payment collection options. But sales calls were not PayPal's core competency. Besides Omaha's ad hoc outbound squad, we did not even have a sales team. Our business development group traditionally focused on signing distribution contacts and pushing PayPal to other companies as a partner, not as a service provider.

With little internal fanfare, Peter reorganized a portion of the business development team to begin targeting the gaming space exclusively.

The group moved into a set of cubes adjacent to the product area where Paul and I sat, and their constant chatter on phone calls to the Caymans meant I soon had their sales pitch down pat: "PayPal isn't just a cost effective way to collect money from customers, it's also a convenient way to make payouts!"

As the newly created sales force began to make inroads into the gaming market, the executive team also looked at potential acquisitions of payment services already in the arena as a means to accelerate our growth. A round of particularly serious talks with a publicly traded North American company was held at the offices of one of PayPal's directors. I suppose a public company showing interest in being acquired by a private dot-com was reason enough for concern, but the company's fast-talking, Ferrari-driving officers and questionable financial records quickly soured Peter on the proposal. When even our own investment bankers advised against the deal, Peter decided to steer clear of the existing payment providers in gaming and have PayPal build up its own customer base.

Notwithstanding the occasional dealings with shady characters, PayPal's foray into gambling did not cause a large degree of controversy within the company despite the presence of a fair number of conservatives on the staff. While perhaps not thrilled to be supporting a vice industry, most of our conservative employees agreed that, even if gaming was not a harmless amusement in all cases, it was harmless enough to remain a person's own business. There was no need for our company to oppose something that was generally no worse than a pastime to the majority of bettors, especially given the urgent need to diversify PayPal's business. Internet gaming was a vice we thought we could live with.

◊

The same was not true for the XXX market. When the prospect of servicing the pornography industry first came up in the second half of the year, it set off a forceful internal debate. Colloquially referred to as the Internet's most profitable business, adult Web sites were projected to generate about $1 billion in annual revenue in 2002,[30] making their appeal to PayPal's business model obvious. But the unsavory nature of an industry viewed by many to be exploitative of young women and having a corrosive effect on society was too much for many of PayPal's employees to bear.

Peter tended to be a libertarian on most social issues, but he took the concerns of his employees seriously. While he didn't take a poll on every decision he made, he still felt it was important to consult with his personnel on matters that they thought were significant. Since he wanted the company's workers to be empowered and speak their minds, he knew that listening was a critical part of his job.

On this sensitive topic there was much for him to hear. One afternoon he took a dozen employees, including me, to lunch at a nearby Chinese restaurant. He asked everyone to go around the table one-by-one and let him know their thoughts on the subject. Since the attendees generally opposed the move for one reason or another, the round-table quickly provided a litany of reasons to avoid the adult marketplace.

"It's wrong to help out this immoral industry," one colleague asserted. "And that's exactly what we'd be doing—helping pornographers make money. We can't plead innocence as 'just a payment provider' if we're doing that."

"I really love coming in to work at PayPal—it's such an exciting place," someone else added. "But if I knew that part of our company was pursuing the pornography business, I'd feel much less comfortable being here."

While I personally agreed with this cultural critique, I also found myself concerned about the business implications of entering this market. "We can't ignore the potential damage this will do to our brand," I ventured. "If PayPal becomes known as a leading processor of adult payments, it stands to hurt adoption on small merchants' Web sites and even on eBay."

"I appreciate hearing from everyone," Peter replied, after giving all of us a chance to speak our minds. "I'm definitely going to think about everything I've heard today. PayPal's most important asset really is its people, and because of that it's critical that PayPal remain a great and comfortable place to work.

"But I also ask that everyone understand that I've got to examine this from two sides. There's also the potential that people's jobs might be at stake, which could be a risk if we opt to stay out of this market. In trying to decide what the moral thing to do is, I've also got to weigh this consideration."

About a week later Peter settled on a compromise that kept PayPal from pursuing an unfettered Las Vegas strategy. We would service adult Web sites that sought us out and opened accounts on our Web site, but we would not actively pursue merchants in this sector. This meant the company would not devote resources to obtaining this kind of clientele while still allowing PayPal's users to transact in an essentially libertarian marketplace where the company would not impose its values on them.

Given both our company's financial risks and the pressure from the board, limiting our participation in the adult market was a bold move by Peter. If it wasn't obvious before, this was another clear demonstration of Peter's concern for his employees. His marketplace of ideas was big enough to allow dissent, and he took that diversity of thought into consideration when laying out the company's policy on this hot-button issue.

◊

As the late summer months rolled in to Silicon Valley, they brought hot weather and a slower work pace. Even frenetic PayPal enjoyed a slight lull as employees took long overdue vacations and extended lunch breaks at the golf driving range across the street.

The summer doldrums came during a pause in our hostilities with eBay and on the heels of stellar second quarter financial results. Payment volume was up 16% from the prior period to about $8.2 million per day. Aggregate accounts reached 8.8 million, and gross margins on payment volume continued to rise, hitting 0.79%. These soaring payment margins, coupled with our steady growth in volume, shrunk our operating losses for the quarter by one-third to $8.3 million, a drop in the bucket compared to the company's $124 million in cash on hand.

August also marked a significant personal milestone. With friends, family, and a number of my PayPal colleagues looking on, Beatrice and I wed on a beach in Southern California. While further details of the event have little bearing on this story, I'll inform the reader that at one point during the reception the author's mother succeeded in ushering a reluctant Peter Thiel onto the dance floor for the twist.

Following the wedding I enjoyed an unheard of three weeks away from the office. Beatrice and I flew off to Italy, my bride's native land, for another reception and our honeymoon. After returning to PayPal early in September for a few days of catching up, I accompanied Beatrice on a short business trip to Chicago. Our plane touched down at O'Hare in the late evening of September 10, 2001. It was the last carefree day for many months.

◊

Unlike my sleeping colleagues on the west coast, I watched as monsters rammed the second jet into the World Trade Center. I had returned to our hotel room after seeing Beatrice off to her meeting and just flipped on the news while waiting for my laptop to boot up. The first shining tower was already ablaze, and ten seconds later a fireball engulfed its sister. As the events of that morning unfolded and thousands of people were incinerated on live TV, I watched in tense agony. After the hasty cancellation of her meeting, Beatrice burst through the door just as the second tower collapsed; I embraced her, turning her view away from the jarring images on the television while whispering in her ear of the horror I had just witnessed.

The skies outside our O'Hare hotel became eerily quiet as the FAA grounded all commercial air traffic. PayPal's corporate spats rightly seemed insignificant at that moment. I let my laptop sit unused on the desk for the rest of the morning, my eyes transfixed on the television while I spoke on my cell phone with anxious friends and family. After finally tracking down an unaccounted friend in Manhattan and seeing my wife off to her rescheduled afternoon session, I tried to focus on some business, though it was not an easy task.

In the face of such evil, I wondered, might PayPal be able to do some good? It seemed that we certainly were set-up to do so. An untold number of New York and Washington families would need financial support. And just as they had during earlier disasters, the American people would rally to help these victims. With 9 million customers and a system built exclusively to move money, I reasoned that we were in a unique position to empower people to provide assistance.

I called Paul and suggested using PayPal to collect donations for the victims. He feared that such a donations drive might be viewed as opportunism, but promised to think it over and get back to me. I was considering calling Sacks directly when an e-mail from Vince Sollitto arrived outlining a similar plan. He and Sacks had met earlier in the day and decided to pursue this strategy on behalf of a charity. The American Red Cross's national leadership, not just our "Charity Robot" friends at the Palo Alto chapter, had given Vince permission to let us raise funds for them. With some speedy work a Red Cross disaster relief donation button was added to PayPal's Web site the next day, and an e-mail was sent around to our users to notify them of the option.

The response of PayPal's customers amazed us. Donations began to pour in immediately. All told, PayPal collected $2.4 million in contributions from more than 60,000 individuals.[31] While less than the amounts collected by more established online presences Yahoo and Amazon, our users' generosity rightfully earned positive mentions in several news articles summarizing the Internet's role in responding to the tragedy.

Unfortunately the same could not be said for eBay. Soon after the disaster the auction giant seized headlines with its "Auction for America" (AFA) campaign, a program to let users auction off items for charity with the proceeds going to various victims' relief funds. Claiming to be in response to a direct request from New York Governor George Pataki and New York City Mayor Rudy Giuliani, eBay promised AFA would raise $100 million in one hundred days.[32]

As admirable as the undertaking sounds, AFA attracted flak as soon as eBay unveiled the details. Sellers complained that the charity auctions, which received special designation on eBay's site, were hurting their business by competing with their everyday auctions for bids. Moreover, AFA required the seller to pay to ship the item, a cost usually borne by the buyer in regular auctions. Sellers found themselves asking why eBay wouldn't just let people donate money instead of flooding the marketplace with these goods.

Yet even more upsetting to our users were AFA's payment guidelines. Not only was PayPal excluded from being a payment option on these charity auctions, but Billpoint was mandatory. EBay justified this move by saying that Billpoint involvement was the only way the company could ensure that funds were collected and actually dispensed to a charity. Just as we had witnessed during the SYI preference change, our mutual customers rebelled at what they perceived as favoritism of Billpoint. "They're doing it to sign people up for Billpoint," eBay seller Sandy Siemers complained to CNET. "PayPal has the same options. Why can't we use PayPal?"[33]

Unlike the scrap over the SYI preferences, however, this time we opted to keep a low profile. After completing the grueling 2,000 mile drive from Chicago back to the San Francisco Bay Area, I met with Sacks and Vince to discuss our communication strategy regarding AFA. Publicly criticizing eBay's charity effort for excluding PayPal would have been risky—we didn't want to be perceived as exploiting this sensitive issue. Besides, customers were already drawing these conclusions without our encouragement. Instead, I suggested that we make Red Cross donation logos for sellers to paste into their regular auctions. This provided civic-minded users with an alternative to the Billpoint-only AFA without forcing us to comment on eBay's charity efforts.

In the end, Auction for America fell short of its $100 million expectations. The effort raised only $10 million despite corporate sponsorships from Taco Bell and Wells Fargo, and eBay's own $1 million donation.[34]

EBay had put itself into a difficult position with AFA. Although at the time we worried that AFA was another calculated Billpoint promotion, upon reflection it seems that eBay's intentions with Auction for America were basically good. Judging from the lengthy intervals between major eBay product launches (recall that eBay chose to buy Half.com because it would have taken its team nine months just to replicate the same fixed price functionality), Billpoint probably was the only option eBay could engineer into the AFA process on such short notice. And no matter how unfair some of its hardball tactics against PayPal seemed, I have no reason to think that eBay would try to profiteer off such a highly publicized relief effort. From a business perspective alone, Meg Whitman is far too shrewd a guardian of eBay's brand to allow her executives to try anything so reckless.

Yet the general customer suspicion was in fact that eBay designed AFA to shill for Billpoint. Our aggressive response to the SYI preference change several months earlier likely biased many users towards this conclusion. Whatever the reasons, it was clear that PayPal and eBay's shared customers were increasingly taking sides in the bitter custody dispute being waged across cyberspace, and they were choosing us.

CHAPTER NINE

EARTH VS. PALO ALTO

SEPTEMBER 2001 — FEBRUARY 2002

SEVENTEEN DAYS AFTER the devastating attacks in New York and Washington, PayPal announced plans that startled both Wall Street and Silicon Valley. On September 28, 2001, our company filed a registration statement with the Securities and Exchange Commission for an initial public offering.

It was not a spur of the moment decision. When Peter Thiel accepted the blue hair challenge at the parking lot meeting several months earlier, his goal was to motivate employees to make the final push to get the company's operations in the black, a necessary precursor to going public given the post-bubble stock market. In late August, as the company's financials continued to improve, the board concluded that after six quarters of operating losses totaling $137 million it was at last time to begin the IPO filing. With our net margins rising and profitability lurking just a quarter away, an IPO would provide PayPal with the opportunity to reward its patient investors and employees, get an $80 million infusion of cash, and increase its public awareness in the process.

But then came the terrorist attacks, which in turn caused the public equity markets to crash. The chill on stocks was so all-encompassing that September 2001 became the first month in twenty-six years without an IPO.[1] In the face of this uncertainty, Peter and the board did not panic but coolly stuck to their strategy, knowing that the turmoil would eventually pass. The IPO process takes a considerable amount of time, generally a minimum of three to four months, long enough for a company's bankers, lawyers, and accountants to learn enough about its business so they can describe it to other bankers, lawyers, and accountants. It stood to reason that the stock market could stabilize by then, providing PayPal the chance to float its shares and strengthen its market leadership.

Of course, the majority of the business media didn't see it that way. Still gripped in the collective obsession with disparaging all businesses related to the Internet, the press received our announcement with skepticism. And since they had long since exhausted their dot-com puns—how many recycled titles with "dot-bomb" or "dot-con" can even the most uncreative editor get away with?—PayPal's announcement was a welcome breath of fresh air. Or, more appropriately, fresh meat.

In a piece called "PayPal Faces Long IPO Odds," a CNET reporter quoted several unnamed analysts as saying that filing for the IPO was nothing more than management's way of putting PayPal on the shopping block. Our competitive environment, the phantom analysts reasoned, and the claim that management "[didn't] foresee black ink anywhere in the future" meant that an actual IPO would be far-fetched.[2] *BusinessWeek* called our valuation target of $700 million a stretch,[3] and the *Wall Street Journal* dwelled on the risk factors outlined in our SEC filing.[4]

And those were the nice articles. A column titled "Earth to Palo Alto," featured in *The Recorder*, a California-based legal publication, put them all to shame. Nearly every word penned by Silicon Valley lawyer George Kraw oozed condescension as he attacked the credibility of PayPal's service, business model, and management team:

> What would you do with a 3-year-old company that has never turned an annual profit, is on track to lose a quarter billion dollars and whose recent SEC filings warn that its services might be used for money laundering and financial fraud?… If you were the managers and venture capitalists behind Palo Alto's PayPal, you'd take it public. And that is what they hope to do in an $80 million offering that will test the limits of investor tolerance and financial market gullibility.[5]

After challenging Peter's libertarian love of freedom for not fighting alongside U.S. soldiers in Afghanistan, the columnist suggested that "drug dealers and domestic terrorists" were the perfect target audience for our original Palm Pilot software. The critic concluded "there was insufficient adult supervision around PayPal to prevent its Sept. 28 S-1 filing with the SEC."

Of course, neither Kraw nor most of his media peers seemed to understand PayPal's business model, otherwise they would've realized that our improving transaction margins meant imminent profitability. Unfortunately for us, Depression-era federal laws prevented us from correcting this confusion.[6] We had entered the mandatory pre-IPO quiet period when we filed the registration statement, meaning that neither Vince Sollitto nor anyone on the executive team could comment to journalists, even to clarify a misconception or to rebut an unfair claim. While the original intent of this legislation—to prevent companies from hyping their stock offerings to investors—was undoubtedly good, the Internet's unbridled flow of information meant that everyone was allowed to talk about PayPal but us. So as the media decreed that our flying McLaren had transformed into a rocket ship and was blasting away into the stratosphere, we had no choice but to hold our tongues.

◊

As the preparation for PayPal's IPO began, events in another corner of planet Earth provided a powerful reminder of the need for PayPal to fulfill its original vision of global currency liberation. Given our pressing competitive realities this was a vision that we spoke of less frequently than during the company's early days, but it was still a mission that we all remembered. My fateful direct mail campaigns may have initiated the sequence of events that transformed eBay into our first stop on the road to "world domination," but neither I nor anyone else in the company assumed it would be our last. The IPO and the benefits it promised would be another destination on our long march toward this goal.

Unfortunately for the people of Argentina, in late-2001 PayPal had not yet reached the point where it could wrest the control of currencies away from corrupt and incompetent governments. Just a few years earlier Argentina would have seemed like an unlikely locale for an economic crisis. In 1991, after decades of economic decline, Argentina had pegged its currency, the peso, to the U.S. dollar. This caused its previously high inflation rate to subside and the country enjoyed several years of strong growth. But by the decade's end the economy soured. The currency devaluation of its neighbor Brazil put downward pressure on regional prices, yet Argentina's lavish farm subsidies, state-sanctioned monopolies, and protectionist trade policies kept domestic prices high, driving the country into recession. Rising public spending and the soft economy caused the government's debt to skyrocket. Foreign bondholders grew nervous as the economic minister seized control of the central bank and raised the specter of devaluing the peso as a cheap way to pay off Argentina's mounting debts.

During the second half of 2001, Argentina's citizens acted on these fears by emptying their bank accounts and converting their pesos into dollars. Instead of making the difficult choices needed to address the underlying economic problems, the government tried to put a stop to the bank run with a 1,000 pesos-per-month limit on withdrawals. Argentines took to the streets in protest, prompting a stream of officials, including the president, to resign. But the withdrawal limit remained in place, and at the beginning of 2002 the government ended the peso's peg to the dollar and defaulted on its debt. Over the next three months the peso fell 70% against the dollar while prices soared by 20%, eroding the purchasing power of the money frozen inside bank accounts.[7]

Rather than cutting spending or liberalizing its trade policies, Argentina's government addressed its debt liquidity crisis by eviscerating the savings of its own people. This was exactly the kind of scenario that Peter and Max had envisioned PayPal preventing. With a fully functional multi-language, multi-currency international service, people in Argentina would have been able to use PayPal to whisk their nest eggs away to safety at the first sign of trouble. They also would have been free to transact electronically with their countrymen in the stable currency of their choice. The government, knowing that this threat existed, would have faced additional pressure to act as a good steward in the nation's interest. Otherwise the people could have simply stopped using the national currency and instead replaced it with foreign alternatives beyond the reach of the government's control.

But this was all just in theory—in reality PayPal could not help the Argentines. Our competitive race to achieve dominance on eBay and our desperate efforts to fix our broken business model had kept us from building multi-language and multi-currency features, and the newly prioritized goal of promoting off-eBay transactions meant that they would not be built anytime in the immediate future. Of course, the still limited penetration of Internet access in Argentina would have blunted a fully functional PayPal's ability to intervene anyway.

The events in South America may have been beyond our ability to alter, but the message they delivered to the company was clear. We needed to execute on the IPO, continue to expand our business, and plot an international course if we were to achieve our founders' original vision. Little did we know that at the same time our most powerful competitor was preparing a campaign that could put all of those plans at risk.

◊

Jeff Jordan's tacticians were preparing a final offensive for 2001. The year had been a mixed one for Jordan, the head of eBay's U.S. division. Despite his group's victory over Yahoo Auctions and successful fee increases, it was difficult to ignore the problems surrounding the eBay Stores, Billpoint preference change, and Auction for America fiascoes. In each instance his squad had rolled out a critical modification to the U.S.

auction Web site to advantage Billpoint, and each time PayPal had either forced significant concessions or seized an outright victory.

The stakes were undoubtedly high for Jordan. Many in Silicon Valley speculated that he held the inside track to be crowned Meg Whitman's successor when the CEO eventually decided to step out of the spotlight. Notwithstanding CTO Maynard Webb's high profile achievement of restoring stability to eBay's beleaguered Web site, Jordan's 1999 appointment to head the company's largest division put the former Reel.com executive at the top of the list to become Whitman's heir apparent.

Given this, it's not surprising that Jordan would look for a way to recoup some personal equity following his year-long string of disappointments. And hearing that PayPal was preparing for a public offering, he likely envisioned a closing window of opportunity to propel Billpoint into online payments leadership. To take advantage of this possible last chance, his engineering and product team personnel worked around the clock to ready a major new feature for an unusual launch during the sales-heavy pre-holiday season.

"Checkout" debuted on the U.S. eBay site in late October. Calling it a feature to minimize confusion after an auction ended, the company began inserting a large gray button at the top of all closed listings with instructions to the buyer to click on it to arrange payment. Clicking took him to a form that collected his address information, which was then forwarded on to the seller for shipping.

While on the surface it sounded harmless, closer examination revealed that Checkout mimicked a method eBay used when it launched the Buy It Now feature. After obtaining the buyer's address, Checkout presented marketing materials promoting Billpoint and even dumped the buyer on a Billpoint payment form if the seller had a Billpoint account. If the seller didn't use Billpoint, a page appeared that encouraged the buyer to contact the seller about the matter, suggesting it was a problem that needed to be addressed. To make matters worse for PayPal, eBay decreed Checkout to be mandatory on all U.S. listings, saying that the need to provide an improved and consistent buyer experience superseded the right of sellers to control their auctions.

The usual panicked scene played out in our Palo Alto offices when we learned of the details surrounding Checkout's launch. "Oh my gawd," David Sacks burst out before slumping back in his chair as Paul handed him printouts of the new auction process. "We're screwed!"

I shared our vice president of product's dismay. After eighteen months of ad hoc efforts to advantage Billpoint, the auction monopolist had concluded that promotional gimmicks and preference changes weren't powerful enough to convince sellers to abandon PayPal's fledgling network. Instead, eBay turned its Web site into a weapon. Since Checkout appeared at the top of each listing, it meant it would vie with PayPal's tiny logos in the auction's description for the attention of every single eBay buyer trying to figure out what to do next after an auction closed. If the buyer naively selected Checkout and its Billpoint-favored flow, the odds that he would even be aware that PayPal was an option dramatically decreased.

Regardless of the short run damage we would suffer from lost transactions, the longer term risks of Checkout were even greater. Checkout tried to train buyers to return to eBay's Web site when their winning item closed, a behavior that would make it more difficult for a third party like PayPal to get involved in any end-of-auction process. From there, eBay could use its own Web site to steer buyers toward Billpoint, pre-empting the need to ever come to PayPal's site to send money. Over time, as eBay swayed more and more buyers to return to its site to go through Checkout, we would have fewer chances to convert winning bidders into PayPal customers.

Reid Hoffman lodged our customary complaint, but unlike the eBay Stores flap, this time he received no sympathetic reply. Sensing that the fate of our IPO and perhaps even the long-term viability of PayPal hung in the balance, Peter demanded a list of strategic responses from Sacks, Reid, Paul, and me. We didn't have much to tell him; we had few weapons in our arsenal to fight this integration. Yet, over the next few days, as we struggled for suggestions on how to respond to eBay's home court advantage, a solution presented itself.

EBay's own discussion boards had long been a hotbed of rowdy and sometimes oratorical user commentary, but in the wake of the Checkout launch, they would serve as the source of PayPal's salvation.

Soon after Checkout's appearance, sellers began to gripe. The initial complaints centered around user resentment of Checkout's mandatory status—sellers wanted a choice over the status of their auctions. But as buyers began to use the feature, malcontent sellers tended to focus on functionality. Since most sellers already had their own personalized end-of-auction processes in place to contact buyers, collect shipping information, and provide payment instructions, the appearance of Checkout diverted many buyers from using sellers' preferred steps. Power sellers, who often use third-party shopping carts to check out their buyers, blamed Checkout for throwing their back office functions into disarray just as the holiday shopping season was hitting full stride. And numerous sellers reported writing "Do NOT Use Checkout" instructions in the descriptions of their auction listings to keep buyers from going through what they regarded as a dead-end flow.

User backlash was in and of itself nothing new to eBay. After weathering the Million Auction March and several similar past uprisings, it would certainly take more than a few stray discussion board comments to persuade eBay to alter its strategy. But Checkout was different. After several days, the discussions showed no signs of burning out; instead, the grumbling on the community boards gradually grew louder. EBay's customer service employees tried to put out the fire by directly replying to user comments on the boards, insisting that Checkout was a response to "community requests" to improve the buyer experience and that it was optional because buyers weren't required to use it after an auction closed. This spin only served to generate additional friction, causing already angry customers to become more strident as they demanded to know who had submitted these requests.

The full-scale user revolt evident on eBay's boards escalated to the point where even PayPal's critics in the press couldn't miss it. CNET quoted auction seller Michelle Carter's assertion that eBay was lying about the new feature: "...eBay is not going to fix the one thing that everybody is complaining about: They say it's optional, and it's not."[8] The investor-focused Web site TheStreet.com quoted several sellers threatening to take their business back to Yahoo and mused that this customer rebellion could put pressure on eBay's revenue.[9]

Sellers also pointed out to journalists that the mandatory Checkout didn't just deprive them of control over their buyers' end-of-auction experience, but it also favored Billpoint over PayPal. Stephanie Stoughton of *The Boston Globe* penned a damning allusion to the Netscape affair: "...[Sellers] say eBay keeps promoting Billpoint and, a la Microsoft, makes it difficult for people to pay through PayPal."[10] EBay spokesman Kevin Pursglove, caught in the middle of this unexpected hurricane, could only concede that the company realized that Checkout needed additional unspecified improvements and was working on it.

The intensity of this grassroots customer uprising came as a surprise to eBay. For the third time in six months eBay's actions forced our mutual customers to choose sides, and for the third time they aligned with PayPal. Sensing that eBay's moves had only served to strengthen the bond between PayPal and its users, Sacks and I discretely sought to reach out to them and in the process toss fuel on the fire. While being careful not to attack eBay or even Checkout directly, we crafted a marketing campaign to our sellers to provide clarifications about using PayPal with the new confusing Checkout feature.

In mid-November, three weeks after Checkout's debut, customer sentiment triumphed and eBay acquiesced. Announcing the immediate removal of Checkout from its site, eBay said that it would shortly return as an opt-out feature. "About one-third of the sellers hated it. They puked on it," Jordan would later tell *Fortune* magazine about Checkout, adding that the debacle was a personal "lesson in humility" and a reminder that eBay could not force features down the throats of its users.[11]

For our part, we didn't sit around hoping that eBay would remember this lesson. Sacks instructed Paul Martin and JoAnne Rockower to build a "turn off Checkout" function for sellers to use from their PayPal accounts to make sure it was simple to deactivate any future Checkout reincarnation. By collecting our sellers' eBay login information and using it to disable the opt-out version of Checkout on their behalf, our tool would ensure that Checkout could not easily reach high usage levels once it returned to eBay's site.

The most ferocious user rebellion in eBay's history ended in a major victory for PayPal. Thanks to our customers we had fended off eBay's final attack of the year, and in the process cleared the way for our IPO to move forward.

◊

The march toward becoming a public company brought organizational change with it. Peter and Sacks caucused with me in October to discuss a reorganization that would create a full-fledged marketing department reporting to Sacks. I had long been a proponent of giving marketing its own department alongside product. Besides what I felt was a need to scale up our marketing efforts beyond my small three-person team, I also had the selfish goal of cutting back my typical fourteen hour workday. After two years of this heavy-lifting, and an increasing focus on crisis management, I was eager to get some help.

The manner in which Peter asked us to scale up was also a relief—he wanted the new group to report to Sacks. Knowing that my trusted boss would ultimately be in charge was reassuring, given that he had proven his ability to chart strategy time and time again. So, on those positive notes, I joined Sacks and several other managers on an executive search committee to locate marketing's new vice president.

The search brought in a varied cross-selection of applicants, some of whom were overqualified for the position, a commentary on the dreadful state of Silicon Valley's post-crash economy. We ultimately decided on Bill Onderdonk, a marketing consultant who had already been working for PayPal for several months. Bill, who ironically had once run a company funded by Confinity's estranged investor Idealab, was an easygoing California surfer in his early thirties. He displayed an ability to analyze situations quickly and visualize responses to problems, traits that an issues-focused marketing department would need in order to deal with the more process-centric product and Web site design teams.

Upon taking the reins, Bill inherited several employees from throughout the organization. In addition to me and my team, Peter assented to message board specialist Damon Billian, strategy analyst Vivien Go (author of the fateful branding survey), and auction seller JoAnne Rockower moving into the marketing group. With their arrival and the opening of several additional job requisitions, for the first time since the merger marketing began to look like a real department.

But as the marketing crew was coming together, one of PayPal's earliest employees decided to depart. After playing the role of vice president of strategy for the prior year and a half, Luke Nosek declined an offer to join the reconstituted marketing department in favor of taking what would turn into a permanent sabbatical.

While saddened to see my exuberant former boss go—especially since we had worked so closely during my first half year with PayPal—his decision didn't surprise me. The company's internal growth in recent months had forced the organization to implement new rules and processes. While still a far cry from the bureaucracy I had to deal with at Andersen, PayPal had definitely become more corporate than it was during its early days and Luke did not seem at home in this environment. Seeking a stark change of pace, the high-spirited young man embarked on a tour of the world, occasionally e-mailing back photos from his stops in Europe and South America. Luke was one of the first entrepreneurs to flee our gradually maturing company, and he would not be the last, but he was certainly one of the most special.

◊

If the creation of a formal marketing group hinted at PayPal's movement from a startup to an established company, our financials supplied the final proof. After posting total losses (excluding non-cash expenses) of $137 million over the six quarters between January 2000 and July 2001, the second half of the year brought a breakthrough. Although we wound up just short of becoming cash flow positive in August—robbing us of the opportunity to see our CEO sport a blue mane—we rebounded from the temporary decline in user activity following September 11 and reached this milestone for the month of October. After trimming our losses to $1.9 million in the third quarter, we booked an operating profit of $2.8 million in the fourth as our revenue soared from $30.2 million in Q3 to $40.1 million in Q4.

PayPal was profitable! In the midst of so much Silicon Valley despair, the words sounded like music. Eight quarters after I naively joined a startup bent on revolutionizing the world's financial systems, and five quarters after Peter started the process of overhauling the business model, the company was finally in the black. Well, sort of.

While not one to parse language, in this case it depends on what the meaning of the word "profitable" is. Caveat emptor: throughout this narrative I've used a calculation for operating profits that excludes the non-cash expenses of stock-based compensation and the amortization of goodwill, the same measure we used internally at PayPal to gauge our own progress. Including these figures, however, puts our bottom line for Q4 at $18 million in the red, a stark difference of $21 million. While not the GAAP definition of profitability, backing out these two items from the income statement more accurately reflects the financial state of PayPal's operations and emphasizes the company's newly positive cash flow.[12]

Profitability wasn't our only accomplishment in the second half of 2001. Peter's focus on diversifying our revenue also began to yield results. Non-auction payments grew from 30% of total volume in the first half of the year to 33% in Q3 and 36% in Q4. Gaming transactions comprised only one-tenth of this non-auction volume but were rising at a fast pace. Our eBay payment volume continued to climb, too, albeit slower than non-auction payments. Despite eBay's repeated efforts to disadvantage PayPal, auction transactions leaped from $523 million in Q2 to $618 million in Q3 and $772 million in Q4, or roughly one-quarter of eBay's gross merchandise sales. Perhaps more amazing, though, was that our aggregate number of users reached 12.8 million after just twenty-six months of operation. To put this into perspective, eBay, which launched its service on Labor Day of 1995, took more than four years to reach 10 million accounts.[13]

Our customer service outlook continued to brighten, as well. The woes that had plagued us throughout our first year of business were largely behind us. Calls to our operations center in Omaha were typically answered in less than a minute, and e-mail inquiries generally led to resolutions within 24-48 hours. After getting labeled "unsatisfactory" by the Better Business Bureau for unresolved customer complaints in January, PayPal restored its good standing with the watchdog group by September.[14]

PayPal had become a profitable business, decreased its dependency on eBay, beaten back the con artists and improved its customer service—all while growing at one of the fastest rates in business history. But if you think that members of the press tripped over themselves to sing our accolades, guess again. Instead, nearly every story on our pending IPO mentioned our $18 million Q4 GAAP loss and repeated the mandatory dire warnings included in our prospectus ("we have a limited operating history, are not currently profitable and may not become profitable").[15] Thanks to the pre-IPO quiet period, Vince was unable even to explain to reporters how to read our income statements, a lesson some evidently needed. The only positive mention of PayPal in the press was the scant coverage of a survey by market researcher Gartner that suggested that two-and-one-half times more online users trusted PayPal than Billpoint.[16]

The media's unfounded pessimism didn't carry over to Wall Street, though, and Peter began the road show in early-2002 to great enthusiasm. The market remained weak as the NASDAQ gave back ground from its post-9/11 rebound, but Salomon Smith Barney, our investment bankers, had no trouble lining up would-be investors. Salomon priced our offering of 5.4 million shares (out of a total of 60 million for the entire company) in the $12-$14 range, valuing PayPal $720-$840 million. With a tentative date set for February 7, we moved forward with our final preparations.

◊

After failing to derail our public offering with its Checkout offensive, eBay observed our progress with heightened scrutiny. San Jose had resigned itself to living with PayPal, an affliction that up until only a few months earlier Meg Whitman had hoped to remove. But after witnessing

Jeff Jordan stumble in his efforts to jump start Billpoint, Whitman realized that a profitable, publicly traded PayPal would not easily be dislodged from her online community. Billpoint remained largely unpopular with users, who failed to adopt the "eBay Payments" brand and criticized its rudimentary product as inferior to PayPal's. To make matters worse, eBay had sullied its own reputation with users on several occasions by trying to coerce our shared customers into abandoning PayPal.

It was clear to Whitman that auction users had chosen PayPal over Billpoint. For the chief executive of a company that lauds its online community as its cornerstone, this grudging realization must have come as a blow. It certainly highlighted the risk of continuing to battle PayPal — success for Billpoint seemed increasingly unlikely, and the danger of further customer backlash against eBay was high. Whitman could only acknowledge that her original strategy to promote Billpoint had failed, and considered her alternatives. That left one obvious solution.

At the end of 2001 Whitman quietly approached Peter with an offer to purchase PayPal. EBay's CEO pledged to shut down Billpoint and make PayPal her company's official payment service. This cash offer, at a price slightly below the range of our expected IPO valuation, tempted Peter. As his focus on diversification indicated, Peter was acutely aware of the "eBay risk" in our business model. And, in the months since registering for an IPO with the Securities and Exchange Commission, PayPal had begun to attract increased attention from various state regulators. Although no major developments had emerged on this front, the potential for government meddling to damage our business was not lost on PayPal's leader.

Peter spent the weekend deliberating with the board. Elon Musk, who had long since repaired his relationship with Peter, extolled him to roll the dice and attempt the IPO. In the end, Peter and the board decided to forego eBay's offer. While less risky, accepting the proposal would've discarded the company's upside potential and forfeited our independence at a point when we had yet to see if the investing public would embrace PayPal.

Both sides discretely kept the offer out of the headlines, but Peter's refusal nonetheless chilled the momentary thaw in relations between the two companies. We heard little from the chastened and rejected eBay team for several months.

With the IPO looming, the company had no time to dwell on eBay's advances. Instead, Peter stressed the importance of us learning from one mistake eBay had made during its own IPO process back in 1998. In the months leading up to its public debut, founder Pierre Omidyar and some of the company's more community-focused executives lobbied to allow eBay's customers to purchase pre-IPO shares. Omidyar claimed that, as an individual investor, being shut out of an earlier IPO was one of his motivations for building eBay in the first place—he wanted to design a platform where big firms enjoyed no special advantages over the little guy. But despite his good intentions, eBay's founder was overruled. Management opted against allowing customers to participate in the IPO, blaming its reluctant investment bankers and citing a concern that many users would not be considered sufficiently sophisticated to invest in pre-IPO shares anyway.[17]

Peter didn't settle for the same outcome. He wanted to ensure that we got shares into the hands of our most valuable customers as a way of rewarding them for their loyalty through our tough times and for standing by us during our conflicts with Billpoint. He pointed out that this would also help us align our incentives; customers who owned shares would be encouraged to stick with us and provide suggestions to help PayPal improve its service.

Peter pressed Salomon Smith Barney until they devised a plan to set aside as large a portion of shares as possible for our customers. April Kelly's outbound call team in Omaha, working off a script approved by our bankers and lawyers, called nearly 10,000 users with an invitation to participate in PayPal's IPO. Many of them eagerly signed up, thrilled to have an opportunity to join in a process generally reserved for high-powered insiders.

Once again, PayPal had outmaneuvered eBay in winning the hearts and minds of our mutual customers, and this time we positioned some of them to make a few dollars in the process. But the apparent calm in our conflict with eBay obscured the fact that other forces were silently amassing against our IPO. And what they were about to unleash would make our competitive struggles seem trivial.

◊

"After over two years of fighting for this, I can't believe it's finally going to happen tomorrow," I mused aloud. Bill Onderdonk nodded his head and smiled. It was early evening on Wednesday, February 6, and my new boss and I sat in his cube, enjoying a lull to reflect.

"I guess they should finish pricing it sometime tonight," Bill replied, adding, "Shouldn't you be getting out of here soon?" This kind of a suggestion was relatively new to PayPal—a work-life balance had been almost impossible just a year earlier.

"Yeah, I'm supposed to take Beatrice out for dinner tonight," I replied, standing up and strolling the several feet of carpet separating our two desks, before adding a small rib, "You should do the same with your wife once in a while, too."

Bill replied with a quip about certain lifestyles not mixing with young children, but a message in my inbox had already caught my attention. "What on earth?! Did you see this?" I exclaimed, reading on for more information. In the grand tradition of PayPal bombshell e-mails, a member of our PR team announced that the IPO had been delayed.

A company named CertCo, a payments consultancy, had filed a lawsuit against PayPal two days earlier alleging that our core payment infrastructure infringed one of its patents.[18] By asserting that the company was entitled to a potentially large amount of compensation for damages, CertCo's lawsuit exposed PayPal's shareholders to a new risk not previously articulated in our IPO prospectus. The by-the-books SEC administrator assigned to our case ruled that this legal attack meant we needed to amend and redistribute the prospectus to potential investors before the shares could finally be priced and floated on the open market, making an IPO the following day logistically impossible.

CertCo's suit wasn't the first intellectual property threat that PayPal received—another company called Tumbleweed Communications had sent us a letter the prior month suggesting our technology violated two of its patents[19]—but the timing seemed suspicious. Neither I nor anyone on the marketing and product teams had even heard of CertCo prior to this lawsuit, and we certainly did not consider them a competitor. Having them appear on the scene hours before our IPO hardly seemed a coincidence. Several analysts later publicly stated what our shocked employees suspected, that CertCo timed its suit to gain leverage in hopes of disrupting our IPO and forcing a lucrative settlement.[20]

Stunned and crestfallen by this unexpected delay in our IPO, I set out on my nightly drive home to San Francisco. I turned the radio on for distraction, only to hear the details of PayPal's postponed IPO repeated as the lead business story. I called Beatrice from my cell phone to break the news to her, which prompted her to ask what this meant for the company's future. I didn't know what to answer—this development caught the entire company off guard, making the situation all the more stressful. If the IPO fell apart, it would certainly damage PayPal's reputation. Worse still, it would rob the company of the $80 million in funds we expected to receive, leaving us with a smaller war chest for our competition with Billpoint. It would also mean that our existing shareholders, already squeezed by a pair of consecutive years of dramatic stock market declines, might demand that the board find a new exit strategy, which could result in putting PayPal up for sale to eBay or some other competitor.

After seeing our company's fortunes rise over the past year and a half following so many close calls, having our public offering jeopardized at the last minute by a legal spat wasn't just frustrating, it was scary.

The following day the executive team responded by going into crisis mode. Our lawyers returned CertCo's legal fire by filing a motion in court to declare the suit an exceptional case, a move that would force CertCo to reimburse our legal fees. Our finance group also raced to comply with the SEC's request to disclose the new development in a regulatory filing that made a point to denounce CertCo's "tardy allegations and rush filing of its unmeritorious lawsuit."[21] While neither action resolved the underlying dispute, they did clear the way for the IPO to move forward again. The bankers assured our management team that investors remained confident in our offering, meaning that the IPO was back on.

But CertCo was just the beginning of the flood. No sooner had the ink dried on our CertCo motion than, that very same day, we received notice from the General Counsel of the Louisiana Office of Financial Institutions ordering us to cease providing our service to the state's residents until we received a money transfer license.[22] This regulatory injunction was a shock — it was the first of its kind in PayPal's several years of operation. Safeguarding PayPal from surprise rulings by state regulatory bodies was precisely the reason Peter had his legal team proactively look into garnering federal trust bank status for PayPal more than a year earlier. Our ultimate failure to obtain that regulatory classification meant we would have to continue to be regulated on a state-by-state, as opposed to a federal, basis. While this outcome guaranteed more red tape and bureaucratic wrangling, we could never have guessed that it would come back to haunt us at the worst possible time.

As with the CertCo suit, members of our finance team believed the timing of Louisiana's order was no coincidence. They speculated that our friends at the SEC, fact-checking the claims in our prospectus, likely called on numerous statehouses to ask if investigations into our regulatory compliance were forthcoming. This none too subtle poking at the hornets' nests stirred up Louisiana's order, which would later be accompanied by a similar request for more information from New York authorities.[23]

In and of itself, our business faced little risk from the Louisiana order since the state accounted for only 0.9% of our payment volume.[24] Our IPO prospects were a different matter. With the appearance of yet another unanticipated bump in the road and the threat of additional states coming after us, would the institutional investors committed to the IPO begin to get squeamish? Peter worried as much.

"We need to have the lawyers get in contact with every state!" he exclaimed the following afternoon from Sacks's nearby cube. "Every single one of them!" the typically staid CEO repeated for emphasis. "Promise to file their paperwork, pay their fees. Just get in touch with them and show that we're working with them. Don't give any of them a reason to hit us with another order like this!" He paused a moment before adding ominously, "My sense is that this deal cannot withstand another surprise like this—the whole thing will just come apart."

Except that wasn't the final snag. At the same time we became aware of the Louisiana order, administrators at the SEC accused us of potentially violating the section of the Securities Act governing IPO quiet periods—an ironic charge, given how hard we had tried to comply with this antiquated rule. At issue was the previously referenced Gartner survey that found that more consumers trusted PayPal than Billpoint. The SEC indicated that PayPal's interactions with Gartner could be interpreted as PayPal using a third party to promote our pending public offering.[25] The warning stemmed from a $25,000 research fee PayPal had paid to Gartner the previous October and Vince Sollitto's receipt of a preliminary copy of the research.

This charge may have had some basis on coincidence, but not on fact. While PayPal did pay Gartner for private research (as did many other Silicon Valley companies), we did not commission the study in question. Nor did Vince try to influence the straightforward findings of the analysis, much less request that it be released prior to our IPO. Most importantly, this flap was over a survey that revealed no new information. By concluding that auction users vastly preferred PayPal to Billpoint, this study simply told the same story as the data already published in our prospectus!

The SEC's assertion, if validated, stood to make PayPal liable for potential losses suffered by investors in case of a stock price collapse.[26]

Even if we faced little real likelihood of that, this SEC accusation and the Louisiana flap forced us to revise the prospectus yet again and to add further disclaimers to a document that already included thirteen pages of risk factors.

This torrent of attacks blindsided our company. While Roelof Botha and Ken Howery remained in New York to try to restore order by getting the IPO rescheduled, a tension not felt since the management clash in September 2000 descended on our Palo Alto office. Employees huddled in the hallways for hushed conversations, seeking the latest news. Friends and family sent quizzical e-mails, asking if something bad had happened. Both management and PR tried to be frank with employees, yet no one could predict what would transpire next.

These legal and regulatory blows seemed all the more confounding since they were a challenge our entrepreneurial company was fundamentally unaccustomed to facing. Squaring off in a competitive match with eBay was one thing—at least in that situation we could adjust our product and marketing and then allow the marketplace to decide. Even combating the Russian mafia was within our comfort zone; we could challenge them head-to-head with our wits and our moxie. But trial lawyers and regulators drawn to our pending success were an entirely different type of opponent. The entrepreneurial traits of creativity, energy, and flexibility might not be enough to get us out of these jams.

Between CertCo, Tumbleweed, Louisiana, New York, and the SEC itself, the entire world suddenly seemed allied against us. This was more than a mere communication from "Earth to Palo Alto," it was a declaration of war—Earth *versus* Palo Alto. With our IPO at risk and our morale damaged, I could almost hear columnist George Kraw and his colleagues in the business media laughing, watching as the first Internet IPO since September 11 began to fall apart just as they had predicted.

◊

As our public offering teetered on the razor's edge, Peter grew all the more determined to get it out the door as quickly as possible. Knowing that any additional bombshells would force us to scrap it altogether, he called upon a tactic that had served him well when closing the $100 million venture round as the NASDAQ crashed—he sacrificed money for speed. Instead of maximizing the company's cash infusion by pushing for a higher valuation on an IPO that was originally vastly oversubscribed, Peter stressed to the bankers the need to get the deal out regardless of the exact price.

PayPal's bankers, lawyers, and finance group kicked their efforts into overdrive. As our legal team strived to keep state regulators at bay, our investment bankers held the hands of our institutional investors while their brokerage counterparts worked around the clock to contact the thousands of customers, friends, and family members registered to purchase shares. After several days of welcome quiet, the pieces of the puzzle fell into place toward the end of the following week. Salomon priced the shares at $13, the midpoint of the announced range, on the evening of Thursday, February 14, Valentine's Day. The shares were set to begin trading on the NASDAQ under the ticker symbol PYPL after the market opened the following morning.

Despite the IPO's rescheduling, the atmosphere at the PayPal office that evening remained hushed and cautious. After all the dashed hopes of the prior week, employees wearily avoided mentioning the topic for fear of having their expectations crushed once again. I followed this code of silence, too, not as much for fear of jinxing the deal but because my closest confidant, Paul Martin, was out of town. When he scheduled his trip to the 2002 Winter Olympics in Salt Lake City months earlier, Paul had no way of knowing that he and his new bride would be missing one of the tensest moments in PayPal's already stressful history.

I woke up early Friday morning and turned on CNBC's business report as I hurriedly dressed, listening to find out if any new obstacles to the deal had appeared overnight. With all quiet, Beatrice and I hopped in the tiny Ford Focus and picked up Starbucks beverages as we set out on the drive south. We had planned a weekend getaway on the coast, but I insisted on stopping by the PayPal office on our way there to hear the latest developments. It turned out that we didn't have to wait that long. I had just merged the car onto the freeway when a financial update on the radio delivered the long awaited confirmation—PYPL was trading! And if that news was a relief, the quote was a shock. Our share price spiked to $18 in its opening minutes. After giving Beatrice a one-armed hug and phoning my parents, I gave my partner in so many PayPal adventures a celebratory call.

"Paul, Paul—it's me!" I cried. "Eighteen dollars! Eighteen dollars!"

"What?" came the bewildered reply from somewhere in Utah.

"The IPO happened! The stock is trading and it's already up to eighteen!" No further explanation proved necessary; I could hear him ecstatically repeating the news to his wife.

When Beatrice and I arrived at the PayPal offices a party was already brewing. It was not quite ten yet the office was already full—even the nocturnal engineers had rolled in early to celebrate. The flat screen monitor over the entrance to the kitchen that typically displayed usage statistics instead showed a Bloomberg chart of our stock, which by now had soared past the $20 mark. Music blared from several cubicles while a handful of programmers danced on their desks. Even David Sacks wore a large smile as he chatted with colleagues. The strain and tension of the past week were forgotten.

Unlike eBay's management team, who spent the day of their IPO in New York with their bankers,[27] PayPal's executives partied with their employees. Peter ordered kegs of beer and snacks for some afternoon fun in the parking lot, and later provided the entertainment by engaging in ten simultaneous chess matches against the rest of the executive staff. (Of those ten competitors, only an exuberant Sacks managed to beat the former U.S. Chess Federation national master.)

Celebration consumed the rest of the day and a sense of achievement filled the air. Our youthful entrepreneurs reveled in their collective achievement. The instantly created wealth was certainly one reason for reveling, but that was not the topic on everyone's lips. It was public justification. After so much ridicule and doubt, after fending off internal strife and external threats, we had just proven to the world that PayPal was something special. Earth had pulled no punches, but Palo Alto had prevailed.

Our shares got in on the action, too. The price peaked at around $22 before ultimately closing at $20.09, a 55% one day increase. In a valley that had witnessed weekly dot-com public offerings just a couple of years earlier, we literally partied like it was 1999.

The skeptical press chose not to join us. Dow Jones News Services later mused that such a surge in stock price by a "money-losing" company like PayPal could only be explained by demand from small investors who liked our brand.[28] *The Los Angeles Times* warned that PayPal "face[d] a cloudy future," and quoted an analyst who noted the obvious by saying that legal and regulatory issues cast a "long and dark shadow as to what [was] going to happen with this company."[29] Not to be outdone, *The New York Times* cited an analyst who called us an anachronism.[30] And while a reporter from *The National Post* wrote a largely positive piece on our success, his editor slapped on the title "Don't Bank on PayPal."[31]

But we paid the sour grapes no mind. Our public debut added millions of dollars to the company's coffers and lifted employees' spirits. It was a great showing for an IPO that almost didn't happen. And at the time little did we know just how close it came to not happening.

That proverbial other shoe waited until the following week to drop.

CHAPTER TEN

TO THE BRINK

FEBRUARY–JUNE 2002

"EBAY THROWS DOWN the Gauntlet to PayPal." The news article's title said it all.[1] Six days after we dared to breathe a sigh of relief and celebrate our IPO, eBay paid $43.5 million to buy out Wells Fargo's 35% stake in Billpoint. Coming as it did on the heels of our offering, analysts and media pundits alike viewed the transaction as a precursor to eBay—no longer needing to seek consensus with Wells Fargo on strategy—moving aggressively to claim control of the online payments business. Billpoint CEO Janet Crane promised "increased integration of Billpoint and eBay over time."[2]

The market believed her. PayPal's stock price, which had already given back some of its IPO froth, tumbled 15% to $15.01 on the news, dropping our market capitalization back below the $1 billion threshold. While most of the market's reaction certainly reflected concern about PayPal's ability to respond to future eBay threats, the moderate $125 million valuation of Billpoint didn't help to the extent investors took it as a sign that PayPal was overvalued.

In a sense the timing of the announcement underscored the precarious circumstances surrounding PayPal's IPO. It's not clear as to when eBay and Wells Fargo began discussing the Billpoint transaction in earnest, but given the speed with which large companies tend to move, the talks likely began weeks, if not months, earlier. The closing of the deal might have come at any time. Had the companies reached terms just a week sooner, this—coupled with the CertCo, Louisiana, and SEC disputes—most certainly would've rattled institutional investors and doomed our already delayed public offering.

Public perception of the buy-out aside, whether eBay's complete ownership of Billpoint would indeed pose additional risks for PayPal remained unclear. By now most of us had trouble imagining what else eBay could conjure up. Billpoint already enjoyed integration on eBay's Sell Your Item, Search, and My eBay pages, and had benefited from promotions such as the free listing days, free Visa, and Auction for America. Checkout had just taken Billpoint's advantages to a whole new level. I doubted the removal of Wells Fargo from the decision-making equation would make much difference. From our perspective, the bank seemed to be a silent partner that went along with eBay's aggressive integration plans.

If eBay's move didn't present an obvious new threat to PayPal, it did provide an opportunity. With Wells Fargo out of the way, eBay could potentially resume talks with a newly public PayPal to turn us into its official payment service. I hoped that eBay might be persuaded to sell Billpoint to us or simply shutter it and replace it with PayPal once a revenue-sharing contract could be negotiated. While hypothetical, these scenarios suggested that eBay might approach the Billpoint-PayPal conflict with more ability for compromise than in the past. Of course, given the intensity of our two year competition and our rejection of eBay's prior acquisition offer, anything less than a continuing struggle seemed unlikely.

◊

With a swarm of legal opponents and regulatory foes coming out of the woodwork prior to our IPO, Billpoint's ownership change amounted to little more than a momentary distraction. The company needed a way to resolve these lingering pre-IPO issues without diverting internal energy from our core operations.

Peter and the management team addressed two of the three eleventh hour surprises in short order. Our strong legal response convinced CertCo to drop its patent infringement lawsuit two months later without the cash windfall it sought; the settlement included only a "non-consequential payment and mutual release."[3] And the SEC's reprimand for our potential violation of the quiet period never amounted to anything, given the flimsy facts and the stock's consistent trading range above the $13 offer price.

The third roadblock, Louisiana's unexpected threat to ban our service, was not so easily circumvented. Since abandoning our earlier attempt to be recognized as a federally regulated trust bank with authorization to act as the custodian of individuals' funds, in 2001 our lawyers had repositioned the company's strategy. Accepting the inevitability of dealing with regulators on a state-by-state basis instead of answering to a single federal authority, our legal team shifted its focus to receiving a money transmitter classification in the three dozen states with pertinent laws. A majority of states signed off on the claim, but several holdouts—including Louisiana, New York, California, and Idaho—resisted, unsure of what to make of our novel service.

In an attempt to prove their point to these state regulators, our lawyers requested an advisory opinion from the Federal Deposit Insurance Commission indicating that PayPal was not practicing commercial banking.[4] Since PayPal did not make loans or pay interest on account balances like a commercial bank, and since our optional money market service was managed by a regulated third party, our legal group believed that the FDIC would take our side of the debate. We had good reason to pray they would. Had PayPal been classified as a bank by regulators in any state, hefty fines, endless rounds of paperwork, and a new slew of requirements would have accompanied the ruling. And besides the brand damage we'd have suffered from being categorized as an unauthorized bank, such a finding by one state posed the risk that others would follow its precedent, creating a regulatory snowball.

Given the stakes, Peter's eagerness to resolve these lingering regulatory issues is understandable. But so was the management team's suspicion that state regulators would not come to the right decision without us doing everything we could to argue our case. As Nobel Prize-winning economist Milton Friedman once put it, "Agencies established in response to [consumer protection] movements have imposed heavy cost on industry after industry to meet increasingly detailed and extensive government requirements."[5] Our executives feared Friedman's generalization was beginning to apply to PayPal. If regulators continued to hound our young company in the name of consumer protection, it could compromise our ability to offer any service to consumers at all.

Louisiana's actions suggest this concern was not just paranoia. With no regard for the thousands of Louisiana residents who depended on PayPal to buy and sell online, much less for our company's diverse stakeholders, the state's Office of Financial Institutions threatened to pull the plug on our service. Its regulators offered no accusation of corporate malfeasance or graft, nor did they explain why preventing Louisiana's own residents from voluntarily using PayPal was in the best interest of those same residents. They weren't even claiming to be protecting citizens from anything—they simply wanted to stop us from doing business until they finished deciding what label to apply to us.

This lack of an accusation of wrongdoing makes the regulators' motives look more than a little self-serving. No one stood to benefit from the decision, except possibly the Office of Financial Institutions itself. The agency might have hoped that its heavy-handedness would give it a reputation as tough player for other companies to reckon with. If nothing else, it would certainly put it in the national spotlight—something that I suspect otherwise seldom happens to Louisiana state agencies.

Impugned motives aside, the problem still had to be resolved. PayPal's lawyers took a pragmatic stance that masked any hint of our private indignation. The legal team met with state officials soon after the IPO and threw in some behind-the-scenes lobbying, just to be sure. The approach ultimately worked and the state rescinded the threatened ban and, in late March, granted us a money transmitter license. At the time, a regulator from the Office of Financial Institutions commented, "We're trying not to be unreasonably hard on those folks. Our goal is to get all of those licensed that are required to be licensed."[6] (If imposing an outright embargo prior to a company's IPO with no provocation and without prior warning isn't considered "unreasonably hard," one can only wonder what these people would call playing hardball.)

It later turned out that Louisiana officials weren't the only trigger-happy regulators, nor was PayPal the only online payment company targeted. An article from CNET revealed that many of the same state administrators hounding PayPal began to train their sights on Billpoint.[7] Specifically, Oregon, California, Illinois, and, not surprisingly, Louisiana, sent inquiries to eBay suggesting that Billpoint needed to obtain money transmitter licenses. While reluctant to wish a regulatory hell on any business, even our tenacious competitor, I'll admit that everyone at PayPal enjoyed seeing Billpoint bedeviled with a similar set of problems to our own.

The same CNET article also gave the first public hint about a possible catalyst for this growing regulatory trend. While some state officials certainly took their cue from Louisiana, at least one special interest group was apparently acting behind the scenes to fan the flames against the online payments industry. The article quoted a giddy director from the American Bankers Association (ABA) who cited a growing sense among banks that payment services like PayPal and Billpoint should be categorized as commercial banks—surprise, surprise—and gleefully suggested that regulation was the only way to ensure that customers would be protected. Evidently our old economy competitors in the banking sector saw nothing wrong in encouraging government to do for them what they could not, derail a nimble young competitor.

This was the ideal of "creative destruction" turned on its head. Instead of competing against a new technology in the marketplace, commercial banks were prodding state governments to quash potential upstarts in a field where they had experienced trouble competing. Bank One and Citibank's disappointing payment ventures coupled with Wells Fargo's divestment of Billpoint must have served as a clarion call for the industry. If they wanted to stop innovative upstarts like PayPal from dominating online payments and potentially reinventing the financial industry in the process, they would have to enlist state regulators to help them out.

Fortunately the ABA and its members received a setback in mid-February when the FDIC responded to our prior request and conceded that PayPal was not engaged in commercial banking under federal law. Citing that "PayPal [did] not physically handle or hold funds placed into the PayPal service," the agency concluded that PayPal did not accept deposits but only passed on funds to banks or other users on the behalf of our customers. While not binding on the decisions of state regulators, we used our first press release at the end of the quiet period to tout the FDIC ruling, calling it a useful precedent for the individual states.[8]

This news from the feds did indeed spur the remaining states into action. In addition to Louisiana, Idaho granted PayPal a money transmitter license and California finally accepted our application, signaling that an approval would be forthcoming. New York followed suit in June by agreeing that PayPal was not a bank, a decision which effectively ended our odyssey to classify PayPal's business and allowed us to avoid suspending operations in any states.

Much to the chagrin of the banking industry, our payments company was out of the regulatory woods—at least regarding the threat of being classified as a bank. Other hurdles would eventually follow, but for now an entirely different development was about to take center stage.

◊

"We've agreed to sell to eBay." The blood drained out of my face and my eyebrows involuntarily arched upwards. Fortunately I was already seated on the black leather couch in Peter's office when Andrew McCormack, Peter's executive analyst, hit me with the news.

"R-Really?" I stammered. "I can't say that I saw that coming." I knew that Whitman's camp had approached Peter following the buy-out of Wells Fargo. During the first half of April due diligence talks had consumed both companies, and I had been involved in preparing several analyses. But I had still doubted that it could result in a sale of our company. With the strained history between the management teams and the failed acquisition efforts of the past, good faith negotiations promised to be a challenge. And with our company now profitable and publicly valued at over $1 billion, PayPal's price tag was far greater than when the companies had last spoken. If anything, it seemed possible that eBay might be convinced to exit payments by selling its unprofitable division to us, an option it could not have easily pursued while Wells Fargo remained its equity partner.

From what I'd just heard from Andrew, clearly this analysis was off the mark. As I collected my wits I managed to ask, "What are the terms?"

I sat listening to my colleague describe the deal with mixed thoughts racing through my head. The benefits to the company were immediately clear. We could finally put the bloody corporate rivalry behind us and turn PayPal into the official eBay payments system. This would remove a major risk to our business model at a time when legal and regulatory challenges were increasingly endangering the company; in fact, eBay's household name and established lobbying apparatus could probably help PayPal deal with these problems.

Personnel also stood to benefit. An end to the constant state of crisis management would aid the quality of life for every employee, and a clause in our stock option agreement that granted all employees a one year acceleration of their grants held a financial allure, as well.

On the other hand, giving up our independence was a scary thought; there was no way to know whether the entrepreneurial culture created by Peter and Max would survive. When control was turned over to X.com's executives following that merger, it nearly destroyed the company's culture. While I had little insight into the internal workings of eBay's organization, its pace of product development seemed more ponderous than ours, and its recent miscues suggested it had less of an understanding for its customers' needs than we did. In short, there were reasons to be apprehensive.

Beyond those business reservations, tying our valuation to eBay's also suggested a limit on our stock's upside, presuming that our younger company held a potential for faster growth and, hence, faster share price appreciation than the auction giant. Moreover, in terms of vision, we couldn't guarantee that eBay would embrace the same audacious goal of empowering individuals by revolutionizing world currency markets. If eBay's vision was limited to commerce on its own site, it meant that PayPal would never be the "Microsoft of payments."

"Is your schedule free two nights from now?" Andrew asked, snapping me back to reality, before adding, "Peter wants you and a few of our other auction strategy leaders to attend a reception at Meg Whitman's house." I couldn't believe it! Just a few months earlier I had hung up an illustrated likeness of Whitman from the *Wall Street Journal* in Paul's cubicle as a practical joke. Now I faced the prospect of mingling at a cocktail party at her house as a future employee.

After accepting the invitation and leaving Peter's office, I bumped into Bill Onderdonk, who gathered from my pale complexion that something significant had taken place. I repeated the news in a hushed tone, prompting his jaw to drop before he began asking me the same set of questions I'd just posed to Andrew. I relayed what little I knew to my stunned boss before we both crept silently back to our seats, keeping the news under wraps from the rest of the team until a company-wide announcement could be made during the following days.

Sitting at my desk, I reflected on these now-familiar emotions—they mirrored the impressions that raced through my mind when Luke told me the news of Confinity's merger with X.com. This time the benefits to such a deal were far more apparent, but it was impossible not to feel conflicted over the decision. For the rest of the day I struggled to focus on the tasks at hand but couldn't help pondering the dramatically changed prospects for our young company. For better or for worse, we seemed poised to bow to external pressures and once again hand control of PayPal over to an outside organization.

◊

Events beyond PayPal's control rendered further soul searching unnecessary. Shortly after I found out about the tentative agreement, so did Wall Street. Our stock price mysteriously began drifting up, and soon thereafter the financial station CNBC publicly broke the story of a potential eBay-PayPal deal.[9] This news, coupled with speculation that we would exceed our first quarter earnings projections, boosted our stock price by 8% the first day and another 13% to $26.05 the next.

Since its debut two months earlier, our stock had always been volatile. Only 5.4 million out of the 60 million total shares could be traded on the market—the rest belonged to insiders, venture capitalists, and friends and family, meaning they were "locked up" for either 90 or 180 days after the IPO. This short supply caused large price fluctuations when demand picked up or cooled off. In this instance, the spike in demand caused the price of PYPL to soar, a factor which Wall Street observers noted could ironically damage the deal's prospects. "It would make sense for eBay to pursue PayPal," a Morningstar analyst told the *E-Commerce Times.* "I'm sure they wish they bought PayPal [the] last [time] they had a chance. Now, they have to decide whether it's worth the current price." Fluctuations in either share price, the analyst added, would impact the ability of both parties to reach an agreement.[10]

These prognostications proved accurate. The run-up in PayPal's stock strangled any remaining chance of a deal. With shares of EBAY trading in the low fifties, PYPL's surge into the mid-twenties meant the agreed-upon exchange ratio would be the same as selling PayPal for less than its fair value, something Delaware corporate law prevented the board from doing. The source of the leak remained unknown, but it cast a pall over acquisition talks that had already begun to fall apart. Mutual distrust and diverging stock valuations caused the tentative deal to collapse and Meg's cocktail party was abruptly cancelled, signaling a resumption in corporate hostilities.

The following week, Peter used our Q1 earnings call with analysts to keep the door open for future negotiations with eBay while still remind-ing the world of PayPal's own remarkable business model: "Obviously, [the] two companies share quite a few customers, and there could be some interesting synergies. [But] PayPal at the same time is a stand-alone business that makes sense and quite a bit of money…"[11] And, for once, no one could disagree with our claim of profitability. With the goodwill created by the Confinity-X.com merger completely amortized and gone from our balance sheet, the company posted a GAAP profit of $1.2 million for the quarter on revenues of $48 million. Excluding non-cash expenses our profit from operations stood at $6.3 million. With 15.4 million total accounts on the books and an average of $16 million in daily payments, PayPal continued to grow at an amazing pace.

◊

"Now is the time to kill off Billpoint," I told Paul Martin. In the days following our scrapped talks with eBay I found myself challeng-ing the company's emphasis on diversification. The imperative of decreasing our eBay dependency had become almost gospel around the office, yet I sensed that the aborted acquisition signaled that PayPal's hand had recently strengthened. I increasingly felt that if we could take advantage of it, we might shift the auction payments scene once and for all. With these concerns on my mind I approached my good friend for his feedback.

"Look, we know how little traction Billpoint is getting," I continued from my perch on the side of his desk, "and its entire team must be demoralized after eBay gave it a vote of no-confidence by trying to buy us. It strikes me that now is the perfect time for us to go back on the offensive. If we devote serious resources to this effort and put further distance between PayPal and Billpoint, eBay will start to feel pressure from investors to ditch this drain on its bottom line."

After a pause, Paul offered a measured reply. "Well, I don't know what else we can do. We've just built AuctionFinder and now I've got all three of my engineers working on the shipping feature." Auction-Finder—a new auction tool—allowed buyers to type in their eBay username into PayPal and have us present them with a pre-populated payment form for their recently won auctions. Buyers immediately latched onto it as a convenient time-saving option.

The shipping feature, by contrast, was a seller-targeted product that would integrate PayPal into another end-of-auction process by letting sellers print UPS shipping labels directly from their PayPal account. Although valuable as a way of increasing seller loyalty to PayPal, it was also the engineering equivalent of climbing Mount Everest. "Shipping is really complicated and it's going to take several months to finish because of all the interaction with UPS," Paul added, removing his glasses and pressing his palm to his forehead.

"I think there are a lot of valuable features that we should build," I said, searching for alternatives. "Is it possible to revisit the timing for shipping, or maybe get you some additional engineering support?"

"You'd have to convince Sacks about rescheduling shipping," he replied with a wisp of a sigh. "As for resources, I don't know who could help us. I only have three engineers and no other producers, and it's not trivial to get someone up to speed on something as complex as our auction features."

Paul's response hit at the heart of the problem. The company had scaled up in recent months, but its auction product team had not. The strategic shift in the middle of 2001 to emphasize diversification had meant increasing the manpower of the merchant services product team, a group that now had three producers and a half-dozen engineers. To some extent, this move did produce results. Growth in Web site payments and gambling soon outpaced auctions, causing our non-auction volume to reach 39% and 41% of total payments in the first two quarters of 2002, respectively—up from just 30% over the same period a year earlier. Gambling alone accounted for 8% of volume in Q1, double its share of the prior year.

But our non-auction efforts were also a mixed bag. The company still was not what could honestly be called diversified since eBay-related transactions accounted for three out of every five payments. And, because of the allocation of resources toward our non-eBay initiatives, it would prove difficult to obtain sufficient support at a time when we needed to focus on the auction market again.

I took my case for increasing our auction-focused resources to Sacks. Calling this perhaps our last chance to break Billpoint's back, I argued for a dramatic shake-up to move manpower back to the auction team. My request received a lackluster response. Sacks acknowledged that Paul was understaffed and noted HR had opened a job requisition for an assistant product manager to help him out. I pushed for more but left with no further guarantees. Needless to say, it wasn't quite the paradigm shifting reaction I'd hoped for; a product-led offensive against Billpoint would have to wait.

Sacks, for his part, had reason to have his mind elsewhere. Peter had recently promoted him to chief operating officer, placing him in charge of our Omaha operations center and sales team in addition to marketing, product, and Web site design.[12] The decision to move Sacks to the newly created COO slot was both well-deserved and logical; Peter oversaw affairs at a very high level, and Sacks had more than proven his ability to manage the details of our business over the prior two years. But this increase in responsibility also forced Sacks to focus a disproportionate amount of energy on customer service, an area of the company that—while vastly improved from our early days—still needed to scale up to meet the needs of our ever-climbing number of users.

The creation of a COO position highlighted just how much our company had grown over the preceding months. As of May, we tallied 760 full-time employees, an addition of more than 20% from our total only five months earlier.[13] Reflecting our emphasis on customer service, 541 of these employees worked in Omaha, a number that had jumped from 418 in December. This rapid expansion in Nebraska-based personnel forced us to seek new office space. In June the company purchased land on the outskirts of Omaha to begin construction of a new state-of-the-art customer service center. This came on the heels of another relocation for our corporate headquarters. In early May we traded in our gray cube farm outside of Palo Alto for a downtown office in Mountain View, the next city to the south. Unlike the pair of cramped downtown Palo Alto offices occupied by Confinity and X.com, the new three-story Mountain View site sported underground parking and bright, spacious cubes for our 200 California employees. But the multi-level building also came complete with a new and distinctly corporate feeling. The company issued employee identity badges for the first time, and access cards were required to move between floors on the elevators. Besides these corporate formalities, the floors themselves subtly altered the atmosphere of the company. Product, engineering, and design occupied the third floor, while my marketing group, along with business development, finance, and legal, wound up on the second. The new layout would take some getting used to, but unfortunately we ended up having very little time to break it in.

◊

In the weeks following the collapse of the April negotiations and our transition to the new corporate headquarters, Billpoint, as if it sensed the distractions we faced, made its move. After months without any improvement of its product, Billpoint launched a carbon copy of our seller protection policy. Similar to PayPal's program, it promised to remove the risk of credit card reversals for sellers who followed a series of risk-reducing steps. The strategy made good sense—I had used Billpoint's lack of chargeback protection as a major theme in our competitive marketing to sellers, and this decision to replicate our program nullified our advantage.

Within two weeks eBay also introduced another aggressive product placement for Billpoint by inserting payment buttons directly into a new, faster version of its end-of-auction (EOA) e-mails. These official e-mail receipts went to winning bidders after the auction closed. But, as with other aspects of eBay's occasionally shaky technology platform, distribution of EOA e-mails had been so slow—sometimes thirty to sixty minutes after the auction ended—that PayPal's own notification e-mails arrived first. By speeding up the process and getting Billpoint payment buttons into buyers' inboxes faster, eBay hoped to erode our conversion to its favor.

Were these attacks made possible by eBay's Billpoint buyout of Wells Fargo? The EOA notices likely were not. This feature mirrored the numerous integration steps taken during the period of shared owner-ship of the venture, and frankly it was less obvious than Billpoint's embedding into Auction for America or Checkout. The chargeback protection program, though, might have been facilitated by the pur-chase. It's possible that the more conservative Wells Fargo didn't want the exposure to chargeback risk on the books, although it's also likely that eBay waited until it could review several quarters of PayPal's public data to estimate the approximate cost of replicating our protection policy.

Regardless of the cause, eBay's latest series of volleys reinforced my conviction that PayPal needed to refocus its energies on the auction market. After drafting some potential product initiatives, I took them to Bill Onderdonk and Keith Rabois, our VP of business development, for feedback. Keith, a shrewd Stanford alumnus who previously wrote speeches for Dan Quayle, shared my tilt toward pro-growth product strategies; he'd also known Sacks for over a decade which promised to be an asset as I readied to make my case. After a few rounds of collabo-ration our trio hammered out an offensive strategy that revolved around several themes: inserting more logos and counters into auction descrip-tions to attract increased buyer attention, developing loyalty-inducing features that helped our sellers' back office processes, and creating a user reputation service similar to eBay's feedback system to enable eBay sellers to move their business off of the auction site.

While the list of recommendations also called for a handful of infra-structure modifications such as improving our scan tools to enhance our reporting capabilities, the majority of suggestions were for user-facing products designed to accelerate PayPal's growth. After putting the finishing touches on our proposal, we sat down with Sacks and Paul to review it. This time Sacks seemed receptive to the majority of the plan and quizzed Paul about potential timelines for implementing several specific ideas. After offering a few suggestions about ways to increase the auction product team's bandwidth, the always-brief COO dismissed the meeting.

My spirits buoyed by this new development, I walked out feeling we finally had a chance at revving up a counter-offensive against Billpoint. Yet as the day wore on and I reviewed the events of the meeting in my mind, I recalled that during our discussions the typically opinionated Paul had remained largely quiet. Had my proactive push for a new auction strategy alienated my friend? It wasn't until a couple of weeks later that I discovered the disturbing source of his preoccupation.

◊

In mid-May Paul Martin added to the rich library of PayPal bombshell e-mails with a notice of his own, "Hiking the Appalachian Trail all the way back to Stanford." Paul announced he was leaving PayPal immediately to go on a six month sabbatical to hike the fabled Appalachian Trail from Maine to Georgia with his wife. Afterward, he planned to return to Stanford to finish his studies and receive his degree before moving on to whatever the next stage in life would hold.

When Paul pulled me into a conference room several days earlier to deliver the news personally, I slumped into a chair, dumbstruck with sadness and shock. But as we talked through his decision it became apparent that my young colleague was not guilty of a rush to judgment. Ever since I convinced him to drop out from Stanford, Paul had always intended to return to complete his degree. And his desire to hike the Appalachian Trail was more than a passing whim; on several occasions he had described it to me as a personal dream. This was an opportunity for him to combine those two goals, he pointed out, and in the process enjoy a once-in-a-lifetime experience.

But he also confided in me that there were additional reasons, beyond these publicly stated ones, for his departure. The product team, Paul insisted, had become increasingly bureaucratic since Sacks abdicated its full-time management. He now found the corporatism that drove Luke Nosek out of the company becoming an obstacle to the part of his job that he loved most—creating new products. An entrepreneur at heart, Paul had no stomach for red tape. Given the personal goals he wanted to accomplish outside of PayPal, he said the process-driven rigidity he had to contend with every day convinced him that leaving was the right decision.

After he presented his case, I realized that I would not be able to talk my sure-minded friend out of his plan. From what I could tell, his job had become more bureaucratic over the past half-year, a fate which my marketing team fortunately had not shared. While his job was still a far cry from the conditions that I had toiled under during my days at Andersen, if he no longer found it engaging what argument could I put forward in favor of postponing his hike and return to Stanford? Instead I offered him a handshake and a smile, wishing him the best of luck. My actions masked my true feelings. Though genuinely excited for him, it was impossible not to have a sense of melancholy seeing my steadfast partner in so many struggles and schemes depart. But following him out the door never entered my mind.

Paul's departure came at a critical moment—a point when we needed to seize the offensive against our competitor yet increasingly seemed to have difficulty doing so. Losing one of our hardest working, most entrepreneurial employees in the midst of this situation could only damage our prospects.

Peter and Sacks understood this and vigorously tried to convince Paul to change course. Though both officers were duty-bound to try to retain such a valued employee, I sensed they also had a personal desire not to lose Paul. He was the first *Stanford Review* alumnus to leave PayPal, something Peter took to heart, especially since the ten alumni from that newspaper had played a vital role in shaping the direction of the company. Sacks, for his part, had formed a close bond with Paul soon after the creation of the product team, a bond that was set in stone when Paul stood by him during the rebellion against Elon. For these reasons both men genuinely hoped to persuade Paul to stay and were all the more downcast when he declined.

His mind made up, two weeks later Paul set out for the mountains, leaving the rest of us lost in the wilderness.

◊

Tension settled on the office during the weeks following Paul's announcement. His decision forced the producers to retrench. To get up to speed, the entire product crew participated in a mandatory Auctions 101 session to compare notes after buying and selling on eBay. The former head of the merchant services group assumed Paul's role and promptly hired two assistant product managers to help him.

Meanwhile, Peter, Roelof Botha, and the rest of the executive team grew weary as PayPal's auction payment volume began to stall for the first time in the company's young history. According to our daily eBay scans, PayPal's listing share remained constant at around 70%, suggesting that something else was driving down our payment volume. Either another behind-the-scenes round of Billpoint integration was damaging PayPal's buyer conversion, or eBay itself was going through a seasonal slump that pulled our numbers down with it.

Unfortunately our less-than-perfect market intelligence rendered it impossible to determine what was the cause of the current slowdown. For more than a year we had discussed a major upgrade to our scanning tool that would allow it to track closed auctions in addition to the live ones it currently sampled. Live auctions told us PayPal's listing share; to estimate conversion we needed to know how many auctions closed successfully. But our constant state of war had made infrastructure improvements an understandably lower priority than bringing new products to market. As a result we now found ourselves missing the data that would have clarified our situation.

Still, in a continuation of PayPal's string of bad luck, the competitive situation wasn't our only problem. In the months following our IPO, trial lawyers began to sprout up wielding their weapon of choice against deep-pocketed corporations—the class action lawsuit.

The use of class action litigation—where an attorney represents multiple plaintiffs allegedly harmed by the same defendant—exploded during the nineties. Over the course of the decade federal filings of these suits grew by 300% and cases in state courts soared by an astounding 1,000%.[14] One form of class-action lawsuits, shareholder suits against corporations, rose by one-third just in 2002 alone.[15] While many of these complaints might very well be justified, the very nature of the class action lawsuit encourages lawyers to hunt for "victims" of minor disputes; even if the individual plaintiffs might only stand to win a few dollars each from the defendant, a large case might generate millions in attorney's fees. Given the incentives, it's no wonder that many companies targeted by this form of litigation often pay to make it go away rather than opting to defend themselves. With the country's total legal bill now topping $200 billion per year, and over half of this amount going just to legal fees, lawsuits have become a very significant cost of doing business.[16]

Given the litigious atmosphere and the attention our IPO attracted, it was only a matter of time until PayPal was targeted by a class action suit. But over a four month period we suddenly found ourselves defending not one but four separate class actions that alleged that the company improperly restricted access to its accounts. [17] At issue were our anti-fraud technologies that blocked suspicious accounts from removing disputed funds from the system. Our tools had prevented the mafia and petty criminals from ripping off our users and bleeding PayPal dry, but now these lawyers alleged that PayPal had gone too far by illegally holding the funds of innocent customers for its own benefit. As the situation unfolded it began to escalate from just a distraction for our legal team into a significant threat to our company's brand. It received a predictably large amount of coverage from the media,[18] prompting some concerned users to worry aloud on eBay's message boards about whether it was safe to keep money in PayPal.

All of this glum news came at about the same time that our stock price began to slide. After once trading as high as $30 a share, a June 13 announcement of a secondary stock offering sent the price into a steep decline. Because of our extensive private financing as well as the poor equities market in early-2002, at the time of the IPO the company had opted to sell less than 6 million shares to the public. This secondary offering was to be comprised of an additional 6 million shares belonging to executives and venture capitalists, effectively doubling the number of PYPL shares available to traders in advance of the expiration of the 180 day lock-up period.[19]

Peter and the management team felt the secondary offering would benefit all shareholders. Without it, 53 million of our 60 million total shares would have become available for trade on August 14, a supply that might have overwhelmed demand and caused our stock price to crash. Instead, the secondary offering was designed to let major share-holders sell some of their holdings in June in exchange for having the rest of their holdings locked-up through mid-November, effectively spreading the release of the 53 million shares across three dates instead of one.

Though intended to preserve shareholder value, this distribution of lock-up release dates drove the already volatile share price down by 7% on the day of the announcement as investors speculated that manage-ment was cashing out of an overvalued stock. In the following two weeks it would continue to tumble before settling near $19 in late June.

With morale in danger of sagging under this crop of newfound risks, departmental re-orgs, and declining share prices, Sacks and Max Levchin mustered the troops for a Patton-esque performance. Sacks, never one to mince words, peered intensely through his wire glasses as he told employees that recent whispers heard through the Silicon Valley and Wall Street grapevines suggested eBay was planning a major offensive for Billpoint. While unsure of the details, he said it promised to be the auction giant's most aggressive yet, giving us no choice but to be ready to respond as needed. When Max took the podium, he warned his engineers in particular of the road to come, pledging "Feature for feature, back and forth, this is going to be a long fight."

While striking a note of confidence that we would ultimately prevail, this rally conveyed a far different message than Peter's "world domination" speech two and a half years earlier. The prospects of a long, hot summer caused downcast employees to sulk as they filed out of the conference room. Didn't the IPO mean that we had succeeded? I heard some grumble. A return to war-footing was taking a toll, and with eBay's unknown surprise still waiting in the wings, exactly what constituted a victory for PayPal seemed more ill-defined than ever.

◊

"So what are we doing for eBay Live?" Hearing the question, I spun my seat around to face David Sacks.

His appearance surprised me. It had been a long time since Sacks had stopped by my desk. While his unannounced visits were a daily event during our startup days, my meetings with the COO were now typically confined to his private office after scheduling an appointment, through his secretary, days in advance.

"It's in about three weeks," I replied, speaking of eBay's upcoming convention in Anaheim, California. Billed as a three day community celebration, the auction giant had organized eBay Live to allow users to mingle with employees, attend workshops, and swap tips with each other about online trading. An eBay executive admitted to the Associated Press that the company hoped the convention would boost its sagging customer relations,[20] which clearly had suffered due to our ongoing struggles.

The eBay Live event was a minor item on our marketing agenda and a late addition at that. Responding to my request, Reid Hoffman surprised everyone when he convinced his eBay contacts to allow PayPal to participate as a vendor. While our company seldom spent time or money on trade shows, the marketing team felt that having a few employees at this convention would offer a valuable opportunity to interact with the 5,000 customers expected to attend. Given the recent flak over the class action lawsuits and our users' ongoing worries that eBay would try to ban PayPal, our appearance at eBay Live would let us address these concerns to active members of the community.

"We've got a small booth with the other vendors," I said, giving Sacks his requested update. "With our budget of $4,000 we are planning on sending down only about six people." Even after the IPO we continued to practice a tight-fisted approach to marketing expenses. Auctions still provided a steady stream of new customers, shielding us from the need to purchase advertisements, and most of the strategy, analysis, and communication work that my team performed involved no cash outlays. This meant marketing worked off of a lean budget, so getting the modest expenditure for eBay Live approved had been a major development.

"That doesn't seem big enough," Sacks huffed in reply. "Can't we try to have a really high profile? I think we should have a party or something. People should come away from eBay Live liking PayPal better than eBay!"

While unaccustomed to having Sacks tell me to spend more, I saw where my boss was going with this. Our recent malaise and the rumblings of a pending eBay offensive had clearly elevated the importance of the conference in his mind, and he now saw it as a chance to do something proactive for us, to take matters into our own hands.

"Sure, I think we've still got time to do that," I replied, glancing over at JoAnne Rockower, my eBay Live collaborator, seated in the next cube. "We can put together a reception or something, but we'll need to send more employees down. And that means we'll need a bigger budget."

"Go spend whatever you have to," he replied. "I don't care, just make it good!" With that the COO shot me a smile, spun 180 degrees, and strode off as suddenly as he had appeared, satisfied with having delegated this problem out to a trusted subordinate.

I wasted no time in calling together my marketing colleagues to plot out our strategy. If management wanted PayPal to use eBay Live to make a statement, we realized that the only way we could do this was by involving our loyal users.

We decided to schedule a party for the first night of the conference and to invite our customers to mingle with employees over free food and drinks. But while word of a large turnout at our reception might reach eBay's management, we wanted to make sure that we delivered a message that our competitor couldn't overlook. We opted to give a free PayPal T-shirt to everyone who attended the reception, and those who wore the shirt to the convention the following day would be eligible to win a $250 prize. This would ensure that hundreds of conference-goers would be sporting the phrase "New World Currency" emblazoned in PayPal-blue across their backs.

As soon as we distributed an invitation e-mail to PayPal's legions of auction customers, thousands of online RSVPs began to pour in to the point where Omaha had to assign additional head count to compile the reception's guest list. In an article entitled "PayPal Crashing eBay's

Party, Again," a reporter for *The Motley Fool* Web site mused that our T-shirt promotion meant Meg Whitman, giving the eBay Live keynote address, would see "a lot of what she [has] begrudgingly seen on her own site over the years—lots and lots of PayPal."[21]

The long, hot summer was about to heat up.

◊

Sacks's instructions to think big turned out even bigger than we could have hoped. Over two thousand enthusiastic customers packed into our rented hotel conference hall for PayPal's reception, and on Saturday morning, the second day of eBay Live, about one-in-four of the auctioneers filing past me into the convention center wore our white and blue shirts. Nearby several young eBay employees assigned to crowd control, easily distinguishable in their company-issued green and yellow button-up shirts, watched in disbelief.

Having just arrived at the main hall, I spotted a group of my PayPal colleagues amidst the throng of eager conference-goers and headed over to join them by the entrance to the auditorium. Meg Whitman was scheduled to give the keynote address in just a few minutes, and from the looks of things she had generated a strong turnout. I was about to strike up a conversation regarding *The Motley Fool*'s amusing prediction when I noticed a solemn look on Bill Onderonk's face.

"I just heard from Sacks that Billpoint is up for sale," the VP of marketing said, before adding the name of a major financial institution rumored to be in talks to make the purchase. After pausing, he continued, "The understanding is that this bank would turn Billpoint into a free service. Billpoint would keep its status as eBay's preferred payment method, and the bank would turn it into a bank account acquisition tool and run it at a loss."

It felt like déjà vu. Once again, and out of the blue, eBay threatened to flex its corporate muscles and endanger our young company. Even if our network could withstand Billpoint becoming a permanently free service, our already weakened stock price would tumble as soon as investors heard the news. The secondary offering, now just days away, would fall apart, and our company's suddenly brittle morale would be shattered.

"D-do we know if this is true?" I stammered, stunned at this dramatic turn of events.

"Sacks said the news came from contacts on Wall Street, so I guess it's impossible to be sure," Bill replied, his gaze drifting on members of the crowd filing past us. "Anyway, we think there's a chance that Meg is going to announce this in her speech now, so we've got to be prepared to have a response to both the media and customers who will be stopping by our booth."

Our group filed into the auditorium, glancing nervously at each other as we took a section of seats toward the back of the cavernous room. Giant television screens flanked the bright stage decorated in primary colors. My heart pounded as a PR man opined about the ways that eBay changed its users' lives. We heard how eBay helped indigenous peoples sell their crafts to the industrialized world while struggling shop owners saved their businesses by moving them online. (How the indigenous peoples or the shop owners received the money for their goods was left unmentioned.) Then, his build-up complete, the pitchman invited Whitman out onto the stage, accompanied by a rock star's welcome.

EBay's CEO looked anything but the part of a rock star. In her mid-forties and sporting straight blonde hair, Whitman wore a pair of khaki slacks and the same button-up yellow blouse issued to the rest of eBay's female staff. As the music quieted and Whitman launched into her speech, the entire PayPal delegation started scribbling frantic notes. After first praising the community and thanking everyone for attending, she began a State of the Union-style laundry list of promises for upcoming improvements. New Power Seller tiers would make it easier to reach this coveted status but also differentiate the high volume sellers from their smaller counterparts. EBay would make health insurance available for self-employed auctioneers to purchase. And a new Buy It Now-only listing format would debut later in the summer.

Missing from Whitman's compilation was any reference to Billpoint. As she wrapped up her remarks and the crowd started to disperse, everyone in our group breathed a sigh of relief—including Sacks, who had been sitting next to me during the speech. Given what a high profile development the sale of Billpoint to a major bank would have been, Whitman's failure to mention it during the keynote address suggested that the announcement would not be made during the convention.

As our employees exited the auditorium and fanned out to man our booth in the exhibition hall, we soon caught another glimpse of Whitman. Touring the booths before they opened to the general public, she made her way around the room to chat with each of the exhibitors. Well, most of them. With the PayPal booth as her next scheduled stop,

Whitman smiled, threw us a polite wave, and kept on walking. I glanced at several of my colleagues before we all burst into laughter. Evidently the CEO did not find it amusing that so many of the attendees at her convention wore PayPal's colors.

The rest of the weekend contained memorable and often petty exchanges between personnel from the two companies. EBay personnel bartered with attendees to get them to ditch their PayPal T-shirts, offering them eBay trading cards and shirts in return.[22] Olympic speed skater Apollo Ohno posed for pictures at the Billpoint booth, but customers wearing our T-shirts were asked to hold up a Billpoint flier in front of the shirt's PayPal logo. During the executive question and answer session on Sunday a customer asked why eBay refused to provide PayPal with a level playing field, prompting eBay U.S. head Jeff Jordan to ask, "Is that question from David Sacks? David, are you in the audience?"[23] And a pair of female eBay employees, sitting in the front row while I delivered a presentation on the uses of PayPal, rolled their eyes and loudly chattered back and forth.

We paid the slights no mind—the accolades that poured in from the event's attendees more than compensated for it. A dense crowd constantly surrounded the PayPal booth as excited customers lined up three and four deep for a chance to speak with our employees. They thanked us for coming to the conference and eagerly passed along their product suggestions. Many made a point to mention that over the course of the weekend they had told eBay employees, and sometimes Whitman herself, that they wanted eBay to make peace with PayPal. The corporate bickering, they said, often made them feel trapped in the middle, concerned about how to run their businesses as the two companies they depended on the most quarreled. But they also uniformly recognized that any peaceful arrangement between PayPal and eBay would have to be initiated by our larger competitor; until eBay welcomed PayPal on its auction site, they understood that we'd need to keep fighting for survival, and they urged us to keep working hard on their behalf.

What eBay's executives would do with this customer feedback remained to be seen. The only thing certain was that PayPal had clearly crashed eBay's party, and our hosts were not amused.

◊

The next week tales of our eBay Live success buoyed the mood in our northern California office. *USA Today* provided an exclamation point by publishing a color picture on the front of its business page of Meg

Whitman signing an autograph for a fan wearing a PayPal T-shirt. Our investment bankers also released the secondary offering without a hitch, removing another source of angst. But any joy from these developments was short-lived as additional reports trickled in that eBay continued its negotiations to sell Billpoint to a major financial player who would turn it into a free service. Some of us began to muse whether our efforts at the convention only succeeded in making eBay's executives all the more convinced that they could not do business with PayPal.

Sensing that the conflict was about to escalate, the company's legal team followed through with plans to file a federal complaint that eBay had engaged in anti-competitive acts toward PayPal.[24] Even if officials at the Justice Department and Federal Trade Commission discounted the filings as competitive posturing, our management team hoped the move would pressure eBay to show restraint when deciding whether to use its person-to-person marketplace monopoly to advantage its payments service. While philosophically reluctant to get the government involved, Peter recognized that the company's increasingly unstable competitive situation, coupled with its legal and stock market woes, posed a risk too great to ignore and consented to filing the complaint.

We also sought ways to bolster PayPal's public image, including potentially adding popular former New York Mayor Rudy Giuliani to the board. While this move never came about, the proposal itself demonstrates the degree to which management was concerned about our company's future.

With this as a backdrop, I approached Sacks with an idea that I had first dreamt up six months earlier. At a high level, the plan called for PayPal to build a new polling feature that would proactively and publicly pit eBay against the will of its own users. The polling tool would collect customer data in such a way that it could then serve as the basis for an aggressive PR campaign highlighting the auction company's disregard of its community's simple request to use PayPal. With demonstrable user support for PayPal's position made public, it would force eBay to respond by either ceasing its attacks against PayPal or acknowledging that it would not honor the wishes of its community. In either case, our hand would be strengthened.

At the time I first conceived it, consensus had deemed the plan too risky to implement. A public assault—and one that was more obvious than our behind-the-scenes maneuvering with the Billpoint preference change and Checkout—ran the risk of damaging relations between the two companies beyond repair. But given our new circumstances, it seemed like a gamble worth revisiting. By uncorking public criticism against its anti-PayPal bias, I reasoned, we just might make a brand-conscious company like eBay reluctant to turn around and launch another blatantly pro-Billpoint initiative. And it could give Billpoint's prospective acquirer a PR reason to think twice.

Without a doubt this was a "doomsday" weapon; once unleashed, it would set in motion a chain of events that could not be undone. But if we had no other option than waiting to see if the Billpoint deal went through, I argued, what did we have to lose with a preemptive strike that could potentially scuttle the transaction?

The auctions product team—which by this point had largely regrouped following Paul's departure and already unveiled several new features—lined up behind the idea, as did marketing. Bill and I presented it to Sacks as our nuclear option, something to consider only if every last diplomatic solution failed. Given the uncertainty of our situation, Sacks acquiesced, giving us the green light to build the feature.

Whatever the outcome of the next few weeks, PayPal would not go down quietly.

CHAPTER ELEVEN

SELL OUT

GETTING OUT OF BED on July 8 was difficult. Beatrice and I had just returned home after celebrating the Independence Day weekend in Los Angeles, and I dreaded the thought of joining the slow motion parade of cars that would already be waiting for me along Highway 101. Stepping out of the shower, I allowed my mind to drift back lackadaisically to holiday fireworks and barbeques, putting off any thoughts of potential crises waiting for me at the office. Then the ringing telephone snapped me back to a reality about to be turned upside down.

"Why'd you do it?!" demanded Paul Martin.

"Paul?" I replied, surprised just as much by the question as I was at hearing my friend's voice. He and his wife had left just a few days earlier to visit her family in New Mexico before setting out on their multi-month hike. "Do what?" I asked, struggling to grasp what was going on.

"Sell out to eBay!" he cried with an audible mix of anger and frustration. "I just read a press release about it. It's all over the news down here."

I hesitated, unable to find a suitable reply. Judging from Sacks's instructions the prior week to wait for his word before deploying the secret weapon, I had guessed that some form of high level discussions were in the works. But the speed and outcome of those negotiations left me stunned. "I didn't know... I mean, I knew we were talking with them, but I didn't know what had come of it..."

"So even *you* didn't know?" Paul asked, inadvertently giving me a compliment and a put-down in the same sentence. "Here's what the press release says—'eBay to acquire PayPal for $1.5 billion.' It says eBay is going to shut down Billpoint and run PayPal as an independent unit."

Shocked, I stumbled toward our apartment's kitchen table and slumped down in a chair. How can this be? I asked myself. How could any agreement have been reached so quickly? The only indication I'd received that talks were even under way came at the end of the prior week; up until that point we'd all labored under the assumption that Billpoint could be sold to its banking suitor within a matter of days.

As the news gradually began to sink in, I instinctively sought to confirm what Paul had told me. I pulled my company laptop out of its case and plopped it on the kitchen table, telling Paul I would call him back later that afternoon. After waiting for what felt like an eternity for the machine to boot up and connect to the Internet, I went straight to the headlines for PYPL. Sure enough, there were already a dozen of them heralding exactly what Paul described.

The first item from the list, a press release put out over the business wire, confirmed the details of Paul's account:

> In a move that will help millions of Internet users buy and sell online, eBay, Inc., the world's online marketplace, today announced that it has agreed to acquire PayPal, Inc., the global payments platform. The acquisition, which is subject to various stockholder, government and regulatory approvals, is expected to close around year-end 2002...
>
> PayPal, which will continue to operate as an independent brand, is a leading online payments solution... eBay's current payment service, eBay Payments by Billpoint, will be phased out after the close of the transaction...
>
> PayPal will continue to provide a variety of consumer services, including its popular Web Accept product, which makes it possible for independent online merchants to accept payment directly at their Web sites. In view of the uncertain regulatory environment surrounding online gaming, eBay plans to phase out PayPal's gaming business after the transaction closes. [1]

It was true! Evidently some record-setting negotiations had gone on during the Independence Day weekend. Management had signed off on an all-stock transaction for the same exchange rate the two companies had first discussed back in April. Billpoint would soon be history, and eBay was already making strategic plans for running PayPal once the deal was completed.

I turned on the television to be greeted with the same news. Business channel CNBC played it as its top story. I shook my head in stunned amazement. Even though eBay's purchase of PayPal had been a possibility for some time and had nearly happened three months earlier, the vitriolic events since then had made any reconciliation seem impossible.

Still in a state of disbelief, I rose from my chair and trudged into the bedroom to wake up Beatrice.

◊

My heart thumped loudly throughout the gridlocked drive down to the office. I anxiously surfed AM radio stations to catch any additional word about the deal. Several channels played brief recaps of what I'd already read online without providing any new details. Those would have to wait until I arrived.

To any unsuspecting employee who hadn't listened to the news that morning, the company's underground parking lot should have provided a clue that something significant had just transpired. I found it nearly full at ten minutes before nine. For a Silicon Valley company that employs dozens of engineers, this was a sure sign that things far from the ordinary were going on.

I rode up in the elevator with another shocked colleague. After exchanging brief comments regarding our mutual surprise at the announcement, he remarked, in a tone almost suggesting relief, that he couldn't believe it had *finally* happened. It was at this moment that the ramifications of the deal sunk in—PayPal's competitive war had ended. Our constant state of conflict, of wondering what eBay would do to us next, was over. But so too was our independence.

A few minutes later I joined the rest of PayPal's employees in our large, downstairs conference room—nicknamed the "Arctic Circle" in honor of the one at our former office with the broken thermostat—for a company-wide meeting. Peter Thiel stood off by the entrance, talking with some members of the executive staff, while employees noisily filed in. The entire room had the atmosphere of a junior high math class when a substitute teacher walks in the door—a steady din rising from a sea of happy faces.

Peter strolled up to the podium in the front wearing his characteristic PayPal T-shirt and jeans. "OK, let's get this started," he said before finishing the motion of swinging the microphone around to face him. "I guess you've all heard the news by now."

Someone in the first row snickered and pointed at the podium. Peter leaned over the front of it to glimpse a makeshift placard that read "Meg Whitman" spelled out in multi-colored, eBay-style letters. "See what I have to put up with?" Peter joked through a broad smile. "That's the real reason I'm selling the company." Everyone laughed.

"As you know, today we announced an agreement to sell the company to eBay. It's going to be an all stock transaction—0.39 shares of eBay for every share of PayPal.

"It will probably take about six months for the deal to close and for the acquisition to be official. Until that time, everything will stay the same and the two companies will continue to be run separately. After the sale is complete, PayPal is going to remain an independent unit within eBay with the current management team left intact.

"Also, before anyone worries, this doesn't mean that anybody's going to lose his or her job. There's not really any functional overlap between the two companies; our specialty is payments and eBay's is auctions, so no positions will be eliminated."

"Except," he continued, after a slight pause, "for Billpoint." Chuckles erupted from around the room. "Once the deal is complete, Billpoint will be closed down and PayPal will be integrated into eBay's Web site." Employees burst into applause.

"The reason this makes a lot of sense is that we have so many shared customers," Peter continued. Up until that point, he reminded everyone, our relationship with eBay had been a back-and-forth battle, causing us to waste many cycles worrying about what eBay would be up to next. This distraction, he claimed, prevented us from focusing on building new tools and services for our users.

"They made us a pretty good offer—we get an 18% premium over the current stock price of the company," he said, responding to a comment about the acquisition price. "There's always some question as to whether or not these kinds of deals make sense. But given that we got a good valuation and removed a huge risk from the company, I think it does."

As the meeting let out, employees streamed out the side doors of the Arctic Circle and headed back toward their desks. I rendezvoused with my marketing colleagues by our work area on the second floor.

"I guess we won, didn't we?" one of them commented. "Although, being bought, it just doesn't feel like it." I nodded in agreement. After fighting on the front lines of a corporate war for so long, it proved difficult to view the former enemy as a new ally just because the shooting had stopped. And, in this case, that former opponent would be more than just a friend, it would be PayPal's new owner.

◊

At noon Meg Whitman strolled up to the podium that Peter occupied just three hours earlier. In contrast to Peter's casual attire, she wore slacks and a button-up blouse, formalwear by Silicon Valley standards. To her left stood Peter, Max, Sacks, and Jeff Jordan, the head of eBay's U.S. Web site.

"Welcome. I'm Meg Whitman, the CEO of eBay," she said, an unnecessary introduction since her visage was already unmistakable to most PayPal employees. Realizing that she needed to strike a conciliatory note, Whitman donned a PayPal cap on her head before tossing a few eBay T-shirts into the audience. "It's really great to be here," she added.

"So, how many people here have bought or sold on eBay?" The vast majority of employees in the room raised their hands. "That's great! Now, how many have over one hundred feedback?" JoAnne Rockower and a few other colleagues lifted their hands into the air. Whitman chuckled. "You know, this morning we had a meeting at the eBay offices and I asked our employees how many of them had used PayPal. Ninety-eight percent of them raised their hands."

Having warmed up the crowd, Whitman enthusiastically walked us through a PowerPoint slideshow providing an overview of eBay. Much of it was the same information we'd seen at eBay Live only a few weeks earlier. A computer is sold on eBay every two minutes, and a collectible car every half hour. She noted with some glee that eBay posted greater than 50% year-over-year growth in its Books and Movies & Television categories, compared to "only 9% up there in Seattle," a thinly veiled reference to Amazon.com.

Whitman concluded her slideshow and resumed her impromptu talk with another compliment to PayPal's employees. "You should be very proud of the company that you've built, in spite of us sometimes putting up some roadblocks." I couldn't help but chuckle, thinking how many times what she called roadblocks were seen as life or death crises for our young company.

At this point, Whitman paused to thank Sacks and Jordan, whom she identified as the driving forces behind the agreement. She said that they had been the first to resume talks following eBay Live, an event that she credited with helping both sides fully grasp their interdependence. Our mutual customers, she claimed, were the ones that had wanted this deal to happen; seeing thousands clad in PayPal T-shirts and hearing requests from many of them to reconcile with us had driven this point home.

Whitman also noted with a smile that this deal had been brought to completion despite the fact that both CEOs had been on vacation—she had been in southern California and Peter had been in Hawaii. I later confirmed that her description of the amazing circumstances surrounding the acquisition was accurate. Sacks informally called Jordan the prior week as rumors of the Billpoint sell-off reached fever pitch. The two agreed that the sale of Billpoint, which would be accompanied by a contract guaranteeing preferential integration on eBay's site, would mark a point of no return, preventing any future reconciliation between PayPal and eBay. If any deal could be struck, this was the last chance.

When Sacks informed Peter of his conversation, Peter instructed him to take the lead in hammering out an agreement with the help of CFO Roelof Botha and our investment bankers. Since the two companies had completed in-depth due diligence just two months earlier, it was just a matter of coming to mutually acceptable terms. Peter, fearing that his outspoken role in the previous aborted discussions might have created mistrust on the part of eBay's executives, hopped on a plane to Hawaii and ignored the investment bankers' calls for the next several days. His hands-off gamble worked.

If any lingering tension existed between Peter and Whitman, it was not evident during her breezy and comforting presentation. Afterwards, she called on the audience for their questions. The first one was predictable: "What's going to happen to Billpoint?"

"Billpoint will be closed, but we will try to find places for those folks elsewhere in our organization," she answered. "Except for Janet Crane, no one at Billpoint knew about this before this morning," she added, making sure to underscore how difficult it was when she broke the news to them. "Everyone there has worked really hard, but they were trying to do with fifty people what you've done with five hundred. Payments are not our core competency." While such a personnel comparison wasn't accurate since Billpoint outsourced its customer service and fraud functions, no one bothered to correct her.

And so Whitman continued, lauding PayPal's accomplishments while stressing that eBay was an incredible company that would be a powerful partner for us. Her performance was on the mark. Her combination of praise and optimism about the future was exactly what the audience of employees needed to hear—in that way it mirrored Peter's memorable reconciliation speech to the company after the leadership change in October 2000. Whitman also conveyed excitement over the prospect of officially joining the Web's leading marketplace with its top payment service.

Whitman's comments had reassured most of PayPal's employees that the acquisition would be a smooth process, and they gave her a vigorous round of applause as she concluded her remarks. Alternatively looking relieved and giddy, they snatched up eBay T-shirts from a box near the conference room's exit as they trickled out.

My own reaction was more somber. Even if a majority of my colleagues' fears were alleviated by the end of PayPal's conflict with eBay, something in my intuition told me to be concerned. It certainly had nothing to do with Meg Whitman's speech—she had said all the right things. But I had a lingering sense that dramatic change was about to unfold for our young company, that the entrepreneurial adventure I naively joined as Peter and I strolled through San Francisco's marina district many months earlier was now coming to an end.

I left from the Arctic Circle's back exit and steered clear of the T-shirt box.

◊

The day's meeting marathon continued at three o'clock in Sacks's office. The marketing, design, and international teams, about twenty people in all, packed into his sparse and functional workspace.

Sacks began with a nervous chuckle and a couple of informal remarks. He then addressed the reasons behind his push to resume negotiations with eBay, characterizing them as a response to feedback from within the company. He shared that numerous employees had approached him following eBay Live and had encouraged him to make new overtures toward eBay after seeing its dynamic community and marketplace in person.

"We had to break this destructive cycle," he said. He emphasized the importance of doing a deal at this point rather than continuing down the combative path of the prior two years. Our product and marketing battles, he stressed, coupled with our behind-the-scenes political lobbying, would soon have led both sides to a point of no return where any future compromise would've proven impossible.

"We simply can't permanently sustain a war-like environment. Doing this merger will let us create as opposed to just bracing for the next onslaught.

"There's also some question as to whether or not we're giving up," he added. "I actually don't think it's clear who would've won. In these cases, if it's clear then a deal usually cannot be struck. Victors wouldn't want to be acquired because they'd know they were going to win, and losers wouldn't be able to convince anyone to acquire them."

He was also quick to defend the agreed-upon valuation, saying he had seen eBay's internal estimates on how much it would be able to part with for a payment service. "We got about the best their models would allow them to spend," he noted.

The session remained informal and he solicited questions from the group. I asked him what had happened to make this round of talks successful when others had failed. Sacks responded it was a willingness that had not existed before on both sides to do a deal; going to the brink of all out corporate war had forced both parties to reassess the situation.

In answering a question about job security, Sacks struck a calming tone: "To do anything to you, first they'd have to get through Peter, then through me, then through your boss, so it's not something you should worry about. It's certainly in their interest to keep everyone happy and keep all our employees here. They just paid $1.5 billion for our company and our company is our people."

Sacks's confident reassurances suggested that life at PayPal after the acquisition would carry on much as it always had. I remained skeptical—even if the executive team had no intention of going anywhere, it was no guarantee that PayPal would be allowed to continue as a stand-alone entity. But I also realized it was beyond my ability to influence the matter.

With day-to-day tasks seeming trivial, I made a point to head home earlier than usual that evening. For the first time since dotBank and X.com emerged to challenge Confinity, I left the office not worrying about a competitor. Whatever lay ahead for PayPal, at least our days of competitive warfare with eBay were over.

◊

While the majority of PayPal's employees seemed relieved, our most important constituency, our customers, displayed mixed feelings about the announcement. Some looked forward to increased integration between PayPal and eBay's Web sites, but others worried that eBay would change PayPal for the worse. On the OTWA discussion boards, posters fretted about numerous features, including the debit card, being phased out after the deal closed. User "dblumenfeld" mused that "certain PayPal features won't make much sense after the merger, e.g. the 'PayPal Preferred' program... Then of course there's the issue of whether the PayPal name will be retained, and if so, for how long."[2] A poster named "ShelbyBoy" on *The Motley Fool* Web site echoed that sentiment: "PayPal seems to be able to introduce new features that are simple to understand and use and the introduction doesn't seem to anger a ton of users. EBay doesn't seem to be able to pull that off on a consistent basis... [My] concern is eBay's culture will prevail and ruin a good thing called PayPal."[3]

A far less valued but predictable constituency—the business media—began to denounce the sale for a different set of reasons. While media criticism of PayPal was nothing new, this time the pundits speculated on the unspoken reasons for the deal. The online edition of *The Wall Street Journal* ran an article titled "Questions Linger about eBay's Bid for PayPal."[4] It quoted a securities analyst who had forecast PYPL shares at $32 as saying "It's fair to say that a lot of us thought there was considerably more upside to the stock." Another analyst was quoted as suggesting that "selling to eBay may have just been the easy way out." The news agency Reuters, in a piece called "PayPal and Its Owners Partying Like It's 1999," alluded that Peter and Max were lured by the temptation of pocketing a combined $111 million in EBAY shares in deciding to sell-out.[5] A columnist with *CBS MarketWatch* claimed that the acquisition by eBay meant "only a few people—namely early investors, management and investment bankers—[were] left richer."[6]

Meanwhile, a handful of shareholders filed a pair of class action lawsuits attempting to block the sale to eBay. Calling the price inadequate, the suits asserted that the board neglected its fiduciary duty by accepting eBay's offer.[7] Based on stock prices the last trading day before the announcement of the deal, when PYPL closed at $20.00 and EBAY at $60.54, the acquisition represented an 18% premium for PayPal. But these shareholders contended that eBay should have paid a larger premium for the company.

Given my own mixed feelings, I sought to understand Peter's reasons for accepting this latest overture from eBay. At a lunchtime conversation the following week I asked him what was his primary motivation for finally doing the deal. Peter replied that it was a "sense that this constant state of war was wearing people down." The conflict, he claimed, coupled with our already volatile stock price, exposed us to a risk of employees leaving the company from either burnout or low stock prices. But, he hastened to add, combining with eBay also created value.

"We want PayPal to be the currency for the Internet," he said. "And the most important driver for that is the number of people using the system. EBay has 46 million users. There's a huge amount of room for us to grow within that customer base. And once we take off on eBay, it's going to lead to further expansion off eBay. Whether it's inside or outside of eBay, I really think that this move puts us in the best position to achieve world domination."

Clearly there was value to ending our struggle with Billpoint. PayPal had taken on so many vested interests over the years that our company now had a long list of enemies. Our clashes with the credit card associations, the banking lobby, state regulators, foreign Mafioso, and litigation-happy lawyers were tiring enough without having to worry about being shut out of our primary market. And the onslaught had significantly increased after our IPO, an event that ironically was meant to strengthen the company's position. This rogue's gallery of foes collectively exposed PayPal's business to more danger than Billpoint alone ever could. By taking our eBay risk off the table, Peter was significantly reducing the total amount of peril facing PayPal and its stakeholders.

A development soon after the deal was struck corroborated this point. New York's headline-grabbing state attorney general, Eliot Spitzer, resurfaced with a subpoena for PayPal. Spitzer had spent most of 2002 showing up the SEC by taking the lead in prosecuting the bevy of public companies involved in accounting scandals, and now he had a new high-profile corporate target in his sights. His subpoena demanded information regarding PayPal's use in online gaming. Hinting that this aspect of our business might be in violation of New York's gambling laws, the subpoena arrived within a day of our public announcement of the eBay acquisition.[8]

While our lawyers believed that Spitzer's interpretation of the laws in question lacked merit, eBay's decision to buy PayPal and phase-out online gaming fortunately made his inquiry more or less moot. But, to Peter's point, without the sale to eBay this investigation might have sent our stock price into a nose dive. Gambling represented 8% of PayPal's total payment volume and was growing briskly. Had Spitzer ultimately found a court to agree with him, PayPal would have had to abandon one of its most successful non-auction business lines, a possibility that certainly would've scared investors away from our stock.

Spitzer turned out to be the first but not the only official to launch an investigation. Several months later the U.S. Attorney of Missouri's Eastern District claimed that our gaming business violated the PATRIOT Act, the federal anti-terrorism enforcement act passed in the wake of the attacks in New York and Washington.[9] While Congress obviously had no intent of regulating PayPal's gaming operations when it wrote and approved the PATRIOT Act—recall that Rep. Leach's bill on the topic never even made it to the House floor for a vote—the U.S. Attorney's office contended otherwise. It asserted that the law's provisions against transmitting money to terrorists also applied to Internet gambling.

Regardless of the merit of the U.S. Attorney's claim, when viewed alongside the Spitzer case it was becoming obvious that a growing number of regulators were willing to take action in spite of ambiguous laws governing Internet gambling. This in turn could have snowballed by causing wary states like Louisiana to rethink issuing money transmitter licenses to PayPal.

Between hearing Peter's case and watching the Spitzer incident unfold, it was clear even to a pro-growth marketing hack that PayPal now faced many challenges outside of the marketplace. Entrepreneurial nimbleness may have helped us survive both the company's post-merger internal turmoil and Billpoint's fierce competitive charge, but these new threats would require a different approach. An eBay-owned PayPal, shielded from stock market fluctuations, would be able to spend more energy confronting these kinds of issues. While not a guarantee that all of our regulatory woes would be resolved, the deal did mean that our company would be better equipped to address the ever-present regulatory risks to our business.

◊

In late July the company assembled at a winery nestled in the foot-hills of the Santa Cruz Mountains for PayPal's annual offsite retreat. The executive team chose this site in the rolling, golden hills that form the western edge of Silicon Valley to review major business issues in a relaxing setting away from the busy office.

In some ways this perch—looking down on the Valley—was an appropriate setting for a dot-com that had accomplished as much as ours. PayPal survived the NASDAQ crash, outmaneuvered its myriad competitors, slugged its way to profitability, signed up millions of customers, became the first dot-com to IPO following September 11, and had just negotiated a blockbuster sale to an established company. By all accounts, PayPal had reached the pinnacle of Silicon Valley success, and now it was time to reflect on the company's next steps while also pausing to celebrate its accomplishments.

Following a series of presentations on the state of the business by Max, Roelof, and Sacks, employees were dismissed to an outdoor terrace for wine, *hors d'oeuvres*, and sumo wrestling.

The sumo ring resembled an oversized version of a child's inflatable wading pool, and the chunky, head-to-toe bodysuits looked like cartoon versions of sumo wrestlers. Many of the smaller-framed employees who strapped the costumes on for a mock sumo match found themselves unable to get up once knocked off their feet. With some coaxing—and some wine—Peter, Max, Sacks, and Roelof donned the hefty suits and entered the ring in an executive free-for-all. Employees screamed with delight as Max sent Peter to the canvas with a head-first charge.

The day's events wrapped up with a buffet served on a patio on the edge of the hill. As the winery staff began offering after-dinner coffee to the seated employees, Peter took to a microphone for a few closing remarks. Speaking above the clink and clatter of cups and saucers, he thanked everyone for their hard work and went on to applaud the excellent financial results from the second quarter. Then, instead of moving on to discuss the acquisition, he abruptly switched themes.

"Sometimes we've said it feels like the entire world is really against us," he said, pausing for effect, "Well, it is!

"First they thought that banks would put us out of business. And when that didn't happen, they said our customers would stop using us. And, when that didn't happen, they called on the rest of the earth to join them."

"Here, let me read a piece from February 2001, 'Losing Faith in Pay-Pal,'" he said, pulling out a piece of paper. "It says, '...Fraud, consumer backlash, new competitors and an industry wracked by failure all highlight the shaky state of PayPal's prominence and the potential need for more consumer protection.'[10]

"And here's another one, from an article called 'Earth to Palo Alto.' 'What would you do with a three-year-old company that has never turned an annual profit, is on track to lose a quarter billion dollars and whose recent SEC filings warn that its services might be used for money laundering and financial fraud?'"[11]

At this point most of my colleagues chuckled while Peter nodded approvingly. These pundits, Peter charged, weren't trying to attack PayPal—they were simply too narrow-minded to understand what it was we had set out to do. PayPal's mission had been to change the way people move money, and he claimed that this sweeping goal needed to be considered against the bigger backdrop of what was happening in the world.

"There are two major trends of the twenty-first century," Peter continued. "First, the globalization of the economy. The economy is growing internationally and people from all over the world are becoming interconnected. One billion people now live in a country other than their place of birth.

"Second, the quest for security. In this globalized, decentralized world, violence and terrorism are widespread and hard to contain. Terrorism has contaminated all countries, and it's difficult to stop it. The challenge is finding a way to fight violence in the context of an open, global economy.

"In my many trips to Washington over the past six months, I've met with regulators and politicians in attempts to persuade them not to impose new regulations on our company. And from all these meetings I've become convinced that they have absolutely no idea of how to deal with these critical issues.

"Most of the conservatives in DC don't understand that we're in a changing world, that the world is becoming more interconnected and complicated. But the liberals are even worse—they always want to rely on regulation to make things better. Neither side is asking the right questions regarding the pressing needs of the day.

"In our own way, at PayPal this is what we've been doing all along. We've been creating a system that enables global commerce for everyone. And we've been fighting the people who would do us and our users harm. It's been a gradual, iterative process, and we've gotten plenty of stuff wrong along the way, but we've kept moving in the right direction to address these major issues while the rest of the world has been ignoring them.

"And so I'd like to send a message back to planet Earth from Palo Alto. Life is good here in Palo Alto. We've been able to improve on many of the ways you do things. Come to Palo Alto for a visit sometime and learn something. I think you'll find it's a much better place than Earth."

◊

Peter's oration at the winery turned out to be a valedictory address, a bookend to the "world domination" speech he delivered to Confinity's employees some thirty-two months before. His presence in the office became increasingly rare as the weeks following the eBay agreement rolled by, and he tasked Sacks with managing the details of PayPal's pending product integration with eBay's Web site. Employees began to speculate that Peter would leave after the completion of the acquisition and return full-time to the hedge fund he managed before his fateful first meeting with Max Levchin.

Although he denied that he was planning such a move, those of us who knew Peter prior to PayPal concluded otherwise. While his leadership had saved PayPal on numerous occasions, Peter seemed most at home dealing with financial markets. If anything, his stint as the CEO of a public company—the lifelong goal of most businessmen—was a brief detour from his career as an investor. And, to be realistic, Peter's talent for focusing on high level business strategy and dealing with the financial markets would no longer be needed once PayPal became eBay's subsidiary.

David Sacks, on the other hand, seemed set to continue on with the company. Peter's appointment of Sacks to head the integration efforts established the COO as his natural successor. Prior to a trip overseas to meet with some of PayPal's larger foreign investors, Peter sent out an internal announcement that the rest of the executive team would be reporting to Sacks in his absence, a clear attempt to set employee expectations. For his part, Sacks appeared at ease with his newfound role as CEO-elect. His strong working relationship with Max and Roelof allowed the company to avoid the kinds of executive team squabbles that marked earlier transfers of power, and his presence at the helm promised a sense of continuity once the company belonged to its former competitor.

The matter of readying PayPal for its acquisition took on a heightened sense of urgency when events in late August expedited the timeframe for officially closing the deal. The Justice Department surprised everyone involved by allowing a key deadline for a second request for information to pass without comment, signaling that the federal government would not launch an investigation with the goal of blocking the proposed merger.[12] The two companies' legal teams breathed sighs of relief upon learning that PayPal's prior complaints to the government over eBay's aggressive pro-Billpoint tactics did not wind up complicating the proposed merger. The Bush administration's generally pro-free market outlook evidently influenced Justice to remain hands-off with regard to both our earlier protests about eBay and now our proposed merger with them.

With this hurdle out of the way, shares of PYPL began trading near the 0.39 conversion ratio as the markets assumed the acquisition to be a certainty. PayPal's board set a date for a shareholder vote on the proposed acquisition for the beginning of October, and personnel from both companies worked frantically to prepare the Web sites for integration. As PayPal's head of acquisition-related marketing issues, I found myself immersed in a steady stream of meetings and conference calls with my future colleagues. It was early in this intense process that the differences between PayPal and eBay's cultures became increasingly apparent. At PayPal, as we've seen, decision-making was inclusive yet streamlined. Generally a simple e-mail was enough to gauge the opinion of key coworkers on a given issue. If a consensus failed to materialize when an employee put forward a proposal, all sides would have a chance to make their case before the relevant decision-makers set a course of action. This was often a rough-and-tumble process, but it encouraged employees to put forward bold ideas and—if they survived the scrutiny of their colleagues—to move quickly to implement them. Even though the maturation of the company inevitably slowed down the speed with which we could implement changes, PayPal's nearly 800 employees were still empowered by a flexible system and encouraged to act like entrepreneurs.

EBay's, however, were not. Inside the auction giant it seemed as if nothing got done without a face-to-face meeting—or possibly several, if you were unlucky. And holding a meeting was never as simple as just sending an Outlook "meeting request" and sitting down with key stakeholders. EBay employees seemed trained to make phone calls to everyone who might have even the remotest interest in the matter and invite them to the yet-to-be-scheduled meeting. After at least two dozen invitations had been extended, a meeting time and location would be scheduled about a week in advance. The following day, like clockwork, the meeting would be rescheduled because of a calendar conflict of a peripheral stakeholder. After several rounds of schedule shuffling, attendees filing into the summit would be handed a thick set of Power-Point slides filled with bullet points, tables, and an aphorism or two laid out neatly under a cover page that featured the eBay mascot—a mustachioed cartoon apple-man that bore a striking resemblance to Mr. Potato Head. The duration of the meeting would then be devoted to wading through the voluminous set of slides, with the usual outcome being an agreement to set up a follow-up meeting so that the issues raised by the slides could be further discussed.

This merry-go-round pattern of meetings immediately began to grate on PayPal employees. Whereas our company's e-mail-centric culture had provided us with long stretches of unscheduled time to reply to messages, brainstorm new ideas, and otherwise address pressing issues, eBay meeting requests soon began to fill our calendars as our days were spent driving the thirty minute route between the two offices. (Fortunately, as word spread at eBay that PayPal's office boasted a kitchenette with free snacks, an increasing number of their delegations consented to holding meetings at our building.)

The cultural differences between the two companies weren't limited to eBay's Byzantine meeting protocols. The auction company's employees were typically two or three years older than their PayPal counterparts and more frequently had degrees from business schools. Yet in spite of their education and experience, even my director-level peers generally seemed reluctant to take any action, no matter how trivial, without first unleashing a meeting blitzkrieg or at least checking in for a supervisor's approval. In one instance, our marketing delegation suggested sending a simple e-mail update on the merger to our users; our counterparts, unsettled that this item wasn't on the officially approved marketing calendar, insisted that we hold off so they could figure out how to approach senior management for a decision. Our team ended up discarding the minor project in frustration.

Unfortunately it soon became apparent that this divide extended beyond the middle-managers and rank-and-file employees of the two companies to the management teams, as well. The informality and willingness to delegate power down to subordinates that PayPal's executives displayed was not evident on the other side of the aisle. Their approach more closely mirrored Meg Whitman's demeanor during her speech the day of the acquisition announcement. While reassuring and not condescending, Whitman came across as formal—almost prim— when compared to the easygoing and approachable Peter.

A generation gap could partially explain this divergence. EBay's senior executives—including Whitman, then forty-five; CTO Maynard Webb, forty-six; and eBay U.S. President Jeff Jordan, forty-three—were born at the tail end of the Baby Boom and were on average fifteen years older than their respective PayPal counterparts Peter, Max, and Sacks.

As part of the Baby Boom generation, it wasn't surprising that eBay's executives presided over a corporate culture that kept their Generation X subordinates on a short leash. Boomers and Gen X often struggle to coexist in the modern workplace, and polls suggest that a significant majority of Boomers consider their younger counterparts to be less trustworthy and knowledgeable than their generation.[13] While a generational dichotomy is certainly not a new societal phenomenon, in the case of the business world, it can be a self-serving one. When the Boomers finally replaced their parents on the highest rungs of the corporate ladder, they looked down to see a younger, more tech-savvy generation in close pursuit. Of course, whether or not that was the reason that eBay's Boomer managers structured their company as they did is anyone's guess, but the generation gap between the two management teams was too obvious to overlook. We could only hope that it wouldn't be a source of conflict later on.

◊

As the integration process wore on, I wasn't the only person to notice the cultural gap between PayPal and eBay. My PayPal coworkers certainly did, and many of our future eBay colleagues commented on it, as well. Even Whitman herself later publicly acknowledged that it was not easy putting together these two companies with their different cultures.[14] It came as no surprise that Whitman was not blind to the importance of culture in making a merger work—recall that similar concerns contributed to eBay rejecting Yahoo's acquisition offer in early-2000.

And yet both sides pressed on in spite of these obvious differences. With the Spitzers of the world nipping at our heels, PayPal had a strong incentive to go through with the deal, and our management team remained confident that we would be allowed a fair amount of autonomy following its completion. And eBay, for its part, seemed less concerned with cultural rifts this time than it did with the Yahoo offer (of course, the difference being that this time eBay was the one doing the acquiring).

On the whole, this look under eBay's hood certainly helped explain why Billpoint had been unable to match PayPal's innovations over the years—our nimbler processes, combined with talented personnel who were encouraged to think boldly, had translated into a competitive edge. These traits manifested themselves in the form of faster product development cycles and well-synchronized campaigns.

Although eBay's culture had hindered the company's ability to compete with PayPal, eBay evidently was a swifter, more entrepreneurial place when it launched under the guidance of Pierre Omidyar. When Whitman assumed control, she implemented a practice of hiring

MBAs and former consultants and the company began to change.[15] Written accounts of its early days, corroborated by conversations I had with many of my eBay counterparts, lent credence to this hypothesis. Whether or not it's correct, Omidyar's brilliant online service—the beneficiary of first-mover advantage—snowballed and continued to pick up speed, oblivious to any bureaucratic transformation being implemented by the company's management.

Enjoying a monopolist's clout meant that eBay no longer had to rely on innovation to generate growth—foreign acquisitions expanded the company's worldwide reach while the domestic part of the business was placed on autopilot. Hence, when PayPal's unexpected appearance complicated eBay's plans to graft an in-house payment service onto Omidyar's platform, the company found itself ill-prepared to respond. Instead of seeking to replicate PayPal's entrepreneurial swiftness and compete with us by focusing on feature development, the auction giant periodically tried to wield its market power to reach the same ends.

Since eBay had been decentralized and entrepreneurial up until a few years earlier, it raised the question as to whether PayPal would come to look more like eBay over time. The acquisition made that a possibility, but as I got to know my new eBay colleagues I concluded that PayPal, if left to its own devices, probably would not come to act like the auction giant. While our company had become more corporate-like and process-driven as it matured—enough to drive out some free-spirited innovators like Luke and Paul—it had not abandoned its core culture. The spirit of ownership and the willingness to encourage debate remained in place across the organization. Procedural red tape may have slowed our ability to innovate, but unlike eBay our decision-making had not become centralized and our employees did not feel obliged to be overly deferential to management. Time, it would seem, had less to do with the companies' cultural differences than did their leadership.

In early September eBay's management team gave us a surprise reminiscent of some of their earlier Billpoint campaigns. Whitman announced through the media that she had shuffled her top staff and Matt Bannick, the head of eBay's international division, was to become the new senior vice president for global online payments. EBay's press release indicated that Bannick, a soft-spoken former McKinsey consultant and U.S. diplomat, would ostensibly be responsible for shutting down Billpoint and working with Peter to integrate PayPal.[16]

The news came as a rude awakening. Peter had not been informed of the decision ahead of time, and, public statements aside, Bannick clearly was not going to be moved out of the prominent post of running international operations just to oversee two payments-related projects set to be completed within six months. Quite the contrary, this would most likely be a permanent position for Bannick, whom the Silicon Valley gossip mill was already beginning to mention as Jeff Jordan's chief contender to become Whitman's heir.

The move stunned Sacks, who now faced an unexpected rival in the form of a Whitman lieutenant in his campaign to secure the top spot at PayPal. Both Whitman and Bannick insisted that there was no unspoken motive behind this shuffle, but everyone in our office knew better. Many of our managers began to look for ways to lobby for Sacks, and a few even circulated an eleventh hour petition to make sure Whitman knew where their sympathies lied. But it was too little, too late—eBay's last second maneuvering came at a point when the acquisition process was too far along for our management team to back out even if it wanted to.

The handwriting was on the wall for my friend and mentor David Sacks.

◊

"We will now attend to the one formal item of business to be addressed at today's meeting," said Peter Thiel, seated at a table in front of several rows of shareholders perched on folding chairs at PayPal's old offices on Embarcadero Road. "The only proposal properly brought before this meeting is to approve and adopt the agreement and plan of merger among eBay Inc. and PayPal Inc.

"Since notice was duly given and a quorum is present, a motion calling for a vote on this proposal will now be received."

I raised my hand and responded, "I so move." With those words I heralded the counting of the vote that ushered in the end of PayPal as an independent company.

Vince Sollitto had asked me the day before to be a plant in the audience to make the motion at the shareholders' meeting. The October 3 meeting was just a formality—the outcome of the vote was a foregone conclusion thanks to proxy votes that started arriving in the mail even before Whitman stunned us with her personnel moves. The final tally recorded "yay" votes representing 65% of the total outstanding shares, or an overwhelming 99% of the shares that cast a vote.[17]

When the board's inspector of elections announced the voting results, Peter gaveled PayPal out of existence: "I hereby declare that the proposal to approve and adopt the agreement and plan of merger has been approved."

That afternoon brought word to my desk of Peter Thiel's resignation and the appointment of Matt Bannick as PayPal's CEO. I grimaced upon hearing this predictable news, and, rather than let my mind dwell on it, reluctantly set out to fulfill my duties as PayPal's head of marketing integration. I trudged upstairs to tell the design team to remove Peter's name from the "About Us" section of the Web site while also placing "An eBay Company" logo at the bottom of every page. The content manager cried as I discreetly whispered the instructions. I knew exactly how she felt.

◊

David Sacks announced his departure a few days after the deal closed. He invited me to his office to break the news. Sitting behind a nearly barren desk and in-between stacks of packed boxes, the typically self-assured Sacks looked down at his feet as he mumbled a few words encouraging me to remain with the company. We glumly mused over all the good times we had shared together over the past three years, and I tried to lift his spirits by suggesting that another great adventure for all of us might be just around the corner. He smiled but from the look in his eyes he didn't seem to think so.

Sacks's departure opened the floodgates. Within a few months an exodus of talent followed him out the door, most notably the senior executive team of Max Levchin, Roelof Botha, and Reid Hoffman. And they were just the beginning. Vince Sollitto, our grizzled head of PR; Ken Howery, my Stanford friend; Mark Woolway and Jack Selby, Peter's fundraising experts; Keith Rabois, our head of business development; and a dozen other bright and talented individuals joined them in leaving behind PayPal, an eBay company, for greener pastures.

EBay did little to stop the personnel flight. On the contrary, at the same time that many of our most gifted and entrepreneurial people fled the company, Bannick shipped over a bumper crop of eBay personnel to replace them. And with the replacements came a host of new processes, revised org charts, and the advent of the PowerPoint culture—that is to say, an endless parade of meetings accompanied by an endless show of slides. It was as if the entire scenario had itself been scripted out ahead of time. Just as Whitman knew what she was doing by waiting until the last-minute to appoint Bannick to the global online payments job prior to the merger, so too she knew that a little turnover would quickly remake PayPal's culture in eBay's image.

Watching the company's formerly entrepreneurial culture morph into something closer to Andersen's than Confinity's while also seeing many good people depart made my choice easy. I left PayPal in June 2003 after serving as the interim vice president of global marketing following a reorganization. Even though I'd had a successful tenure under the new management team and had established a good working relationship with the likable Bannick, I opted not to pursue the permanent VP position. Assuming the stable role of a well-paid manager at a big company—what I had envisioned as my ultimate career goal before I joined PayPal—now seemed unthinkable.

Once you've become an entrepreneur, there's no turning back.

CONCLUSION

IN SPITE OF THE MASS EXODUS of talented personnel from PayPal, the combination of eBay and PayPal seems to have energized the short-run financial results of both companies. Revenue from PayPal and eBay soared in the quarters following the merger, thanks to an increase in PayPal's auction volume caused by its integration, which likewise sped up inventory turnover on eBay as money moved much faster. This mutual acceleration strengthened the hands of both the auction giant and its new payment subsidiary.

EBay cemented its position as a monopolist in the person-to-person transactions marketplace. Despite rumblings that search engine Google will find a way to compete in online shopping, eBay commanded 94% of all traffic to auction sites by the second half of 2003.[1] In early-2004 eBay raised its U.S. listing fees for the first time since Yahoo's auction collapse three years earlier; the hike ranged between 9% and 45% depending on the auction's starting price.[2] EBay moved $7 billion in merchandise in the last quarter of 2003—or three-and-a-half times as much as Amazon[3]—making it the undisputed king of Internet sales.

And following the shut down of Billpoint, PayPal looks more dominant than ever. The subsidiary posted a net income in the range of $70-$110 million in 2003. By the end of that year, PayPal had negotiated a deal to become a payment option for CyberSource online merchants, launched a new Web site for users in the United Kingdom, and recorded its 40 millionth user.[4] No doubt these resounding successes helped convince Citigroup, PayPal's last significant person-to-person payments competitor, to throw in the towel and shutter C2it's doors.[5] Yet even this heady string of successes still leaves unanswered the question as to whether PayPal will be able to fulfill the vision its founders laid out for it.

For one thing, PayPal's regulatory woes persist following the acquisition. In March 2004, PayPal's recurring nemesis Eliot Spitzer badgered eBay, Inc., into paying a $150,000 fine because he felt the service's user agreement wasn't clear enough.[6] At the same time, the FTC initiated an investigation into PayPal's practice of temporarily freezing accounts involved in suspicious activities.[7] Add to that the costs of complying with recent federal money laundering requirements and it becomes obvious that government regulation will continue to pose a risk to PayPal into the foreseeable future.[8]

Regulation is only part of the story—recently fraud seems to have reemerged as a challenge. "Phishing" e-mails, spam that poses as official communication from PayPal but redirects the recipient to a counterfeit Web site, have managed to dupe hundreds of unsuspecting users into turning over their passwords in a number of highly publicized incidents.[9] Without the fraud-fighting savvy of Max Levchin, in one instance the company was reduced to distributing panicked warnings ("Your account may be a target for deceptive emails") to customers it thought might have received a fraudulent notice. [10]

Lingering fraud and regulatory problems aside, the post-integration PayPal is certainly better positioned now than it was during its starry-eyed startup days to revolutionize money transfers and wrest control of currencies away from corrupt governments. Whether or not it will follow the path to what Confinity's entrepreneurs playfully called "world domination" is not clear.

Such an observation flows in part from the fact that, in spite of the merger, eBay's objectives aren't the same as PayPal's. While they share millions of customers, eBay is a closed trading platform that profits from growth confined to its site but PayPal facilitates transactions all over the Internet. Without doubt PayPal's decentralized potential will prove unsettling to some at eBay looking for ways to grow their maturing platform. Should there come a time when Whitman's team must choose between committing resources and crafting policies to promote growth on eBay proper or strengthening PayPal's non-eBay business, it's not obvious which they would pick. Reports indicate that some members of Whitman's executive team as well as eBay's board opposed the PayPal purchase.[11] Jeff Jordan, who did support the acquisition, displayed a hint of a "we bought PayPal for the benefit of eBay" outlook in a public statement when he likened the purchase of PayPal to eBay regaining control over its own shopping cart.[12] Then there is eBay's sub par record of managing domestic acquisitions. Billpoint is closed, Half.com is being phased out, and the high-end auction house Butterfields was sold for a purported loss three years after eBay acquired it.[13] Considered together, these factors aren't exactly encouraging.

If the "PayPal is our shopping cart" mentality triumphs within eBay, it's clear that developing PayPal for uses other than auctions will not become an organizational priority. Hopefully such pessimism is misplaced and eBay's intelligent executives, realizing that PayPal's ultimate potential might dwarf even their auction site's, will adopt the vision that Peter and Max first hatched. If eBay labors to build a consumer-empowering way of moving money instead of a glorified auction shopping cart, the positive consequences for people around the world could be profound. Whether a fully developed PayPal will ultimately succeed in plying the control of currencies away from corrupt governments is unclear, but it certainly would give middle- and lower-income citizens worldwide more power over their own finances than they ever had before.

Regardless of Meg Whitman's ultimate vision for PayPal, the fact remains that the sell-out was ultimately the best decision for PayPal and all of its stakeholders. The millions of buyers and sellers who depended on PayPal for their online transactions certainly benefited from having the roadblocks to using PayPal on eBay's site removed. Employees should be able to invest more time in developing skills rather than putting out fires thanks to a stable work environment with fewer competitive crises. And shareholders have removed a large amount of risk from their portfolios while enjoying strong returns as share prices for the combined company rose by 150% in the year and a half following the merger.

This is not to say there are no drawbacks to the acquisition, but I think any fair analysis would conclude that the combination of competitive and non-competitive perils facing PayPal decisively tipped the scale in favor of selling the company. Had we not, it's impossible to say what shape PayPal would be in today, but the odds are it would be worse than the prosperous status quo.

◊

The wide array of threats, many of them non-competitive, that PayPal faced during my three and one-half years there suggest some disconcerting conclusions about the broader environment in which modern entrepreneurs must operate.

The regulatory system turned out to be perhaps the greatest obstacle for our young business. Once PayPal became a publicly traded company, regulators seemed willing to pursue their own agendas whenever the laws were murky. Louisiana's threat to ban PayPal when it couldn't determine how to classify us and the charges over gaming leveled by Eliot Spitzer and the U.S. Attorney from Missouri demonstrate this point. In each case PayPal thought it was obeying existing statutes, but after we became a high-profile company these officials opted to interpret vague laws in a way that justified meting out punishment. From our perspective, many regulators seemed more interested in adding another notch to their belts than in protecting consumers. The regulatory environment surrounding online gambling in particular eventually grew so uncertain that PayPal endorsed the Leach bill in the hope that Congress would finally provide clear rules for companies and regulatory agencies alike.

The legal system wasn't much better. While the courts, like regulators, are a critical institution in keeping the wheels of capitalism turning, today's version seems ominously hostile to people starting a business. As was the case with regulators, we had few legal troubles in the company's first three years of existence, but as soon as we filed for an IPO that situation changed dramatically. A number of intellectual property disputes—including CertCo, Tumbleweed, and later Bank One and AT&T[14]—were leveled against the company, as were the aforementioned host of class-action suits. Without addressing the merits of these individual cases, the timeline suggests that PayPal's success was a major factor behind these complaints. Companies holding broad patents and trial lawyers specializing in class actions must have seen easy money when they looked at PayPal, and without laws to discourage frivolous lawsuits there was nothing to deter them.

Unfortunately there were other external threats beyond regulators and litigation. Along the way we encountered a number of other institutions that proved to have less than ideal calibrations for the purpose of promoting entrepreneurship:

- Shifting monetary policy and a general lack of transparency at the Federal Reserve has riled capital markets in the past and likely contributed to the stock market run-up in the late-nineties and collapse in 2000; such periods of uncertainty make it difficult for entrepreneurs to get financing to start and expand their businesses.

- Law enforcement generally seems a step behind in fighting online crime; if your customers are at risk, evidently you'll need to protect them yourself, and if the Russian mafia targets your company, you're the one who's going to have to defend it.

- The business media certainly can often hinder the dissemination of accurate information; its faddish dot-com coverage was too positive before the NASDAQ crash and too negative after it.

In sum, many institutions in modern America combine to make growing a successful entrepreneurial venture even more difficult than it needs to be. And, make no mistake, it's a tough enough road without them. Schumpeter chose the term "creative destruction" to describe the introduction of new innovations into the economy for a reason—as the case of PayPal shows, it's a strife-filled process. A half-dozen startup competitors were quick to follow PayPal's lead before eBay got in on the act. And that's just representatives of the so-called new economy. The fact that many banks either entered the online payments market directly or lobbied for regulations against it showed that the old guard was not prepared to go silently into the night.

This fierce competition is understandable given the magnitude of the rewards, and it's even socially desirable since it forces companies to move adroitly and respond to their customers' needs. Entrepreneurs starting new ventures have to be prepared to deal with competition—it comes with the territory. But demanding that entrepreneurs also deal with capricious regulators, opportunistic lawsuits, unstable capital markets, and outdated law enforcement is just asking for trouble.

For the past half-century, and the last twenty years in particular, America's economic system has been the world's most dynamic. It's created a host of new industries while shedding old ones, all the while promoting rising standards of living and keeping the nation competitive in the global economy. And yet it's not clear that we can sustain this dynamism without addressing many of the problems that eventually confronted PayPal. If the regulatory system is allowed to become more obtuse, the legal environment more litigious, the capital markets more unstable, and law enforcement less effective, at some point the combined effect is going to overwhelm the efforts of even the most bright and dedicated entrepreneurs. At that point we would have effectively destroyed "creative destruction."

Hopefully this won't come to pass. If lawmakers at the federal and state levels simplify and clarify their laws, the increased certainty would improve the regulatory environment. Tort reform can bring unmerited lawsuits under control. Clear monetary policy pronouncements and investor-friendly tax policies will promote the long-run stability of capital markets. Modernization of law enforcement, coupled with a willingness to partner with companies knowledgeable in security issues like PayPal, will help reduce crimes targeted at businesses and their consumers. And the business media—well, there may be no way to fix that one. Hopefully heightened awareness of faddish reporting will help promote balance in the business press much the same way that Bernie Goldberg's book *Bias* promoted scrutiny of the political press, but beyond that I won't hold my breath.

Fortunately, as anti-business as today's environment can be, there's still one surefire way for entrepreneurs to attempt to cope: hire the best people and empower them. PayPal's original team of entrepreneurs might not have taken the company to the point of global currency liberation as they had hoped, but they still managed to go a lot further than most of the outside world ever expected. Peter, Max, and Sacks accomplished this by leveraging a diverse set of intelligent people whom they trusted to work hard on behalf of the company. Sometimes it was a messy process, and it was almost always turbulent, but in the end it worked well.

The PayPal diaspora has moved on to do amazing things. As a *Forbes* reporter noted in a profile of PayPal's alumni, "maybe there was something in the beer at Fanny & Alexander's,"[15] referencing a bar near Confinity's office on University Ave.

Peter Thiel moved his hedge fund, Clarium Capital, to San Francisco and recruited some of PayPal's brightest—including Ken Howery, Jack Selby, and Mark Woolway—to join him. Peter and Ken later joined with Luke Nosek to create the Founders Fund, a high tech venture fund. Max Levchin started Slide, a company that lets users make digital slide shows. David Sacks created Room 9 Entertainment, a movie production company; his first feature film was *Thank You for Smoking*.

Reid Hoffman and Keith Rabois are the CEO and vice president, respectively, of LinkedIn, a professional networking Web site. Roelof Botha is a partner for Sequoia Capital. Elon Musk is the CEO of SpaceX, a firm developing low-cost space rockets. Paul Martin concluded his studies at Stanford and started an online baby products store named Noss Galen. Chad Hurley and Steve Chen founded online video-hosting service YouTube. Vince Sollitto is a spokesman for California Governor Arnold Schwarzenegger.

David Wallace started a private Christian school named Veritas Academy. JoAnne Rockower is doing marketing for Shop.com. Jeremy Stoppleman and Russel Simmons founded Yelp. Ryan Donahue started the online local advertising company HourTown. Chris Gregory is studying at business school, and Premal Shah is the president at micro-finance lender Kiva. Skye Lee started a fashion accessory company named Skye Lee Designs. Dave McClure helped found the job search site SimplyHired, and Damon Billian later joined the company as a community marketer.

Even with this exceptional cast, Earth versus Palo Alto was no easy contest. While we were not able, in our limited tenure, to fully transform PayPal into the Microsoft of payments, we created a multibillion dollar company, built a highly lucrative business model while most dot-coms went bust, and empowered millions around the globe to move money with the click of a mouse. It may not be "world domination," but, then again, it's not half bad.

AFTERWORD:
GOOGLE CHALLENGES PAYPAL

GOOGLE'S CORPORATE MOTTO may be "don't be evil," and the search engine's offbeat, non-threatening brand may be known worldwide, but no company in Silicon Valley is more feared. And as the Internet era enters its second decade, a confrontation between Google and eBay is in the works, with PayPal in the center of the storm.

As I write this, Google is easily the world's most influential and powerful dot-com. By mid-2006, Google accounted for a staggering 59% of all online searches in the U.S., dwarfing second place Yahoo's 22% market share.[1] Google's extensive ad network powered its revenue to $2.5 billion in the second quarter of 2006, a 77% increase over the prior year,[2] putting the company on track to book $10 billion annually—an astounding amount for a company that was started about the same time as PayPal. Google's rapid revenue growth has caused its stock to soar nearly 300% in the two years since its IPO.

Google's servers have indexed not just millions of pages of content on the Web, but also images, maps, blogs, books, and even videos. By the end of 2005, the company claimed to have indexed over 8 billion pages of content.[3] Google's phenomenal success at cataloguing most of the information known to mankind has prompted a reverent Thomas Friedman—the mustachioed *New York Times* columnist never known to downplay his own importance—to ask, "Is Google God?"[4]

Just as Peter Thiel and Max Levchin understood that people around the globe had an unmet need to move money, Larry Page and Sergey Brin answered a need when they created a search engine that empowers people to find information. And while Google has soared in the two years since I wrote the first edition of this book, PayPal's corporate parent has found itself struggling to replicate its past success.

eBay Inc. booked $1.4 billion in revenue for the second quarter of 2006—a healthy increase of 30% over the prior year, but just 1% over the previous quarter and far below Google's $2.5 billion figure. Growth rates for eBay have slowed over the past couple of years as its core U.S. auction business has matured. In fact, U.S. marketplace revenue posted its first ever quarter-over-quarter decline, slumping from $507 million in Q1 to $490 million.[5] To demonstrate how sharply eBay and Google's paths have diverged, in Q3 2004 both companies had nearly identical revenue totals of $806 million, and since that time Google's share price has quadrupled while eBay's has declined by about 40%.

Some of eBay's slowdown can be attributed to Google's success. The vast majority of the search engine's revenue is from its keyword advertising service, which places clickable classifieds on Google's own Web site as well as those of millions of affiliates. As this new technology has grown to universal acceptance, it has offered a new sales channel to small- and medium-sized merchants, in effect allowing them to sell from their own online stores without having to pay the auction giant a commission approaching 10%. In other words, eBay's former monopolistic might, which crushed Yahoo Auctions just a few years before, now appears to be faltering under a volley of "creative destruction" from Google.

Fortunately for eBay, PayPal has been a bright spot. The one-time startup that bled $10 million per month now has growth rates far in excess of its acquirer's flagship U.S. site, and during some quarters it has even outpaced eBay's foreign growth—an amazing accomplishment given that U.S. auction transactions remain a major subset of PayPal's total volume and thus weigh down its growth rates. The subsidiary contributed $659 million in revenue to eBay during the first half of 2006, a 38% increase over the same period in 2005. PayPal had also soared to 114 million registered users by mid-2006, making those recollections of Confinity's World Domination Index seem quaint, indeed.

But now Google has ostensibly trained its sites on PayPal. The search engine recently unveiled its own online payment service, Google Checkout, to positive reviews. An analysis of the new service prompted a Citibank analyst to chop his target price for eBay shares from $51 to $40 after concluding that Google Checkout was "faster, easier, and less expensive than PayPal."[6] The analyst also added a telling criticism: "As we see it, this speaks volumes about Google product development skills and PayPal's lack of innovation."

This challenge comes at a bad time for PayPal. Most of the deep bench of talent recruited by Thiel, Levchin, and David Sacks has departed, leaving behind eBay's PowerPoint culture for greener pastures. And yet eBay has found it hard to retain even its home-grown talent. In July 2006, Jeff Jordan, the replacement to Matt Bannick as PayPal's president in 2005 and Meg Whitman's long-time presumed successor, announced that he would be leaving the company to euphemistically spend more time with his family.[7] The loss of the aggressive and product-focused Jordan—who ultimately adopted a broader view of PayPal's potential than his earlier "shopping cart" comment suggested—has rightly been called a blow for eBay. Whitman announced she was making her former CFO, Rajiv Dutta, PayPal's fourth president in four years.

While product innovation alone probably won't overcome PayPal's network effect, Google Checkout does have a massive advantage going for it that Citibank's C2it and Yahoo's PayDirect lacked: Google's ad network. Google AdWords provides Checkout with a large installed base of merchants (both advertisers and affiliates), and its continued growth also serves to weaken PayPal's largest market (eBay's auction platform). This double-edged sword ensures that Google Checkout could be PayPal's greatest challenge yet.

Lest anyone thinks that Google—a company with a somewhat geeky image—would hesitate to wage a tough-as-nails competitive war with PayPal, I'll point out that the search engine that once leased Confinity's old office at 165 University Avenue didn't turn its name into a verb by luck alone. It's done it through innovation—and, at times, being just a little ruthless.

Google certainly didn't let its "don't be evil" motto get in the way of one decision to expand its business. In 2005, Google cut a deal with China's totalitarian government to open a Beijing office and launch a new Chinese language site at Google.cn.[8] In return for being allowed access to the millions of Chinese internet users surfing the Web behind the government's national firewall of censorship, Google agreed to block Chinese searches on terms such as "democracy," "religion," "Tibet," and the persecuted religious group "Falun Gong."[9]

While Google is sadly not the only Silicon Valley search engine that's censoring information in return for the Chinese communists' blessing, it is the only one refusing to cooperate with the Justice Department of its own country. When the U.S. government—attempting to comply with a court demand to determine if the Child Online Protection Act (COPA) signed by President Clinton is constitutional—asked several tech companies for anonymous search data, AOL, Yahoo, and Microsoft were able to work out deals that protected their users' anonymity.

Google didn't bother. Instead, it rejected the government's request, opting to fight the matter out in the courts.[10]

(Google's refusal to cooperate with the Bush Administration might have more to do with politics than ethics. Google's management appears to be overwhelmingly left-wing. A study by WorldNet-Daily.com showed that all but six of approximately two hundred political donations by Google employees over a four year period went to Democrats or liberal organizations. CEO Eric Schmidt gave $100,000 to the Democratic National Committee, as well as contributions to Hillary Clinton and John Kerry.[11])

Regardless of one's opinion of Google's decision to cooperate with Beijing communists and stonewall a benign Justice Department request, it should be clear that the company is no pushover. It has talent, momentum, and moxie to spare.

This doesn't mean that a clash between Google Checkout and Pay-Pal is inevitable. On August 28, 2006, eBay and Google agreed to an advertising deal that calls for Google to provide text ads on eBay's foreign Web sites and for the two companies to collaborate on a "click to call" service.[12] But this data point also doesn't indicate that a détente is in the works, either, especially since eBay and Yahoo recently signed a cooperation agreement that intended to hedge their risk against a ubiquitous Google.[13]

Will Google finally be the challenge that topples PayPal? Can the payments network that was built with $10 referral bonuses and auction buttons withstand the challenge of a ruthless 800 pound cyber-gorilla? Only time will tell. Let's hope that the free market, unleashing its gales of "creative destruction," is the factor that ultimately decides the outcome.

— Eric M. Jackson, September 2006

NOTES

Introduction

1. For a concise summary of Schumpeter's life and works, see his entry in the Library of Economics and Liberty's encyclopedia at http://www.econlib.org/library/Enc/bios/Schumpeter.html. Schumpeter's original explanation of "creative destruction" can be found in his book *Capitalism, Socialism, and Democracy* (New York: HarperPerennial, 1976), 81-86.

Chapter 1

1. Lillington, "PayPal Puts Dough in Your Palm," *Wired*, July 27, 1999, http://www.wired.com/news/technology/0,1282,20958,00.html; *International Herald Tribune*, "Briefly: Money Beamer," July 29, 1999, http://www.iht.com/IHT/TECH/tek072999a.html.

2. For a detailed account of how Andersen's focus on growing its consulting business led to the company's involvement in the Enron, Global Crossing, and WorldCom scandals, see Barbara Ley Toffler, *Final Accounting: Ambition, Greed, and the Fall of Arthur Andersen*, (New York, Broadway Books, 2003).

3. Ian Fried, "A Building Blessed with Tech Success," *CNET News.com*, October 4, 2002, http://news.com.com/2100-1040-960790.html.

4. Yardena Arar, "Beam Me Up Some Money, Scotty," *PC World*, November 15, 1999, http://www.pcworld.com/news/article/0,aid,13788,00.asp.

5. Rafe Needleman, "You've Got Money!" *The Red Herring*, January 21, 2000, no longer available online.

6. *PR Newswire – PayPal's press release*, "PayPal.com and Star Trek's 'Scotty' Put the Power to Beam Money in the Palm of Your Hand," December 17, 1999, http://www.findarticles.com/ cf_dls/m4PRN/1999_Dec_17/58288542/p1/article.jhtml.

Chapter 2

1. Lisa Branstein, "Former Intuit CEO Harris Joins X.com," *The Wall Street Journal*, December 7, 1999, sec. B12.

2. Ibid.

3. Stephanie AuWerter, "Free, No-Minimum S&P 500 Fund," *SmartMoney.com*, December 8, 1999, no longer available online.

4. Warren Packard, "From the Ground Floor: Metcalfe's Law Has Some Shortcomings, but It's Still a Pretty Good Validator of the Internet Economy," *Red Herring*, August 2000, no longer available online.

5. For an excellent profile on Luke and Max, see *Computer Science Alumni News*, "Max Levchin and Luke Nosek: Pals and PayPals," Winter 2001, http://www.cs.uiuc.edu/news/ alumni/jan01/lev.html.

6. *EBay, Inc. 2002 Annual Report*, 22.

7. Listings, site traffic, and industry sales data from Wolverton, "Everyone's an

Auctioneer," *News.com*, December 27, 1999, http://news.com.com/2100-1017_3-234885.html; market share data from Sandoval, "Hobby Site Aims to Grab Some of eBay's Glory," *News.com*, November 16, 1999, http://news.com.com/2100-1017-233120.html? legacy=cnet.

8. Cited in various sources. For the most complete and compelling account, see Adam Cohen, *The Perfect Store: Inside eBay* (New York: Little, Brown, and Company, 2002), 5-9, 23-25.

9. These are two of the five core values that Omidyar posted on eBay's Web site. For a lengthy discussion of these values, refer to the commencement address that Omidyar and his wife, Pam, delivered at Tufts University on May 19, 2002, available at http://enews. tufts.edu/stories/052002Omidyar_Pierre_keynote.htm.

10. Wolverton, "Everyone's an Auctioneer."

11. DotBank revamped its referral policy to give users a special auxiliary balance of $500 that could only be used for sending money to non-users. If the intended recipient of the funds decided to create an account, he could retain the funds. However, users could only send up to $5 from this auxiliary balance to any given individual, and unlike the PayPal and X.com services the person making the referral could not earn a bonus.

12. Tim Clark, "EBay Acquires Two Firms," *News.com*, May 18, 1999, http://news.com. com/2100-1017_3-226031.html.

13. Cohen, *The Perfect Store*, 186-187.

14. Ibid, 94-95, 191.

15. Internet Archive query of "payme.com," http://www.archive.org.

16. *Idealab.com*, Web site, http://www.idealab.com/about/index.tp.

17. Troy Wolverton, "Idealab Launches Online Bill Payment Service," *News.com*, Feb. 23, 2000, http://news.com.com/2100-1017-237211.html?legacy=cnet.

Chapter 3

1. Mark Gimein, "Fast Track," *Salon.com*, August 17, 1999, http://www.salon.com/tech/feature/1999/08/17/elon_musk/.

2. Megan Barnett, "Great X-pectations," *The Standard.com*, February 28, 2000, no longer available online.

3. Cohen, *The Perfect Store*, 230.

4. Troy Wolverton, "EBay Gets Set to Accept Credit Cards," *News.com*, January 25, 2000, http://news.com.com/2100-1017_3-236079.html.

5. *PR Newswire - EBay press release*, "EBay and Wells Fargo Join Forces to Create the Standard for Person-to-Person Payment on the Internet," March 1, 2000, http://investor. ebay.com/releases.cfm?Year=2000.

6. Corcoran, "Merger Unites Online Payment Systems," *Forbes.com*, March 3, 2000, http://www.forbes.com/2000/03/03/mu2.html; Dennehey, "X.com, PayPal Merge," *AuctionWatch.com Daily News*, March 2, 2000, no longer available online.

7. Cohen, *The Perfect Store*, 238.

8. *PR Newswire - Yahoo press release*, "Yahoo! Plans to Offer Person-to-Person Payment Solution to Buyers and Sellers," March 23, 2000, http://docs.yahoo.com/docs/pr/release496.html.

9. *PR Newswire - Bank One press release*, "I'll Send It Through eMoneyMail.com," March 8, 2000, http://www.marketwire.com/mw/release_clickthrough?release_id=5722&

category=Technology.

10. *PR Newswire - GMoney press release*, "GMoney.com Launches Online Money-Management Tool with a Splash," March 15, 2000, no longer available online. (I've read this press release a dozen times and I still can't figure out what the point of the bikes was.)

11. Troy Wolverton, "PayMyBills.com Pays Up for PayMe.com," *News.com*, April 12, 2000, http://news.com.com/2100-1017_3-239187.html.

12. *PR Newswire - X.com press release*, "X.com Surpasses One Million Customer Mark," April 5, 2000, no longer available online.

13. Adam Feuerstein, "X.com Raises $100 Million," *Upside Today*, April 5, 2000, no longer available online.

14. Jim Seymour, "The Perils of Betting on 'Concept Companies,'" *TheStreet.com*, http://www.thestreet.com/pf/comment/techsavvy/1139783.html. This story is also delightfully told by Michael Lewis in his classic Silicon Valley tale *The New New Thing*, (New York: Penguin Books, 2000), 91-101.

15. Sam Ames, "Earnings Season May Stabilize Jittery Markets," *News.com*, April 10, 2000, http://news.com.com/2100-1023_3-239062.html.

16. For a recent history of the federal funds target rate, see Federal Reserve Monitor, *The Wall Street Journal*, http://online.wsj.com/documents/mktindex.htm?fedwatch.htm.

17. *Price Waterhouse Coopers*, "Money Tree Survey", http://www.pwcmoneytree.com.

Chapter 4

1. Troy Wolverton, "EBay, Visa Partner in Bill-Pay Deal," *News.com*, March 29, 2000, http://news.com.com/2100-1017_3-238576.html.

2. *The Nilson Report*, August 2002, 8. For the year 2001 Visa accounted for about 52% of all US credit card payments in dollars, compared to 29% for MasterCard and 13% for American Express.

3. Cited publicly in various sources, including Cohen, *The Perfect Store*, 229.

4. Jupiter Media Metrix reports that 70% of online retailers fail to resolve customer service problems within six hours, and 48% of online-only services take more than three days to respond to e-mails. Also see Tiffany Kary, "Online retailers fumble on customer care," *News.com*, Jan. 3, 2002, http://news.com.com/2100-1017-801668.html?legacy=cnet.

5. Ed Ritchie, "Growing Pains for X.com, PayPal," *AuctionWatch Daily*, May 19, 2000, no longer available online.

6. ECircles and AllAdvantage closed shop after the bubble burst, and eGroups became another Yahoo acquisition and eventually was stripped to a shell of its former self.

7. While the debuts of many new eBay features have been promoted by free listing days, to my knowledge this is the only example in eBay's history when it held three such days in a one month interval. I estimate that these three promotions cost eBay $400,000 - $500,000 in contra-revenue charges.

8. *Associated Press*, "California Company to Employ 500 in Omaha," March 27, 2000, http://www.theindependent.com/stories/032700/new_omahajobs27.html.

9. Glenn Simpson and Rudy Kleysteuber, "Dot-Com Firms Learn to Play the Political Finance Game," *The Wall Street Journal*, June 6, 2000, http://online.wsj.com/PA2VJBNA4R/snippet/0,,SB960247331541322798-search,00.html.

10. Alice LePlante, "Zipping Along," *Upside.com*, September 22, 1998, no longer available online.

11. Megan Barnett, "X.com CEO Gets the Boot," *The Industry Standard*, May 16, 2000, no longer available online.

12. *Red Herring*, "The Red Herring 100 Company Profiles," June 2000, 188.

Chapter 5

1. *PayPal secondary offering prospectus*, June 21, 2002, 76.

2. An odd justification, given that Paul's message dealt with a policy clarification that impacted many of eBay's own users. Over the years I observed some of PayPal's smaller competitors blatantly using eBay's boards to shill for their service without apparent repercussions.

3. Martha Woodall, "Launch Weekend a 'Whirlwind' for Half.com," *The Philadelphia Inquirer*, January 24, 2000, http://corp.half.com/pressfiles/phillydailynews01242000.html.

4. Cohen, *The Perfect Store*, 234-235; McCaffery, "EBay Goes All the Way with Half.com," *Fool.com*, June 14, 2000, http://www.fool.com/news/2000/breakfast000614.htm.

5. Holden Lewis, "Paying Online with a Person-to-Person Service is Uncharted Territory: Beware the Scammer!" *Bankrate.com*, August 1, 2000, http://www.bankrate.com/brm/news/ob/20000801.asp.

Chapter 6

1. For example: Sandoval, "PayPal's Outages Disrupt eBay Auctions," *News.com*, May 18, 2000, no longer available online; Ritchie, "Growing Pains for X.com, PayPal," *AuctionWatch Daily*, May 19, 2000, no longer available online.

2. *PayPal IPO prospectus*, January 18, 2002, 10.

3. *PayPal secondary offering prospectus*, June 21, 2002, 71.

4. Adam Feuerstein, "X.com Raises $30 million, Plots Overseas Expansion," *Upside Today*, August 29, 2000, no longer available online.

5. David Baranowski, "PayPal's Plea for Honesty," *AuctionWatch.com*, September 13, 2000, no longer available online.

6. *PayPal IPO prospectus*, 87.

Chapter 7

1. *PayPal IPO prospectus*, 29.

2. *The Electronic Payment Systems Observatory's (ePSO)*, Web site Profile on PayPal, http://epso.jrc.es (displayed on August 22, 2001). EPSO was a project set up by the European Commission's Directorate General in 2001.

3. *PayPal.com*, PayPal interstitial page titled "Notice: New Credit Card Limit for Personal Accounts" (displayed ca. October 3, 2000).

4. Greg Sandoval, "PayPal Cracks Down on Business Customers," *News.com*, October 4, 2000, http://news.com.com/2100-1017-246627.html?legacy=cnet.

5. Christine Costanzo, "Billpoint Sees an Opportunity as Rival PayPal Initiates Fees," *American Banker*, March 15, 2001, http://cma.zdnet.com/texis/techinfobase/+-wo_qos+_8XsXK/cdisplay.html.

6. Penelope Patsuris, "AOL, Citigroup Bid for Web Payment Standard," *Forbes.com*, July 19, 2000, http://www.forbes.com/2000/07/19/feat2.html.

7. Erich Luening, "Citigroup Gets into Online Payment Service Game," *News.com*, October 31, 2000, http://news.com.com/2100-1017-247879.html.

8. Trombly, "Citigroup Launches New E-Cash Service," *ComputerWorld*, October 31, 2000, http://www.computerworld.com/industrytopics/financial/story/0,10801,53153,00. html; Kharif, "Why Citi Is a Credit Card Cannibal," *Business Week Online*, November 16, 2000, http://www.businessweek.com/bwdaily/dnflash/nov2000/nf20001116_ 630.htm; Moore, "Citigroup to Push Ecash into Prime Time," *Business 2.0*, November 28, 2000, no longer available online.

9. Greg Sandoval, "X.com Chief to Step Down," *News.com*, October 8, 2000, http://news.com.com/2100-1017-246741.html?legacy=cnet.

10. *PayPal.com*, Industry Awards and Accolades page, http://www.paypal.com/cgi-bin/webscr?cmd=p/gen/awards-outside.

11. Robert Lenzner, "The Messiahs of the Network," *Forbes*, March 8, 1999, no longer available online.

12. Greg Sandoval, "PayPal Cracks Down on Business Customers," *News.com*, October 4, 2000, http://news.com.com/2100-1017-246627.html?legacy=cnet.

13. Greg Sandoval, "Holiday Traffic Jam Leaves PayPal Users Honking Mad," *News.com*, November 28, 2000, http://news.com.com/2100-1017_3-249107.html.

14. Rafe Needleman, "Baby, You Can Crash My Car," *RedHerring.com*, November 17, 2000, no longer available online.

15. It ironically turned out that *The Red Herring*'s business model bore more of a resemblance to Elon's flying McLaren than PayPal's. Flush with advertising money during 1999-2000, the magazine was forced to shrink its staff, size, and publication frequency during the tech decline of the following two years before folding entirely in early-2003.

16. *PR Newswire - PayPal press release*, "PayPal Tops Five Million Users, $1 Billion Moved to Date," December 13, 2000, http://www.paypal.com/html/pr-121300.html.

17. Calculations of losses used in this text are operating losses that exclude the non-cash expenses of amortization and stock-based compensation.

18. Troy Wolverton, "Amazon Auction Sellers Face New Fees, Rules," *News.com*, January 24, 2001, http://news.com.com/2100-1017-251484.html?legacy=cnet.

19. Yahoo figure from Enos, "Fees Cause Yahoo! Auctions to Drop More Than 80 Percent," *E-Commerce Times*, February 13, 2001, http://www.ecommercetimes.com/ perl/story/7444.html; eBay figure from Kany, "Is Yahoo's Move to Fees Risky Business?" *News.com*, January 3, 2001, no longer available online.

20. Tim Clark, "EBay Plays Hardball with Feedback Rating," *News.com*, June 10, 1999, http://news.com.com/2100-1017-226926.html?legacy=cnet.

21. Cohen, *The Perfect Store*, 259.

22. Troy Wolverton and Jeff Pelline, "Yahoo to Charge Auction Fees, Ban Hate Materials," *News.com*, January 2, 2001, http://news.com.com/2100-1017-250452.html? legacy=cnet.

23. Enos, "Fees Cause Yahoo! Auctions to Drop."

24. Troy Wolverton, "EBay Follows Yahoo's Lead with Auction Fees," *News.com*, January 16, 2001, http://news.com.com/2100-1017-251029.html?legacy=cnet.

Chapter 8

1. Lori Enos, "PayPal Scores $90M in Financing," *E-Commerce Times*, March 7, 2001, http://www.ecommercetimes.com/perl/story/7973.html.

2. Andy Roe, "Mr. Thiel Goes to Washington," *AuctionWatch Daily News*, March 28, 2001, no longer available online.

3. *PayPal secondary stock offering prospectus*, 11.

4. For example, TicketMaster uses a similar test on its Web site to prevent would-be scalpers from creating multiple accounts to circumvent its per-user limits for popular events, and Internet domain registration services also employ it to prevent computers from harvesting massive numbers of domain names.

5. Paul Cox, "PayPal and FBI Team Up to Combat Wire Fraud," *The Wall Street Journal Online*, June 21, 2001, http://online.wsj.com/PA2VJBNA4R/snippet/0,,SB992639123 888198275- search,00.html.

6. Ibid. Cox is citing an estimate by the Gartner Group.

7. Steve Bodow, "The Money Shot," *Wired*, September 2001, http://www.wired.com/wired/archive/9.09/paypal.html.

8. *PR Newswire - PayPal press release*, "PayPal, FBI Join Forces to Boost Online Security," May 22, 2001, no longer available online.

9. Cox, "PayPal and FBI Team Up."

10. Deborah Radcliff, "Cybersleuthing Solves the Case," *Computerworld*, Jan. 14, 2002, http://www.computerworld.com/securitytopics/security/story/0,10801,67299,00. html.

11. Brad Stone, "Busting the Web Bandits," *Newsweek*, July 16, 2001, http://www.paypal.com/html/newsweek-071601.html.

12. Stacy Forster, "PayPal's Popular Service Gets Some Complaints from Users," *The Wall Street Journal Online*, January 16, 2001, no longer available online.

13. Stone, "Busting the Web Bandits."

14. Suzanne Shaw and Steve Willey, "Checkmate, PayPal," *MyPrimeTime.com*, February 7, 2001, no longer available online.

15. Brian Bergstein, "EBay CEO on World After the Dot-com Bust," *Associated Press*, May 28, 2001, no longer available online.

16. Ina Steiner, "EBay CEO Disses Yahoo!" *AuctionBytes.com*, May 29, 2001, http://www.auctionbytes.com/cab/abn/y01/m05/i29/s01.

17. Cohen, *The Perfect Store*, 105.

18. For further discussion of the various auction competitors vanquished by eBay, see Troy Wolverton, "EBay Seeks to Sail into New Territory," *News.com*, July 19, 2001, http://news.com.com/2100-1017-270198.html?legacy=cnet.

19. At some level, the fact that customers could not easily close unwanted Billpoint accounts was the reason eBay was able to exploit this preference change in the first place. I estimate that around 25% of the active eBay sellers who opened a Billpoint account abandoned it but did not officially close it down.

20. Michael Mahoney, "PayPal Gets Itself into Hot Water," *E-Commerce Times*, July 13, 2001, http://www.ecommercetimes.com/perl/story/11968.html.

21. Troy Wolverton, "EBay, PayPal Open New Chapter in Feud," *News.com*, July 11, 2001, http://news.com.com/2100-1017-269808.html?legacy=cnet.

22. Rosalinda Baldwin, "Unethical eBay/Billpoint," *The Auction Guild*, July 14, 2001, updated February 7, 2002, http://www.auctionguild.com/generic.html?pid=63.

23. Wolverton, "EBay, PayPal Open New Chapter."

24. Owen Thomas, "Damon Billian, Customer Attaché," *Business 2.0*, July 2002, http://www.business2.com/b2/web/articles/0,17863,514847,00.html.

25. Bodow, "The Money Shot."

26. For example, credit card providers Wells Fargo, Providian, and MBNA no longer allow cardholders to send payments for gambling, and the American Express and Discover associations do not allow any of their cards to be used for wagers. See Matt Richtel, "A Credit Crisis for Web Casinos," *The New York Times*, January 21, 2002, http://query.nytimes.com/gst/abstract.html?res=F40F12F73F5F0C728EDDA80894DA404482

27. Richtel, "A Credit Crisis for Web Casinos;" Horn, "Point and Bet," *Newsweek*, October 28, 2002, no longer available online.

28. Roy Mark, "Leach Again Bets on Internet Anti-Gambling Bill," *Internetnews.com*, January 9, 2003, http://www.internetnews.com/bus-news/article.php/1567321.

29. Horn, "Point and Bet."

30. Ibid.

31. *PR Newswire - PayPal press release*, "PayPal Community Contributes $2.35 Million to Aid in September 11 Relief Efforts," http://www.findarticles.com/cf_dls/m4PRN/2001_Nov_12/79975916/p1/article.jhtml (displayed on the Red Cross Bay Area Chapter's Web site at bayarea redcross.org, November 13, 2001).

32. Troy Wolverton, "EBay's Charity Auction Upsets Some Sellers," *News.com*, September 18, 2001, http://news.com.com/2100-1017_3-273153.html.

33. Ibid.

34. Troy Wolverton, "EBay's Charity Auction Falls Far Short of Goal," *News.com*, January 4, 2002, http://news.com.com/2100-1017-801366.html?legacy=cnet.

Chapter 9

1. Don Clark, quoting Thompson Financial in "PayPal Files for an IPO, Testing a Frosty Market," *The Wall Street Journal*, October 1, 2001, http://www.online.wsj.com/PA2VJBNA4R/snippet/0,,SB1001792898981822840-search,00.html.

2. Margaret Kane, "PayPal Faces Long IPO Odds," *News.com*, October 19, 2001, http://news.com.com/2100-12_3-274658.html.

3. Ben Elgin, "Can PayPal Pull This Off?" *BusinessWeek*, October 29, 2001, http://static.highbeam.com/b/businessweek/october292001/businessweekebizupstartscanpaypalpullthisoff/index.html.

4. Clark, "PayPal Files for an IPO."

5. George Kraw, "Earth to Palo Alto," *The Recorder*, October 31, 2001, http://www.law.com/regionals/ca/opinions/stories/edt1031_kraw.shtml.

6. U.S. Securities and Exchange Commission Web site, "Quiet Period," modified February 4, 2001, http://www.sec.gov/answers/quiet.htm.

7. For background on the Argentine currency crisis, see *The Economist*, "A Decline Without Parallel," February 28, 2002, http://www.economist.com/research/backgrounders/displaystory.cfm?Story_ID=S')H%2C-PQ_%22!P%23H%0A; for the inflation and devaluation statistics, see *BBC News*, "Argentina Inflation Soars," May 6, 2002, http://news.bbc.co.uk/1/hi/business/1970198.stm; for a biting commentary on the government's actions, see Hanke, "Legalized Theft," *The Cato Institute* Web site, March 4, 2002, http://www.cato.org/current/argentina/pubs/hanke-020304.html.

8. Troy Wolverton, "EBay Revamps Checkout Feature," *News.com*, November 2, 2001, http://news.com.com/2100-1017-275345.html?legacy=cnet.

9. Tim Arango, "EBay Users Up in Arms Over Billing System," *TheStreet.com*, October 30, 2001, http://www.thestreet.com/stocks/timarango/10003236.html.

10. Stephanie Stoughton, "With New Billing Procedures, eBay Not Exactly Everyone's Pal," *The Boston Globe*, November 12, 2001, no longer available online.

11. Adam Lashinsky, "Meg and the Machine," *Fortune.com*, August 11, 2003, http://www. fortune.com/fortune/fastest/articles/0,15114,473553,00.html.

12. I believe that my decision to back out these two expenses from operating profit/loss calculations is pedagogically useful and also defendable from a business standpoint. In recent years the expensing of stock-based compensation has turned into a contentious accounting issue. What is clear, though, is that offering equity to employees in lieu of salary is a sound strategy for a cash-starved startup. Yet expensing this item treats it as tantamount to a cash outlay for salaries, undermining this axiom and distorting the apparent health of the business derived from granting stock to employees. Including amortization in a definition of PayPal's profitability would obscure the business's true condition even more than stock-based compensation. Accounting standards led the company to write down more than $100 million in goodwill prior to January 1, 2002. Conversely, had this deadline been delayed for a year or two, this would have made the GAAP income statements appear far better during this period without benefiting the fundamental performance of our business. Consider that when we were bleeding $10 million a month in mid-2000, debiting all the goodwill in the world wouldn't have rescued our business model.

13. EBay 2002 Annual Report, 22.

14. *PR Newswire - PayPal press release*, "PayPal Surpasses 10 Million User Mark," September 6, 2001, no longer available online.

15. For example, see Kane, "PayPal Gears Up for IPO," *News.com*, February 6, 2002, no longer available online; Grant, "Analysts: PayPal IPO Should Pay Off," *E-commerce Times*, February 5, 2002, http://www.ecommercetimes.com/perl/story/16172.html.

16. *Gartner*, "Gartner Survey Shows PayPal Leading the Online P2P Payment Market; Market Intelligence," February 7, 2002, http://www.gartner.com/5_about/press_releases/2002_02/pr20020205b.jsp.

17. Cohen, *The Perfect Store*, 151-152.

18. *Wall Street Journal Online*, "PayPal Says CertCo Filed Suit to Delay Public Offering," February 11, 2002, no longer available online.

19. Troy Wolverton, "PayPal Moves to Put IPO Back on Track," *News.com*, February 8, 2002, http://news.com.com/2100-1017-832925.html.

20. For example, see Avivah Litan's comments to Elaine Grant, "PayPal Booted Out of State, Under Legal Siege," *E-Commerce Times*, February 12, 2002, http://www. ecommercetimes.com/perl/story/16291.html.

21. Ibid.

22. Miles Weiss, "PayPal Says Louisiana Bars Company Services Within the State," *Bloomberg.com*, February 11, 2002, no longer available online.

23. Weiss, "PayPal Says Louisiana Bars Services;" Wolverton, "La. Asks PayPal to Halt Service in State," *News.com*, February 11, 2002, http://news.com.com/2100-1017-834313.html.

24. Wolverton, *PayPal Moves to Put IPO Back on Track.*

25. Tom Cooke, "PayPal Says CertCo Patent Suit Was Filed To Disrupt IPO," *Dow Jones Newswires*, February 11, 2002, no longer available online.

26. Weiss, "PayPal Says Louisiana Bars Services."

27. Cohen, *The Perfect Store*, 147.

28. Raymond Hennessy, "IPO Outlook: In PayPal, Brand Strength Beat Net Profile," *Dow Jones News Services*, February 19, 2002, no longer available online.

29. Josh Friedman, "PayPal Jumps 55% on Stock Offering," *The Los Angeles Times*, February 16, 2002, http://pqasb.pqarchiver.com/latimes/108317110.html?did=108317 110&FMT=ABS&FMTS=FT&date=Feb+16,+2002&author=JOSH+FRIEDMAN&desc=Pa yPal+Jumps+55%25+on+Stock+Offering%3b+Internet:+After+a+one-week+IPO+ delay, +the+online+payment+service+makes+a+strong+debut+amid+%27anemic%27+market.

30. Matt Richtel, "Internet Offering Soars, Just Like Old Times," *The New York Times*, February 17, 2002, http://query.nytimes.com/gst/abstract.html?res=F20E17F6385B0C 758DDDAB0894DA404482.

31. Paul Kedrosky, "Don't Bank on PayPal," *The National Post*, February 16, 2002, no longer available online.

Chapter 10

1. Heather McLean, "EBay Throws Down the Gauntlet to PayPal," *Silicon.com*, February 22, 2002, http://www.silicon.com/networks/webwatch/0,39024667,11031526,00.htm.

2. Keith Reagan, "PayPal Tumbles as eBay Buys Back Billpoint Stake," *E-Commerce Times*, February 22, 2002, http://www.ecommercetimes.com/perl/story/16463.html.

3. Ina Steiner, "PayPal Settles Patent Lawsuit with CertCo," *AuctionBytes.com*, May 1, 2002, http://www.auctionbytes.com/cab/abn/y02/m05/i01/s01.

4. *PayPal secondary offering prospectus*, June 21, 2002, 76-78.

5. Milton Friedman and Rose Friedman, *Free to Choose* (New York: Harcourt Press, 1990), 191.

6. Troy Wolverton, "EBay's Billpoint Draws States' Attention," *News.com*, March 27, 2002, http://news.com.com/2100-1017-870006.html.

7. Ibid.

8. Troy Wolverton, "Feds: PayPal Not a Bank," *News.com*, March 12, 2002, http://news .com.com/2100-1017-858264.html?tag=bplst.

9. Reuters, "PayPal Mum on Possible eBay Deal," *News.com*, April 15, 2002, no longer available online.

10. Keith Reagan, "PayPal Shares Surge Amid eBay Takeover Rumors," *E-Commerce Times*, April 16, 2002, http://www.ecommercetimes.com/perl/story/17279.html.

11. Keith Reagan, "PayPal Busts Profit Barrier in First Quarter," *E-Commerce Times*, April 18, 2002, http://www.ecommercetimes.com/perl/story/17332.html.

12. *PR Newswire – PayPal press release*, "PayPal Promotes David Sacks to COO," March 19, 2002, no longer available online.

13. Dec. 2001 figure from *PayPal IPO prospectus* (67) and May 2002 figure from *PayPal secondary offering prospectus* (82).

14. *Institute for Legal Reform*, Web site, http://www.legalreformnow.com/newsroom/ factsfigures.cfm.

15. Howard Stock, "Class Action Lawsuits Rise Again: Market Cap Losses During

Plaintiff Motions Have Never Been Higher," *Stanford Law School Securities Class Action Clearinghouse*, March 24, 2003, http://securities.stanford.edu/news-archive/2003/20030324 _Headline03_Stock.htm.

16. Stuart Taylor and Thomas Evan, "Civil Wars," *Newsweek*, December 15, 2003, http://msnbc.msn.com/id/3660738.

17. *PayPal secondary offering prospectus*, 82-83.

18. For example, see Regan, "PayPal Users Sue Over Frozen Funds," *E-Commerce Times*, March 13, 2002, http://www.ecommercetimes.com/perl/story/16751.html; Weinberg, "PayPal Runs Up Against Competition," *Forbes.com*, March 8, 2002, http://www.forbes.com/2002/03/08/0308paypal.html.

19. Joanna Glasner, "PayPal Insiders File to Sell," *Wired News*, June 13, 2002, http://www.wired.com/news/business/0,1367,53172,00.html.

20. Brian Bergstein, "EBay Seeks to Mend Its Ties with Disgruntled Customers," *Associated Press*, June 16, 2002, no longer available online.

21. Rick Munarriz, "PayPal Crashing eBay's Party, Again," *Fool.com*, June 14, 2002, http://www.fool.com/news/take/2002/mft/mft02061402.htm.

22. A juvenile act also noticed by Skip McGrath, *The Auction Seller's Resource* online newsletter, June 2002 edition, http://www.auction-sellers-resource.com/newsletters/2002june.shtml.

23. A reporter recounted part of this exchange. While omitting Jordan's reference to Sacks, he noted CFO Rajiv Dutta's reply that it would be unfair to favor PayPal over other online payment services like C2it. The writer dismissed this answer as "nonsense," adding "...it must be true, after all, that eBay hates PayPal." Keith Regan, "eBay Flexes Its... Friendliness?" *E-Commerce Times*, June 27, 2002, http://www.ecommercetimes.com/perl/ story/18411.html.

24. Troy Wolverton, "EBay's PayPal Bid Under Scrutiny," *News.com*, August 7, 2002, http://news.com.com/2100-1017-948793.html.

Chapter 11

1. *PR Newswire - EBay Inc. press release*, "EBay to Acquire PayPal," July 8, 2002. (Edited for length).

2. *OTWA forum on Andale.com*, Discussion topic "Damon, Whatever eBay Does Ask Them to Keep the Debit Card," July 8-9, 2002, no longer available online.

3. *Fool.com*, Discussion topic "EBay Acquiring PayPal," July 8, 2002, no longer available online.

4. Michael Liedtke, "Questions Linger About eBay's Bid for PayPal," *Dow Jones Newswires*, July 21, 2002, http://www.detnews.com/2002/technology/0207/22/technology-542794.htm.

5. Jeffrey Goldfarb, "PayPal and Its Owners Are Partying Like It's 1999," *Reuters*, July 8, 2002, http://www.clearstonevp.com/news/news_PAY070902.html.

6. Bambi Francisco, "Who Is Really Getting Paid, Pal?" *CBS.MarketWatch.com*, July 9, 2002, no longer available online.

7. Troy Wolverton, "Shareholders Sue eBay, PayPal," *News.com*, July 11, 2002, http://news. com.com/2100-1017-943136.html?legacy=cnet.

8. Beth Cox, "New York AG Takes Aim at PayPal," *Internetnews.com*, July 12, 2002, http://www.internetnews.com/bus-news/article.php/1402511.

9. Gee Lee, "EBay, Inc. Gets Letter from US Attorney of Missouri," *Dow Jones Newswires*, March 31, 2003, no longer available online.

10. This quote is from Damien Cave, "Losing Faith in PayPal," *Salon.com*, February 23, 2001, http://dir.salon.com/tech/feature/2001/02/23/pay_pal/index.html.

11. Kraw, "Earth to Palo Alto."

12. *PR Newswire - PayPal Inc. and eBay Inc. joint press release*, "PayPal, Inc. and eBay Inc. Announce Expiration of Hart-Scott-Rodino Waiting Period," August 20, 2002, http://www.shareholder.com/paypal/releaseDetail.cfm?ReleaseID=114036&Category=US.

13. For example, see Curt Davies and Jeff Love, "Tracking Baby Boomer Attitudes Then and Now," *AARP Knowledge Management*, August 2002, http://research.aarp.org/general/bbattitudes_1.html.

14. David Gardner and Tom Gardner, "Meg Stands by Her Mark," *Fool.com*, September 15, 2003, http://www.fool.com/specials/2003/03091500ceo.htm.

15. Adam Lashinsky, "Meg and the Machine," Fortune, August 11, 2003, http://www.fortune.com/fortune/fastest/articles/0,15114,473553,00.html.

16. Ina Steiner, "EBay Appoints Bannick to Manage Online Payments Services," *AuctionBytes.com*, Sept., 2002, http://www.auctionbytes.com/cab/abn/y02/m09/i06/s03.

17. *PR Newswire - EBay press release*, "EBay Completes PayPal Acquisition," Oct. 3, 2003, http://www.shareholder.com/paypal/releaseDetail.cfm?ReleaseID=114025&Category=US.

Conclusion

1. Carl Bialik, "Failure Rate for eBay Searches Leaves Some Sellers Rankled," *The Wall Street Journal*, October 7, 2003, http://online.wsj.com/PA2VJBNA4R/snippet/0,,SB106 45033 9481909900-search,00.html.

2. Lisa Baertlein, "Web Auctioneer eBay to Raise Listing Fees," *Reuters*, January 5, 2004, http://www.forbes.com/business/newswire/2004/01/06/rtr1199982.html.

3. Leslie Walker, "A Study in E-Commerce Opposites," *The Washington Post*, January 29, 2004, http://www.washingtonpost.com/wp-dyn/articles/A58253-2004Jan28.html.

4. For the CyberSource announcement, see *PR Newswire - CyberSource Press Release*, "CyberSource to Offer PayPal as a Payment Option," October 9, 2003, http://www.cybersource.com/news_and_events/view.xml?page_id=1169; for the UK launch, see *PR Newswire - PayPal Press Release*, "PayPal Available For Users In The UK," October 9, 2003, http://www.shareholder.com/paypal/releaseDetail.cfm?ReleaseID=119722&Category=US; for the user count, see PayPal homepage as of March 20, 2004.

5. Rick Munarriz, "PayPal 1, Citigroup 0," *Fool.com*, October 1, 2003, http://www.fool.com/News/mft/2003/mft03100101.htm.

6. Leticia Williams, "PayPal Settles Charges with NY Regulator," *CBS Marketwatch.com*, March 8, 2004, http://www.marketwatch.com/news/print_story.asp?print=1&guid= {98740489-20DC-46E9-A61D-6CA2649054FA}.

7. *Reuters*, "PayPal Probed for Anti-Fraud Efforts," March 9, 2004, http://www.bizreport. com/article.php?art_id=6415.

8. For a full discussion on the potential impact on PayPal of compliance with the USA PATRIOT Act, see Yochi Dreazen, "Too User Friendly? Legislation Aimed at Stopping Terrorism Could Have a Devastating Impact on an Innocent Bystander: PayPal," *The Wall Street Journal*, October 21, 2002, no longer available online.

9. For example, see Riva Richmond, "Computer Virus Attempts PayPal 'Phishing' Scam," *Dow Jones Newswires*, November 14, 2003, no longer available online.

10. PayPal customer e-mail received March 20, 2004.

11. Mike Tarsala, "Putting EBay's Future Out to Bid," *CBS.Marketwatch.com*, September 18, 2003, no longer available online.

12. *EBay.com*, "Live Chat Event with Jeff Jordan," April 30, 2002, http://pages.ebay.com/event/jeffj/?ssPageName=CMDV:IC0164.

13. Joelle Tessler, "EBay Jettisons Butterfields," *Mercury News*, August 2, 2002, http://www.siliconvalley.com/mld/siliconvalley/3782231.htm.

14. *Wall Street Journal Online*, "AT&T Files Patent Suit Against eBay, PayPal Unit," November 20, 2003, http://online.wsj.com/article/0,,SB106935214758888300,00.html.

15 Rachel Rosmarin, "The PayPal Exodus," *Forbes.com*, July 12, 2006, http://www.forbes.com/2006/07/12/paypal-ebay-youtube_cx_rr_0712paypal.html?partner=yahootix

Afterword

1. Elinor Mills, "Google Gets Nearly 60% of U.S. Searches—Report," *News.com*, June 8, 2006, http://news.com.com/2061-10803_3-6081834.html.

2. *Google*, "Google Announces Second Quarter 2006 Results," July 20, 2006, http://investor.google.com/releases/2006Q2.html.

3. *Google*, "Google Milestones," http://www.google.com/intl/en/corporate/history.html.

4. Thomas L. Friedman, "Opinion: Is Google God?" *CNN.com*, June 29, 2003, http://www.cnn.com/2003/US/06/29/nyt.friedman/.

5. *eBay*, "eBay Inc. Announces Second Quarter 2006 Financial Results," July 19, 2006, http://investor.ebay.com/news/EBAY0719-204302.pdf.

6. Dan Goodin, "Analysts: eBay Faces Competitive Threat," *Associated Press*, July 6, 2006, http://biz.yahoo.com/ap/060706/ebay_s_paypal_troubles.html?.v=10.

7. Mylene Mangalindan, "eBay's PayPal Chief to Step Down, Jolting Investors," *The WSJ*, July 7, 2006, http://online.wsj.com/article/SB115220193310099640.html.

8. *BBC News*, "Google Censors Itself for China," January 25, 2006, http://news.bbc.co.uk/1/hi/technology/4645596.stm.

9. Clive Thompson, "Google's China Problem (and China's Google Problem)," *The New York Times*, April 23, 2006, http://www.nytimes.com/2006/04/23/magazine/23google.html?ei=5090&en=972002761056363f&ex=1303444800&adxnnl=1&adxnnlx=1157425373-ZLn/5BjSP5f4R3xDUudOIA.

10. Arshad Mohammed, "Google Refuses Demand for Search Information," *The Washington Post*, January 20, 2006, http://www.washingtonpost.com/wp-dyn/content/article/2006/01/19/AR2006011903331.html.

11. Joseph Farah, "Google Money Engine for Democrats Only," *WorldNetDaily.com*, May 6, 2005, http://www.worldnetdaily.com/news/article.asp?ARTICLE_ID=44125.

12. Scott Reeves, "Google Dials eBay," *Forbes.com*, August 28, 2006, http://www.forbes.com/technology/ebusiness/2006/08/28/google-ebay-0828markets02.html.

13. Rachel Rosmarin, "eBay, Yahoo! Take on Google," *Forbes.com*, May 25, 2006, http://www.forbes.com/technology/2006/05/25/ebay-yahoo-google_cx_rr_0525ebayyahoo.htm.

INDEX

the former interim Vice President of Marketing for
ed a crucial role in turning PayPal into the world's
yment service and the first Silicon Valley dot-com to
blic offering (IPO) after the terrorist attacks of 9/11.
ent commentator on radio and television programs,
interviewed by Forbes, BusinessWeek, US News &
d numerous other publications. He currently serves as
orld Ahead Media. Jackson holds a degree in econom-
m Stanford University, and he lives with his wife in

Eric M. Jackson is
PayPal. He play
leading online p
hold an initial p
Jackson is a frequ
and he has been
World Report, an
the President of W
ics with honors fr
Los Angeles.